I0560352

The Sacred Teachings of the Orishas

Explore Over Fifty Stories, Prayers, Rituals, and Insights from the Yoruba Spiritual Tradition

Awo Ifagbemi

Copyright © 2025 by Michael Perez
All Rights Reserved.

No part of this publication may be copied, distributed, or transmitted in any form, whether electronic, mechanical, or otherwise, without prior written permission from the Author or Publisher, except for brief quotations used in reviews or other non-commercial works allowed under the fair use provisions of U.S. copyright law.

First Edition: 2025.
Print. ISBN: 979-8-9909018-3-4
LCCN: 2025913144
Published by Michael Perez, Erie, PA, U.S.A.

Disclaimer Notice
By reading this book, the reader acknowledges and accepts the following.
This book describes certain traditional practices of Yoruba culture, including animal sacrifice and divination. The information provided herein is solely for educational and entertainment purposes. It is not intended to replace the advice of a qualified professional in any regulated field, such as medical, legal, or financial services. This information is not intended to diagnose, treat, cure, prevent illness, or predict future events. By choosing to read this book, the reader acknowledges that the Author does not offer legal, financial, medical, or any advice requiring professional licensure. This book does not substitute for such advice. Readers also understand that neither the Author nor the Publisher can guarantee the reliability or accuracy of the information presented in this book. Therefore, readers are strongly advised to consult legally licensed professionals in their respective jurisdictions before attempting any techniques outlined in this book. Furthermore, readers are urged to discuss any alternative remedies, herbal use, or spiritual practices mentioned herein with qualified and legally recognized professionals beforehand. It is essential not to disregard professional advice or delay seeking it due to the direct or indirect influence of the information contained in this book. By continuing to read this book, the reader acknowledges that neither the Author nor the Publisher shall be held liable for any losses, whether direct or indirect, incurred from the use or misuse of the material presented within this publication.

PREFACE
A JOURNEY TO SELF-DISCOVERY

The journey to discovering your true self begins with a deep desire to understand your purpose and connect with the divine forces guiding your life. For many years, I searched for answers through various spiritual practices, hoping to find a path that truly resonated with my soul. I studied ancient wisdom, practiced meditation, and learned from spiritual mentors, with each step offering valuable lessons and revealing deeper truths about who I am. Through this exploration, I came to realize that what I was seeking could not be found outside myself. It was already within me, buried beneath layers of conditioning, fear, and past pain. True growth, I learned, is an inward journey, one of self-reflection, healing, and awakening. It requires listening to your inner voice, trusting your intuition, and honoring the path that is uniquely yours.

As I continued this inner work, I discovered Orisha Spirituality and the transformative power of IFA divination. Rooted in Yoruba tradition, this ancient spiritual system teaches the interconnectedness of all life, the importance of balance, and how to align with one's true purpose. IFA is not about predicting the future; it is about understanding your present state and learning how to realign with your highest potential. Through Orisha Spirituality and IFA divination, I deepened my connection to my inner wisdom and began living with greater clarity, fulfillment, and purpose. The guidance of the Orishas continues to support me as I face challenges, strengthen my gifts, and move through life with balance and grace.

This book invites you to begin your own transformative journey. By connecting with the Orishas and their timeless wisdom, you can uncover the clarity, strength, and guidance needed to live in harmony with yourself and the world around you. The power to unlock your true potential already lives within you. Embrace the path before you and step into a life of purpose, balance, and spiritual fulfillment.

* * *

Contents

INTRODUCTION
WELCOME TO THE WORLD OF THE ORISHAS

In recent years, there has been a growing interest in African traditional spirituality, particularly the Yoruba Orisha tradition. Many people are seeking to reconnect with their ancestors and the timeless wisdom they embodied. As we explore Orisha spirituality, we begin to recognize the sacredness of the natural world around us. We become more attuned to the natural cycles of life that our modern world has largely disconnected us from, helping us rediscover a connection to something much larger than the day-to-day routines of our man-made society.

Long before the rise of modern Western civilization, the Yoruba people of West Africa cultivated a deeply spiritual worldview. Their traditions, centered on the divine beings known as the Orishas, provide profound insights into humanity's relationship with the universe. The natural world reflects our inner world, with the forces of nature embodying the divine beings who guide us toward spiritual harmony. The Orishas are not just deities; they are sacred intermediaries who embody the essence of Olodumare, the Supreme Creator, and serve as a link between humans and the forces of nature, balance, and creation. In Yoruba cosmology, the Orishas are active participants in life. They serve as protectors of the natural world, embodiments of divine wisdom, and guiding forces in human development. This reciprocal relationship between the Yoruba people and the Orishas is built on deep respect and gratitude. Through offerings, prayers, and rituals, humans honor these divine beings, who, in turn, offer guidance, protection, and spiritual growth.

The Yoruba tradition recognizes "400 plus one" Orishas, symbolizing the evolving nature of the spiritual world. This flexibility reflects life's complexities and Olodumare's boundless creativity. The word "Orisha" comes from the Yoruba words Ori (head) and sha (guardian), signifying these entities as wise and powerful protectors. Each Orisha governs specific aspects of existence and natural elements, embodying the intricate balance of the universe. Sacred natural spaces, forests, rivers, mountains, and crossroads, are revered as the homes of the Orishas and remain central to Yoruba spirituality.

These places are seen as conduits for divine communication, where offerings, prayers, and rituals are made to honor the Orishas and seek their blessings. These acts are crucial not only for spiritual alignment but also for preserving the delicate balance of nature.Despite the devastating impacts of enslavement and colonization, Yoruba spirituality endured. It adapted to new realities while preserving its core. In the Americas, enslaved Africans skillfully blended their Orisha traditions with Christianity to maintain their faith under oppressive conditions. The Orishas became symbols of resistance and hope, offering spiritual strength and comfort during one of humanity's darkest periods.

Today, Orisha spirituality continues to thrive, offering a pathway to reconnect with nature, honor ancestors, and restore balance in life. As many people seek alternatives to mainstream religions, they are rediscovering the indigenous practices of their ancestors. Orisha worship centers on living in harmony with the earth, fostering community well-being, and holding a deep reverence for the divine, timeless values that continue to resonate in our modern world.

The Sacred Teachings of the Orishas is more than just a book; it is an invitation to connect deeply with the divine forces that have guided generations. Through the rhythm of sacred poetry and the timeless wisdom, you will discover the world of the Orishas, experiencing their power, presence, and profound teachings.

Each chapter in this book follows a structured format and is divided into three sections as follows:

- **Introduction**: Overview of the Orishas, their roles in Yoruba traditions, and their spiritual and historical significance.
- **Sacred Stories & Legends**: Traditional stories of the Orishas, showcasing their actions, relationships, and influence, presented in a way that is easy for modern readers to understand.

- **Insights, Offerings, Rituals and Spiritual Significance**:
  Insights and lessons from the stories, along with guidance on how
  to embody the Orishas' teachings and energy in daily life.

The Sacred Teachings of the Orishas weaves poetry, myth, and ritual into a
transformative journey, guiding you to deepen your connection with the
Orishas, honor the divine, and realign with the sacred rhythms of the ancestors and of nature.

* * *

1. The Yoruba Spiritual Tradition

THE YORUBA RELIGION is one of the oldest and most enduring spiritual systems in the world, originating in southwestern Nigeria and extending into parts of Benin and Togo. The Yoruba people have preserved a rich cultural and religious heritage for millennia. At the heart of Yoruba spirituality is the belief in a Supreme Creator, Olodumare, who is equivalent to the concept of God in Western religions.

Alongside Olodumare, there is a vast array of divine beings known as the Orishas, who govern all aspects of the natural world, human life, and the balance of the universe. The Orishas are central to Yoruba spirituality and represent divine forces that oversee various aspects of life. They act as intermediaries between humans and Olodumare. Each Orisha embodies unique qualities, energies, and principles, influencing areas such as love, wisdom, wealth, health, and the elements of nature, like water, fire, and earth. The Yoruba believe that through rituals, offerings, and prayers, they can connect with the Orishas to receive guidance, protection, and blessings. The Orishas are divine beings in the Yoruba spiritual tradition, each connected to natural elements like rivers, the ocean, and the sky, as well as animals, forces of nature, and specific colors. Their stories, called patakis, reveal their personalities, powers, and roles in the world. Some Orishas are known for their strength, while others are recognized for their wisdom or compassion. Devotees of the Yoruba religion often turn to them for guidance and help in times of need. Some of the most well-known Orishas include:

- **Yemanja**: The mother of all Orishas and goddess of the sea. She represents motherhood, fertility, and protection, and is often called upon for healing in times of emotional or physical distress.

- **Shango:** The Orisha of thunder, lightning, and fire. He embodies strength, leadership, and justice, and his followers seek his help in matters of power and courage.
- **Oshun:** The goddess of love, beauty, and rivers. Oshun represents compassion, fertility, and creativity, guiding her followers in love, relationships, and personal growth.
- **Obatala:** The Orisha of wisdom, purity, and fairness. Known as the father of the Orishas, he symbolizes justice, clarity, and spiritual enlightenment.
- **Eleggua:** The trickster and messenger, known for opening paths, creating opportunities, and serving as the guardian of the crossroads.
- **Ogun:** The Orisha of iron, work, and war. He symbolizes strength, perseverance, and overcoming challenges, particularly in labor.
- **Orunmila:** The Orisha of wisdom and divination, guardian of Ifá, who guides destiny and life's questions.

* * *

These Orishas, commonly known as the **Seven African Powers** (or *Las Siete Potencias* in Spanish), are among the most widely recognized figures in the Yoruba spiritual tradition. Each Orisha has distinct qualities, stories, and areas of influence, making them essential to Yoruba spiritual practices. The Yoruba connect with these divine beings through divination, music, dance, rituals, and offerings. These practices strengthen their relationship with the spiritual realm and help align their lives with the cosmic order. Yoruba religious practices have flourished for centuries, offering spiritual guidance and a deep sense of interconnectedness between the physical and spiritual worlds. Central to Yoruba belief is the understanding that everything in life is interconnected, and humans are part of a vast spiritual network that includes both the living and the ancestors. This holistic worldview has allowed Yoruba spirituality to endure, even throughout periods of great upheaval.

The Trans-Atlantic Slave Trade and the Survival of Yoruba Spirituality

The trans-Atlantic slave trade had a profound impact on the Yoruba people. Millions were forcibly taken from their homeland and transported to the Americas, where they were sold into slavery. This displacement led to the loss of homeland, language, and family, and threatened the survival of Yoruba religious practices. However, despite these hardships, Yoruba beliefs adapted and endured. The forced migration of Yoruba people led to the creation of syncretic religious traditions that blended Yoruba beliefs with African, Indigenous, and Catholic spiritual systems. These hybrid religions were not merely a survival tactic; they also reflected the resilience and spiritual strength of the Yoruba. By merging their traditional practices with the religious customs of their new environments, the Yoruba were able to preserve their beliefs while adapting to new conditions.

Syncretism and the Yoruba Diaspora

As Yoruba people spread across the Americas, their religious practices merged with other African, Indigenous, and Catholic beliefs. In regions like Cuba, Brazil, and Haiti, these blended traditions thrived, becoming central to the spiritual landscapes of these countries. Some of the most notable syncretic traditions include:

- **Santería (Cuba):** A blend of Yoruba Orisha worship and Catholicism. Yoruba slaves in Cuba associated Orishas with Catholic saints, allowing them to practice their faith in secret. For example, Ogun, the Orisha of iron and war, was syncretized with Saint George, and Yemanjá, goddess of the sea, with Our Lady of Regla.
- **Candomblé (Brazil):** A fusion of Yoruba, Fon, and Bantu spiritual traditions. Candomblé incorporates Catholic saints but retains many Yoruba elements, with Orishas venerated through music, dance, and offerings.
- **Vodou (Haiti):** Combines Yoruba beliefs with African, Indigenous, and Catholic influences. The Vodou pantheon includes many Yoruba Orishas, such as Ogún and Yemanjá, but they are associated with different spirits known as Loa.

- **Umbanda (Brazil):** A syncretic religion blending African, Indigenous, and Christian beliefs, incorporating elements of Spiritism and honoring Orishas alongside spirits of ancestors and other spiritual entities.

These syncretic religions demonstrate the adaptability and strength of Yoruba spirituality. Despite the challenges of slavery, colonization, and forced cultural assimilation, Yoruba religious practices have survived and thrived in the Americas, influencing spiritual practices worldwide. Today, these religions are practiced by millions, and their impact is evident in popular culture and contemporary spirituality.

THE ONGOING INFLUENCE OF YORUBA SPIRITUALITY

While the traditional form of Yoruba religion remains strong in its home-land, its diaspora has had a significant impact on the religious and cultural landscapes of the Americas and beyond. Yoruba beliefs, customs, and practices have shaped new religious movements, social justice initiatives, and artistic expressions like music, dance, and literature. Yoruba spirituality's ability to adapt and thrive in diverse cultural environments speaks to its resilience. Whether through divination, ancestor veneration, or Orisha worship, these traditions continue to create vibrant spiritual communities around the world. Yoruba religion is not just a survival of the past but a living, evolving tradition that continues to shape the spiritual and cultural identities of millions.

CONCLUSION

The Yoruba religion has withstood centuries of historical challenges, from the trans-Atlantic slave trade to the suppression of indigenous African practices. Through it all, the Yoruba people have preserved their spiritual beliefs, adapting and transforming them into new forms that continue to thrive today. The emergence of syncretic religions like Santería, Candomblé, Vodou, and Umbanda shows the strength and flexibility of Yoruba spirituality and how it continues to influence global spiritual practices. As we explore these traditions, it is crucial to remember the deep spiritual connection between the Yoruba people, their Orishas, and their ancestors, and how these practices continue to guide and shape communities worldwide.

2. THE YORUBA CREATION STORY
THE SUPREME SOURCE IN YORUBA COSMOLOGY

IN THE PREVIOUS CHAPTER, we introduced Olodumare, the Supreme Being in Yoruba cosmology, which shares similarities with the concept of God in many Western religions. Now, let's delve into the creation of the universe and gain a deeper understanding of the Yoruba belief system, beginning with a closer look at Olodumare. The Yoruba see Olodumare as the ultimate source of all life, energy, and creation, beyond gender and definition. Olodumare is the creator of the universe and everything within it. Unlike gods in many other religions, who often interact directly with human affairs, Olodumare is understood to be distinct from creation in some stories, while in others, Olodumare is considered an integral part of it. Olodumare exists as a powerful spiritual force beyond human comprehension. The presence of this force is felt through Ase, a divine energy that flows through all living things. To understand Olodumare's role, think of it like the sun: just as the sun provides light and life to everything on Earth, Olodumare provides life to everything in the universe. Honoring Olodumare involves living righteously, doing what is right, and staying aligned with one's divine purpose. The will of Olodumare is carried out by the Orishas, powerful divine beings who maintain balance in the universe and guide humans in fulfilling their destinies. Olodumare is understood in three aspects, each reflecting a different expression of divine power as shown below:

- **Olodumare:** *The ultimate creator, the source of Ase, and the determiner of fate. Olodumare is honored through righteous living and moral actions, rather than direct worship.*
- **Olorun:** *The ruler of the heavens and the spiritual world, associated with the sun and cosmic order. Olorun oversees divine justice and the fate of souls after death.*

- **Olofin:** *The bringer of divine energy into the physical world, working through natural forces and the Orishas to ensure that human actions align with divine law and balance.*

Together, these three forms offer a more complete understanding of how the Yoruba view the Supreme Being.

WHAT IS ASE?

At the heart of Yoruba cosmology is the concept of **Ase** (also spelled **Ashe**), the divine energy that flows through all things. Ase is the power that sustains life, enables change, and maintains universal harmony. It permeates everything, living beings, nature, and unseen spiritual forces, and gives vitality to the universe. Ase is not just an abstract idea; it is a living force that makes rituals, prayers, and sacrifices effective. Every being carries Ase to some degree, but the Orishas, the divine entities of the Yoruba tradition, possess it in greater abundance. Olodumare, the Supreme Creator, is the ultimate source of Ase, granting it to the Orishas so they can shape creation and uphold cosmic balance. Humans can access and strengthen their Ase through righteous living, spiritual practice, and devotion. By aligning with moral and spiritual principles, individuals enhance their connection to Ase, allowing them to fulfill their destiny and live in harmony with the divine order. In Yoruba tradition, Ase is often invoked during prayers, blessings, and ceremonies to empower words and actions. Saying "Ase" at the end of a prayer affirms its power and helps bring it into reality.

* * *

PART 2
THE CREATION STORY

In the beginning, before time and existence, there was only an endless, formless void, silent and dark. There was no land, sky, light, or movement, only stillness, awaiting the spark of life. From this emptiness, Olodumare, the Supreme Being, emerged. With infinite wisdom, love, and power, He began shaping the void, filling it with life and meaning. Olodumare created the heavens, a radiant realm of light and energy where divine beings would dwell. This celestial realm became the foundation of all existence. From the essence of Ase, the divine power, Olodumare brought forth the Orishas, divine beings entrusted with maintaining balance and harmony throughout the universe.

The Birth of the Universe

In the beginning, the universe was born,
With wisdom deep, from night till morning.
Olodumare, through Ase's might,
Shaped the world with radiant light.

The Orishas, tasked to guide and hold,
Balanced the forces, brave and bold.
Their struggles taught of wisdom's way,
Responsibility in the light of day.

Creation's story, powers bestowed,
Transformation's path, in life it flowed.
Through growth and change, we find our place,
Connected to the divine, in sacred space.

The Yoruba wisdom, a guiding star,
For all beings, no matter how far.

* * *

The Elements and the Physical World

After creating the universe, Olodumare formed the elements: Fire, Earth, Air, and Water, to shape the physical world. These powerful forces became the foundation of existence, each with its unique essence and purpose. To maintain balance and harmony, Olodumare entrusted the Orishas with dominion over these elements.

Fire
With Olodumare's will, Fire came alive,
A force of passion, to burn and thrive.
It clears the old, ignites the new,
A beacon of power, strong and true.

Earth

From steady hands, Earth took its form,
A cradle of life, rich and warm.
Its roots, it holds, it nurtures deep,
A mother's strength, a promise to keep.

Air

Olodumare spoke, and Air took flight,
A silent whisper, swift and light.
It moves, it stirs, it breathes, it sings,
A bridge of thought on unseen wings.

Water

From sacred depths, Water rose,
A river of life that ebbs and flows.
It soothes, it carves, it cleanses, it calls,
A force of wisdom that never falls.

* * *

THE DAY THE POWERS FELL FROM THE SKY

As the universe expanded,
the Orishas sought control over it. To settle their rivalry,
Olodumare made a decree: The powers
shall fall like scattered seed.

Whoever catches them first shall reign,
The strongest shall rise, the rest shall remain.
Orunmila announced the fateful day,
The Orishas gathered, eager to play.

From the heavens, the gifts rained down,
And the Orishas scrambled across the ground.
Some were swift, some fell behind,
Yet each received what fate assigned.
Thus, their powers were set in place,
Each Orisha, with divine embrace.

REFLECTIONS

This poem tells the story of a special day when the Orishas, powerful divine beings, must compete for their powers. Orunmila, the wise Orisha, predicts that the powers will fall from the heavens like scattered seeds. The Orishas rush to collect them, some fast and some slow. The strongest ones rise to claim their power, while the others take what fate gives them. In the end, each Orisha receives the power meant for them, and their roles in the world are set. This story relates to the destiny of all people because, like the Orishas, everyone has a unique role and purpose in life. Some may rise quickly to fulfill their destiny, while others may take a different path. Just as the Orishas are guided by fate, each person's journey is shaped by divine order, and we all receive the gifts and challenges meant for us. The poem reminds us that, although we may face different circumstances, our destinies are part of a greater plan.

OBATALA AND THE CREATION OF HUMANITY

After the Earth was formed, Olodumare assigned Obatala the task of creating humans from earth and sand. Obatala began shaping the first human beings and called upon Olodumare to breathe life into them. One day, feeling exhausted from his work, Obatala drank too much palm wine. Under its influence, some of his creations turned out imperfect, missing limbs, or having unusual features. When Olodumare saw this, He was displeased. Obatala, feeling deep shame, admitted his mistake and vowed never to drink again. Olodumare forgave him, and Obatala became the protector of all people, especially those with physical and mental differences, as well as the Orisha of Divine Justice. This story teaches that all creation, even in its imperfections, carries inherent worth and a meaningful role in the world.

THE SACRED BALANCE OF EXISTENCE

In conclusion, the Yoruba story of creation serves as a profound reminder of the delicate balance between divine intention and human existence. From the formless void, Olodumare shaped the universe, endowed the Orishas with power, and bestowed humanity with the gift of Ase. These sacred forces continue to guide the world, teaching lessons of responsibility, harmony, and transformation.

Through growth and change, we find our place,
Connected to the divine, in sacred space.
A path of harmony, for all to see,
A journey of life, where we are free.

* * *

Through wisdom, kindness,
and alignment with divine principles, we can fulfill our purpose and
contribute to the ongoing balance of the cosmos.

* * *

3. THE ORISHAS
THE DIVINE SPIRITS OF THE YORUBA PANTHEON

THE ORISHAS ARE NOT distant beings watching from far away. They are close to us, walking beside us in everyday life. They are part of nature, emotions, and the human spirit itself. Each Orisha has a unique energy, as diverse as the people who honor them. Some shine like fire, others move gently like rivers. Some bring storms, while others whisper through the trees or dance in the market. Although divine, the Orishas have human qualities we recognize. They reflect our strengths and weaknesses, fears and hopes, joys and sorrows. More than just spiritual beings, they are living symbols of life representing emotions, forces, choices, and lessons. Some stand for love, beauty, and sensuality; others for justice, war, or healing.

This variety makes the Yoruba pantheon rich and relatable. Everyone can see themselves in an Orisha, whether in Oshun's kindness, Ogun's strength, or Shango's fiery pride. Each Orisha represents a part of life and offers unique wisdom and guidance. It is believed that each person is watched over by one or more Orishas who help guide their destiny and shape their character. The Orishas resemble humans in many ways. Like us, they argue, struggle, make mistakes, and grow. Their sacred stories, called *patakis,* pronounced (Pah-Tah- Kees), teach moral lessons and reflect life's complexities. The Orishas reveal that, despite their power, even divine beings must actively work to maintain balance, harmony, and purpose. This chapter is just the beginning. From here, we will meet the Orishas one by one, learning their names, symbols, stories, and sacred wisdom. We will see how these ancient spirits still influence millions around the world, reminding us that the divine is not far away but within and all around us. The Orishas are not just echoes of ancient times; they are vibrant and alive today. *They move through the rhythms of nature and human life, guiding us with their wisdom and strength. As we learn their stories and connect with their spirits, we*

11

discover a deeper understanding of ourselves and the world around us. The Orishas invite us to embrace life fully with courage, compassion, and balance, reminding us that the sacred is not distant but woven into every moment we live.

* * *

4. AGANJU
ORISHA OF FIRE, VOLCANOES, WILDERNESS AND TRANSFORMATION

A CLOSER LOOK AT AGANJU

AGANJU IS the Orisha of volcanoes, wilderness, and transformative power. His name, meaning "wilderness," reflects his rule over untamed landscapes, from towering mountains to flowing lava. As a force of destruction and renewal, he clears obstacles and forges new paths, teaching resilience through adversity. Father of Shango, Aganju, passes down his fiery strength and endurance, and is invoked during times of intense challenge for courage and support. Beyond fire and earth, Aganju is a protector of the oppressed, symbolizing liberation and resistance. He guided enslaved people to freedom and is called upon by those seeking to break free from physical, emotional, or spiritual captivity. Travelers, warriors, and all who endure hardship seek his unwavering strength. While his worship may not be widespread, Aganju's influence is constant, representing the unstoppable force of change. He shares a deep bond with Shango, complementing Shango's bold lightning with his steady volcanic power. Together, they embody leadership and transformation. Aganju's energy reminds us that even through destruction, renewal is possible. Those who honor him embrace courage, endurance, and the wisdom to transform through life's greatest trials.

AGANJU, SPIRIT OF FIRE AND EARTH
Poem and Prayer
VERSE I:I

Aganju, mighty, wild, and wide,
You shape the land where mountains rise.

With fire's glow and lava's stream,
You bring to life the strongest dream.

Your name means "wilderness" and flame,
A sacred force no one can tame.
Through rocky cliffs and rivers deep,
You wake the soul from heavy sleep.

Breaker of chains, you bring release,
And fill the heart with strength and peace.
Through storm and heat, you still remain,
A calm, bold fire through joy and pain.

Father of Shango, fierce and wise,
You lift the earth into the skies.
Not rushed, but steady, firm, and true,
Your lessons guide in all we do.

In glowing coals and mountain stone,
We feel your power, sure and known.
You light the way through fear and doubt,
And teach what strength is all about.

Aganju, fire in the land,
Hold us gently in your hand.
Burn away what blocks our way,
And build us strong for each new day.
Ase.

* * *

SACRED STORIES / LEGENDS
SECTION 2

OSHANLA AND THE FERRYMAN
STORY 2:1

Aganju, the Orisha of the earth and volcanoes, was also the guardian of a great river, responsible for ferrying travelers across its vast waters. He ruled his domain with firm authority, ensuring that only those who provided the required payment could make the journey. His role was not merely that of a ferryman but also a keeper of balance, ensuring that all exchanges were fair and that no one crossed without proper tribute. One day, Obatala, the wise and revered Orisha of creation, arrived at the riverbank. Known as the molder of humanity, Obatala was a figure of great dignity and patience. However, he lacked the necessary fare to cross the river. As he approached Aganju, he respectfully requested passage, expecting his status to grant him favor. But Aganju, ever bound to the principle of fair exchange, remained resolute.

He denied Obatala's request, stating that without payment, he could not grant him passage. Obatala, rather than contesting the decision, understood that different forces governed different aspects of the world. Knowing that brute insistence would not change Aganju's mind, he instead chose another approach. Calling upon his divine abilities, he transformed himself into Oshanla, an aspect of his being that embodied beauty, grace, and divine femininity. Now appearing as a radiant woman, Oshanla approached Aganju once more, speaking with a voice that carried the softness of flowing water. Aganju, who had been unwavering in his decision, found himself moved by Oshanla's presence. Her energy was not one of force but of persuasion, a quiet but undeniable power that softened the earth itself. Without realizing it, his resolve shifted. For the first time, he made an exception, allowing Oshanla onto his ferry and guiding her across the river.

During their time together on the journey, a deep connection formed between them. What began as an exchange between ferryman and traveler evolved into something greater, a union of two forces, earth and grace, strength and wisdom. From this union, a child was conceived: Shango, the Orisha of thunder and lightning, destined to be a powerful and revered force among the Orisha pantheon. This story serves as more than a mere account of an event. It illustrates the interplay between rigidity and adaptability, between law and the transformative power of persuasion. Aganju, the unshakable guardian of the river, was not conquered by force but was moved by something greater, divine grace. The encounter between Aganju and Oshanla did not break the rules of balance but rather redefined them, showing that sometimes, the most powerful exchanges are not those of wealth, but of spirit.

REFLECTION & WISDOM

The story of Aganju and Oshanla teaches us that being strong is important, but knowing when to be flexible is just as powerful. Aganju stuck to the rules, but when Oshanla used grace and wisdom instead of force, he changed his mind. This shows us that sometimes, kindness and understanding can be more effective than strict rules. The lesson is that we should balance strength with gentleness and be open to different ways of solving problems. By doing this, we can create better solutions and make stronger connections with others.

* * *

THE PACT OF SHANGO
STORY 2:2

Shango set out on a journey through unknown lands, seeking wisdom. He visited Orúnmila, who told him to continue on his path to discover his true purpose. Along the way, Shango met Eshu, who spoke of a town where the sky was always cloudy and the king, Agayú, remained hidden by the river. Shango entered the town and saw a strange sight: a man surrounded by smoke, with a woman cooling him with water. The people were silent, and Shango soon discovered that Agayú was the king. However, anyone who tried to speak to him turned into stone. Realizing that he needed to help, Shango struck a deal with Agayú. Shango would rule the town, but Agayú's power would remain as a distant, powerful force. To break the curse, Shango taught the people to speak with respect and harmony, understanding that it was fear and disconnection that caused the curse. As the people learned to speak from the heart, the curse was lifted, and they could now communicate with Agayú. Shango's thunder and Agayú's volcanic eruptions symbolized their united strength. The bond between Shango and Agayú restored balance, showing that true power lies in unity.

REFLECTION & WISDOM

This story teaches that true power lies in communication, understanding, and unity. Shango helps lift the curse on the town by teaching the people to speak with respect and harmony. It shows that fear and disconnection can silence us, but through cooperation and sincere communication, balance can be restored.

The bond between Shango and Agayú reminds us that strength comes from working together with wisdom and unity.

* * *

INSIGHTS, OFFERINGS, RITUALS AND SPIRITUAL SIGNIFICANCE
SECTION 3

THE SACRED OFFERINGS AND SYMBOLS OF AGANJU

OFFERINGS TO AGANJU

Aganju is honored with offerings that represent his control over both fire and earth. These offerings include rum, gin, palm oil, yams, cornmeal, roosters, goats, pineapple, and okra. The stones associated with Aganju are lava stone, volcanic stone, obsidian, and thunderstone. Many of Aganju's offerings, foods, and plants overlap with those of Shango. In numerology, Aganju's sacred number is 9. Bananas are considered taboo in some lineages and should not be offered to him. Aganju's colors include brown, red, white, yellow, blue, and orange. He is often depicted holding a staff or scepter, symbolizing his dominion over both fire and earth.

FINAL THOUGHTS

Aganju embodies resilience, leadership, and transformation. His influence teaches us that challenges are not meant to break us, but rather to forge us into something stronger. Whether facing personal struggles or major life transitions, invoking Aganju's presence can provide the courage needed to endure, evolve, and thrive.

* * *

AGANJU'S RITUAL OF FIRE AND STRENGTH

PURPOSE
This ritual is designed to invoke the power of Aganju, the Orisha of fire, earth, and transformation. It is intended to bring clarity, strength, and courage during challenging times or periods of change.

ITEMS NEEDED

- A red or brown candle
- A small stone or volcanic rock
- A piece of paper and pen (for writing down a personal challenge or intention)
- A bowl of water

STEP 1: PREPARE YOUR SPACE AND SET YOUR INTENTION

- Find a quiet and peaceful space where you can focus and perform the ritual without distractions.
- Set the candle on a stable surface in front of you.
- Place the volcanic stone or small rock near the candle.
- Hold the paper and pen in your hands. Reflect on the challenge or transformation you are currently facing. Write down your intention or challenge clearly on the paper.

Light the Candle: Stand or sit before the candle. As you light it, say the following prayer (or create your own prayer).

STEP 2: RECITE THE PRAYER TO AGANJU

Aganju, lord of fire and earth,
Guide me through this time of birth.
With strength and flame, you clear my way,
In your power, I find the day.

Father of Shango, fierce and bold,
In your blaze, my spirit is whole.
Protector of the oppressed, I call,
Guide me through hardships, big and small.

Through the wilderness, I seek your light,
With courage and strength, I rise to fight.
Aganju, I honor your name, in your flame, I find my claim.
Ase!

Hold the Stone: Pick up the volcanic stone or rock and hold it in your hands. Close your eyes, focus on the light of the candle's flame, and feel its energy illuminating your path. Say:

Aganju, powerful force of transformation,
I stand firm in your presence.
Help me face this challenge with courage and resilience.
May your strength be my foundation.
Ase!

STEP 3: READ YOUR INTENTION ALOUD

Hold the paper with your intention and read it aloud. Once you have stated your intention clearly, burn the paper in the flame of the candle. When the paper is fully burnt, carefully extinguish the candle by placing it in the bowl of water.

CONCLUSION

Take the remaining water outside and pour a few drops onto the earth as an offering to Aganju. Use the rest of the water for a cleansing bath, allowing the essence of the ritual to soak into you.

* * *

5. Aje Shaluga
Orisha of Wealth, Money and Abundance

A Closer Look at Aje Shaluga

Aje Shaluga, also known simply as Aje, is the female Orisha of money, wealth, and economic success. The word *Aje* translates to mean *wealth* or *money* in the Yoruba language. She is believed to be the daughter of Olokun, the powerful Orisha who rules the deep ocean. Aje is connected to both material wealth and economic abundance. Her sacred symbol is the tiger cowrie shell, which represents prosperity and good luck. Historically, the Yoruba used cowrie shells as money to trade goods in the marketplace. Even today, cowrie shells continue to symbolize wealth in Yoruba spirituality and are often used in jewelry and art. Aje is honored as the guardian of traders, artists, and entrepreneurs. She guides her followers to success by teaching patience, wisdom, and flexibility in their business and financial decisions. She blesses with wealth those who conduct their affairs with honesty and respect.

Ajé, Spirit of Wealth and Sea
Poem and Prayer
Verse 1:1

Ajé, keeper of cowrie bright,
Your treasures glow in ocean light.
With shells that shimmer, white and small,
You share your gifts and bless us all.

Daughter of Olokun, wise and strong,
You've held the sea's great wealth so long.
You guard the deep where secrets lie,

Beneath the waves, beneath the sky.

You bring abundance, calm and clear,
And guide us when the path feels near.
With gentle tides and wisdom true,
We feel your power flowing through.

Where sea meets sand and stars above,
You teach us truth; you teach with love.
With insight sharp, you light the way,
And help us grow more each new day.
Ase.

* * *

THE POWER OF AJE'S WEALTH
Poem and Prayer
VERSE 1:2

Aje, keeper of gold and light,
You turn our darkness into bright.
With shining shells that softly gleam,
You bring to life our richest dream.

Your blessings open doors each day,
Leading us to a brighter way.
Through you, prosperity grows strong,
In your grace, we all belong.

Aje, queen of fortune's flow,
Guide our steps where blessings go.
Fill our lives with health and peace,
Let abundance never cease.
Ase.

* * *

SACRED STORIES / LEGENDS
SECTION 2

THE GOLDEN PATIENCE OF ORUNMILA
STORY 2:1

Aje was very rich, but no one really liked her. She was not kind, and her manners were bad. Many powerful Orishas, like Sango, Eshu, and Ogun, tried to be with her, but they always left angry. Aje had a strange habit - whenever she cooked for someone, she would put things in their food that they were not allowed to eat. This made the Orishas upset, and they would leave, never wanting to see her again.

One day, Orunmila, the wise Orisha, asked to marry Aje. He was not like the others. He did not care about her wealth - he wanted to help her change. Aje's father, a great king, hoped this marriage would make her better. Before deciding, Orunmila asked Ifa, the sacred oracle, for guidance. Ifa told him: "If you stay calm and never lose your way, your patience will guide you, come what may." Orunmila listened and agreed to marry Aje. But Aje wanted to test him, just like she had tested the others. She put taboos in his food to see if he would get mad. But Orunmila stayed calm and ate without complaining.

Aje was confused. No matter what tricks she played, Orunmila never lost his patience. Then, Aje tried one last trick. She went with Orunmila to visit his mother's grave. While there, she did something very disrespectful - she made a mess on the grave, waiting for Orunmila to get angry. But Orunmila did not yell. He did not get upset. He stood still and watched, calm as ever. Aje was shocked. She expected him to punish her, but he didn't. Instead, something amazing happened - the ground where she had been turned into gold! Aje could not believe her eyes. She finally understood that real power was not in being tricky or rich - it was in being wise, patient, and kind.

She felt ashamed of her actions and wanted to change. From that moment on, she was no longer mean or careless. She became kind and respectful, standing beside Orunmila as a true partner. Together, they ruled wisely, and their land was blessed with wealth and peace. Aje had learned the most important lesson - patience and goodness could turn even the worst mistakes into something beautiful.

REFLECTION & WISDOM

The story of Aje and Orunmila shows the power of patience and wisdom. Aje, once disliked for her mischief, tests Orunmila's composure by provoking him, including adding taboos to his meals and desecrating a grave. Despite these actions, Orunmila remains calm, eventually softening Aje's heart. Through his patience, Aje transforms, and the grave she defiled becomes a source of wealth. The story teaches that patience and wisdom can turn challenges into opportunities and lead to growth and prosperity.

* * *

AJE'S JOURNEY
STORY 2:2

Aje, an Orisha, was about to leave her mother, Olokun. Olokun was worried and sad because she knew the world could be harsh, and she didn't want Aje to face it alone. Olokun called upon Ifa for guidance. Ifa told her that Aje's journey would be long and difficult, and that she would travel without riches or a crown. However, Aje would find her true purpose along the way. Aje started her journey, feeling unsure but determined. She traveled from town to town, dressed in rags and covered in dust. In the first town, Aje hoped to find a place to stay, but the people there were proud and rejected her. She was hurt but didn't give up. She moved on to the second town, only to face the same rejection.

By now, Aje was feeling lost and uncertain about her journey. She wondered if she would ever find a place where she belonged. Then, in the third town, Aje came across an elderly couple who welcomed her with open arms. They treated her with kindness, offering her food and shelter without any judgment. Aje, grateful for their love, revealed her true nature as a goddess and blessed them with a special gift. Aje realized that Ifa's words were true, her blessings were meant for those who showed kindness and love, not for those driven by wealth or pride. She learned that her true home was not a place filled with riches, but in the hearts of people who cared for others.

Aje continued her journey, offering blessings to those who treated her with respect and kindness. When she found people who were warm and welcoming, she stayed with them. But when their kindness faded, she moved on. In the end, Aje realized that her true home was where love and kindness grew.

REFLECTION & WISDOM

Aje's story teaches us that love and kindness are more valuable than wealth or power. Even though Aje faced rejection, she found her true home in the hearts of those who welcomed her with love. This story reminds us that being kind and caring for others brings true wealth.

* * *

AJÉ AND OSHUN
STORY 2:3

A long time ago, in a world so wide,
Oshun, the Orisha, had nowhere to hide.
She was graceful and kind, a spirit so sweet,
But she had no riches and little to eat.

Her only dress was torn and old,
She had no treasures, no silver or gold.
Each day she washed it in the river's flow,
Dreaming of better days, though they came slow.
Ajé-Shaluga, of wealth and trade,
Watched from the water where she stayed.

An orisha of kindness, so giving and true,
She saw Oshun's struggle and knew what to do.
From the river she rose, with love in her heart,
Ready to give Oshun a brand-new start.
With cowries that sparkled and treasures of gold,
She gave Oshun gifts so bold.

Her life was changed, her sorrow was gone,
With Ajé's blessings, she grew strong.
No longer poor, she walked with pride,
For Ajé's love was by her side.

This story shows us, for all to see,
Kindness and giving can set people free.
Ajé-Shaluga, so wise, so kind,
Brings blessings to all she finds.

REFLECTION & WISDOM

This story is about Oshun, the Orisha of beauty and kindness, who once lived in poverty and dreamed of a better life. Even though she was graceful, she had no wealth or comfort, and her only possession was a torn dress. One day, Ajé-Shaluga, the Orisha of wealth and prosperity, saw Oshun's struggles from the river. Moved by love, he rose from the water and blessed her with cowries and treasures, completely transforming her life. Oshun's pride and strength grew. This story teaches that kindness and generosity, like Ajé-Shaluga's gifts, have the power to lift others up and change their lives, reminding us that giving can bring freedom and strength to those in need.

* * *

INSIGHTS, OFFERINGS, RITUALS AND SPIRITUAL SIGNIFICANCE
SECTION 3

OFFERINGS AND SYMBOLS OF AJÉ

Ajé-Shaluga, the Orisha of wealth and prosperity, is honored with offerings that embody abundance, grace, and financial success. Devotees present these gifts with reverence, seeking her favor in matters of fortune, business, and stability. Common offerings to Ajé include pigeons and ducks, symbolizing care and devotion, as well as fresh flowers and water, which invoke her nurturing and purifying energy. Jewelry, coins, and cowrie shells, once used as currency, are placed on her altar as symbols of material and spiritual wealth. Candles are lit to illuminate the path to prosperity, while incense carries prayers and gratitude into the spiritual realm. Traditional food offerings include guinea fowl, honey, bananas, eggs, beans, and palm wine, all of which are linked to sustenance, sweetness, and financial growth. Mirrors are sometimes placed at her altar, reflecting opportunities and offering clarity to those seeking financial success. Ajé's sacred colors include white, symbolizing purity and divine abundance. She is also associated with the numbers five and seven, which are believed to unlock the path to prosperity. However, certain items, such as black palm oil (Adin Dudu), are avoided in her offerings out of respect for her preferences.

THE SACRED TOOLS OF AJÉ

Ajé's power is also represented through specific tools and symbols that embody her dominion over wealth and financial flow:

- **Cowrie Shells (Owo Eyo)** – The most significant emblem of Ajé, cowrie shells were once a form of currency and remain a powerful symbol of wealth, prosperity, and divination.
- **Water and the Ocean** – As the daughter of Olokun, Ajé is deeply tied to the sea, where treasures and abundance lie beneath the waves. Water, in its flowing nature, represents the continuous movement of wealth and opportunity.
- **Clay Pots or Calabashes** – These containers hold sacred offerings or spiritual items related to Ajé, symbolizing stored wealth, preservation, and the safeguarding of financial prosperity.

THE SACRED STONES OF AJÉ

Ajé's energy is also infused within certain stones and minerals that serve as conduits of her blessings:

- **Tiger Cowrie** – A rare and powerful shell closely associated with Ajé, representing financial stability and protection.
- **Pearls** – Symbolizing purity and hidden wealth, pearls reflect the treasures that lie beneath the ocean's surface.
- **Quartz** – Known for its clarity and amplifying properties, quartz enhances the energy of abundance and prosperity.
- **Gold and Precious Gems** – Long associated with power, affluence, and divine favor, these elements embody Ajé's blessings of wealth and success.
- **Herbs associated with Aje Shaluga** include patchouli, clove, basil, cinnamon, mint, and ginger.

Used in rituals, placed on altars, or carried as talismans, these sacred stones help attract prosperity and financial security, ensuring Ajé's guidance remains present in the lives of those who honor her.

FINAL THOUGHTS

Ajé is a powerful force in the manifestation of wealth, success, and abundance. Her presence teaches that prosperity is not only material but also deeply connected to wisdom, intuition, and generosity. Through devotion, offerings, and the use of her sacred symbols, devotees align themselves with the currents of financial flow and opportunity, ensuring that her blessings continue to enrich their lives.

* * *

6. THE AJOGUN
BRINGERS OF MISFORTUNE, SUFFERING AND CHAOS

UNDERSTANDING THE AJOGUN

IN THE YORUBA RELIGION, the universe is filled with spiritual forces that work to keep life in balance. Some of these forces bring blessings, while others bring challenges. The *Ajogun* are spiritual beings known for causing problems such as illness, confusion, loss, and hardship. The *Orishas* are divine forces that usually protect and support humans. When called upon, they bring blessings and help fight off negativity. In contrast, the *Ajogun* are seen as forces that bring only trouble. Some stories say the Ajogun were born when *Ìkú* (Death) was first sent to Earth, during a time when the world was out of balance. Since then, the Ajogun have roamed the Earth, playing a role in maintaining spiritual balance - especially when things begin to fall apart.

Because of this purpose, even the Orishas don't always stop the Ajogun. For example, although the Orishas can sometimes delay death, no one can avoid it forever. This shows that the Ajogun are part of the natural order of the universe. In Yoruba tradition, negative spiritual forces like death, illness, and violence are often called *Osogbos* or *Ibis*. These terms describe different kinds of spiritual imbalance. *Ìkú* (Death) is considered the leader of the Ajogun and the chief among the Osogbos. Some teachings say there are as many types of Ajogun as there are Orishas. Below are some of the most common Osogbos:

- **Ìkú** - *Death*
- **Eyo** - *Tragedy*
- **Ona** - *Suffering*
- **Arun** - *Illness*

- **Òfò** - *Loss*
- **Epe** - *Curse*
- **Ewon** - *False imprisonment*
- **Ìjà** - *Violence*
- **Tiya Tiya** - *Gossip or slander*
- **Akoba** - *Misfortune*
- **Èjó** - *Legal trouble*

* * *

How Ajogun Are Revealed

In Yoruba practice, *divination* is a sacred process used to receive messages from the spirit world. During divination, the presence of an Ajogun may be revealed. These negative forces are often shown as Osogbos or Ibis. When someone is said to be "in *Osogbo*," it means they have gone off their true spiritual path and are no longer aligned with *Ìrè*, which means positive destiny. According to Yoruba belief, every person chooses their destiny and spiritual path before coming to Earth. If someone strays from that path, the Ajogun may appear to warn them or guide them back however; this is often done in a tragic way. The Ajogun can also appear in a person's life because of bad behavior or poor character. This is where the idea of *Iwa Pele* becomes important. *Iwa Pele* means having a good and gentle character. It includes values like kindness, patience, respect, and honesty. People who live with Iwa Pele are seen as walking the right path and are more likely to live a happy and meaningful life.

Having Iwa Pele is also believed to protect a person from negative forces like the Ajogun. Another related concept is *tutu*, which means staying calm, respectful, and morally strong during difficult times. Together, Iwa Pele and tutu help a person stay in balance and avoid spiritual harm. Even though the Ajogun bring pain and struggle, they are not just here to cause harm. Their deeper purpose is to act as spiritual warnings helping people reflect on their actions, grow as individuals, and return to their true path.

* * *

SACRED STORIES / LEGENDS
SECTION 2

HOW DEATH WAS INTRODUCED TO THE WORLD
STORY 2:1

In the beginning, the world was full of peace and harmony. Life was eternal- no one died- and the connection between Heaven and Earth was open. Humans and Orishas could move freely between both realms, and everything existed in perfect balance. Then one day, wealth arrived in the form of cowrie shells. At first, it seemed like a blessing. But soon, greed began to grow in the hearts of both humans and Orishas. This greed led to arguments, jealousy, and confusion. As disorder spread across the world, the balance that once existed started to fall apart.

Seeing the chaos, Olofin -the Supreme Creator- knew something had to change. To protect the universe, Olofin commanded *Eshu* to close the portal between Heaven and Earth. This stopped the free movement between the two realms. Then, Olofin sent *Ìkú* (Death) to Earth, hoping it would restore balance by putting an end to the corruption caused by greed. Ìkú, once an Orisha, was transformed into a powerful force meant to correct the growing disorder. But instead of carefully restoring harmony, Ìkú acted without mercy. It moved across the Earth like a storm, destroying everything in its path. What was meant to bring balance instead brought devastation. Eternal life came to an end, and all of creation was in danger of being wiped out.

When Olofin saw the destruction Ìkú had caused, he understood that its power had gone too far. Though Ìkú had been sent to fix the problem, it had only made things worse. To prevent total collapse, Olofin removed Ìkú's Orisha status and limited its power. From that moment on, Ìkú would no longer act freely. It could only come when truly needed- as part of the natural rhythm of life and death. With this change, the Law of Balance was re-established. Life returned to Earth, and nature began to heal. Death remained with all its manifestations, but it now existed in harmony with life, no longer threatening to destroy everything all at once.

REFLECTION & WISDOM

This story teaches that balance is the foundation of life. Greed disrupted the harmony between Heaven and Earth, and Death was introduced to restore order. But even corrective forces like Ìkú must be limited, or they can cause more harm than good. The re-establishment of the Law of Balance reminds us that life, death, and wealth must exist in harmony. Yoruba teachings, especially through Ifá divination, help guide people back to balance when it's lost.

* * *

INSIGHTS, OFFERINGS, RITUALS AND SPIRITUAL SIGNIFICANCE
SECTION 3

DIVINATION, SACRIFICE, AND DESTINY

WHY DOES DIVINATION MATTER? Divination is a sacred practice that helps us understand spiritual issues and receive guidance. It reveals whether someone is in Ìrè (alignment) or Ìbì (imbalance), often caused by the presence of Ajogun.

WHAT IS THE PURPOSE OF ÈBÓ (SACRIFICE)?

When Ajogun are present, Ifá may prescribe an èbó - a meaningful offering to restore harmony. Èbó is not a bribe, but a spiritual exchange. It may involve food, animals, money, or promises to make a change. Èbó serves to bring blessings from the Orishas and ancestors, reconnect you with your higher self (Ori), calm or remove Ajogun, and remove spiritual blockages.

RETURNING TO YOUR PATH

Everyone is born with a destined path. However, life's challenges - and our own actions - can cause us to stray. Ajogun often serves as a wake-up call. Through divination and sacrifice, we can return to peace, purpose, and our rightful path.

* * *

7. Ayangalu
Orisha of the Drum and Rhythm

A Closer Look at Ayangalu

Ayangalu, also called Ayan Agalu, is the Orisha (spirit) of music and rhythm. He is known as the first drummer and the creator of the talking drum, called the Dùndún. This drum is special because it "talks," connecting the physical world with the spirit world and carrying the voices of spirits and ancestors. Ayangalu guides musicians, drummers, dancers, and singers to use rhythm to honor ancestors, communicate with the divine, and bring healing. He teaches them how music can touch the heart and mind, helping people feel peace and strength. Music is a powerful healing tool because its rhythms calm the mind, lift the spirit, and restore balance to the body and soul.

In traditional Yoruba culture, the talking drum is played during ceremonies, festivals, and prayers. Its beats carry wisdom and messages from the divine. Playing the drum honors Ayangalu and reminds us of the close connection between ancestors and the spirit world. In many African cultures, music is the main way to enter a trance-like state, helping people connect with their higher selves and the spirit world. The drumbeat often sounds like a heartbeat, and some believe it represents the sound of life itself. Music creates a bridge between the earthly world and Orun (heaven), the spiritual realm. Through this connection, people receive important messages, guidance, and wisdom from ancestors and divine beings. The rhythms and melodies reach deep into the subconscious mind, influencing thoughts and emotions in ways words cannot. This power helps heal the body, mind, and soul by restoring balance, easing stress, and opening the heart to peace. Music also brings joy and comfort, especially during hard times like grief or pain. It lifts spirits, soothes worries, and inspires hope.

Because of its healing power and spiritual connection, music is sacred and honored in many cultures as a divine gift.

AYAN'S GIFT: A PRAYER OF HEALING
Poem and Prayer
VERSE 1:1

Great Ayan, Orisha of rhythm and sound,
Your sacred music echoes all around.
Through talking drums, your tales arise,
Of Yorùbá realms beneath the skies.

Through you, the earth's own heartbeat flows,
In every rhythm, our culture grows.
Ayan, we honor your sacred art,
For it binds our spirit and culture as a part.

The drum speaks, a voice so wise,
Reaching the earth and touching the skies.
Its patterns tell of things unseen,
Ayan's whispers were calm and serene.

We humbly ask you, keeper of sound,
Bless the music we create all around.
Let every beat and melody we send
Carry your healing to wounds that mend.

May our rhythms calm troubled minds,
Bring peace and hope to all humankind.
Transform our songs into a light that shines.
In darkest places, healing all who listen.

Guide our hands, our voices, and souls,
So, through our music, the broken are whole.
Let our art be a sacred gift,
A balm that heals and spirits lift.

Ayan, receive the prayer we send,
Grant your blessings without end.
Through the power of song and sound,
May healing and peace all around be found.
Ase.

* * *

SACRED STORIES / LEGENDS
SECTION 2

HOW AYANGALU CREATED THE FIRST DRUM
STORY 2:1

A long time ago, people couldn't hear the Orishas. They wanted to understand their messages, but the world was silent. No one knew how to speak to the powerful spirits. One day, Ayangalu, the Orisha of music and sound, sat by Ogun's River, thinking. As he listened to the world around him, he heard the wind blowing through the trees and the water splashing against the rocks. These sounds gave him a big idea. Ayangalu found a strong iroko tree and carved a frame from its wood. He took a piece of goat skin, blessed it, and stretched it over the frame. When he hit the drum, it made a deep, powerful sound: *bata-bata-bata*. The sound traveled across the land and into the sky. The Orishas like Shango, Yemoja, and Oya heard the sound and were amazed. Even Olodumare, the creator of everything, smiled and said, "Now people can speak to the Orishas." Ayangalu made more drums so that people could share their prayers, feelings, and stories. Every beat talked about beginnings, struggles, and victories.Today, when the batá drums are played during ceremonies, the Orishas still listen and answer. Thanks to Ayangalu, music became the bridge between people and the spirit world.

REFLECTION & WISDOM

The story of Ayangalu shows how one person's creativity can change the world. By paying attention to the simple sounds of nature, Ayangalu found a way to connect people and the Orishas. His drum brought hope, communication, and unity. This teaches us that even small ideas can lead to big changes when we listen carefully, stay creative, and use our talents to help others. It reminds us that music, art, and creativity have the power to bring people closer together and make the world better.

* * *

THE TEST OF SILENCE
STORY 2 2

Long ago, there was a clever trickster who wanted to silence the sound of the drum. He knew that the drums carried the voices of the Orishas, connecting people to the divine. If he could stop their rhythm, he could break that connection. But Ayangalu, the spirit of the drum, would not allow silence to take over. He knew the power of the drum was too important to be lost. Determined, he traveled deep into the land of the ancestors, where the spirits rest. There, he fasted and danced, pushing himself to his limits. For nine long days, Ayangalu moved with grace, listening to the whispers of the sacred forest. On the ninth night, the spirit of the first drummer appeared before him. This ancient spirit taught Ayangalu the rhythm he had once created, a beat so strong it could never be forgotten. As Ayangalu struck the drum, its powerful sound filled the air, breaking the trickster's curse. The silence was gone, and the world was alive again with music. He returned home, his heart filled with strength, and played the batá drum once more. "Bata-bata-bata!" The sound echoed, bringing back light and life. The drums became a bridge between people and the divine, their rhythms connecting every heart.

REFLECTION & WISDOM

This story teaches us that rhythm is more than just sound -it is the heartbeat of life, uniting us all. It reminds us that even when someone tries to break our connection to our culture, our ancestors, or our spiritual path, we can find strength in tradition. No matter how much silence or darkness may try to take over, the spirit of the drum and the power of unity will always bring back the light.

* * *

INSIGHTS, OFFERINGS, RITUALS AND SPIRITUAL SIGNIFICANCE
Section 3

THE TALKING DRUM: VOICE OF THE YORUBA PEOPLE

The talking drum is a unique West African instrument, especially among the Yoruba people of Nigeria. It has an hourglass shape with two drumheads connected by adjustable leather cords, which control the pitch when squeezed or loosened. Skilled drummers can mimic human speech by adjusting the tension and rhythm, allowing the drum to "talk" and convey messages, proverbs, or praises. Traditionally, it has been used for communication, storytelling, and religious ceremonies, especially in honoring the Orishas and transmitting messages. The talking drum is not just an instrument but a vital link between people, spirits, and culture.

* * *

THE CALL OF THE TALKING DRUM

The talking drum begins to speak,
Its rhythms are soft, its pulse unique.
A humming sound, a sacred call,
It weaves a trance that binds us all.

The cords are pulled, the pitch does change,
The drum becomes a voice, so strange.
It mimics words we cannot hear,
But through its hum, the gods draw near.
With every beat, a spirit wakes,
The Orishas come, the earth shakes.

Their presence fills the air with grace,
As sacred rhythms find their place.
The drum's embrace is deep and wide,
A portal where the gods reside.

In every sound, the world transforms,
A trance of music, pure and warm.

So, listen close when the drum does play,
For in its beat, the spirits stay,
And through its sound, we are made one,
As Orishas gather, at night or in the sun.
Ase.

* * *

8. Ayelala
Orisha of Justice, Truth, and Sacred Oaths

A Closer Look at Ayelala

Ayelalá, the Orisha of justice, truth, and retribution, enforces moral integrity and ensures wrongdoers face consequences. She is invoked in legal disputes and sworn oaths, with severe punishment for those who break their word. Her retribution is swift, often manifesting as illness, misfortune, or even death. Feared yet revered, Ayelalá protects those who uphold honesty, granting them peace and prosperity. She restores balance, avenges the wronged, and ensures justice prevails. Her name is called upon in daily speech as a reminder of divine justice, and in rituals, oaths are sworn with water and a knife, symbolizing purity and truth. She also communicates through dreams, revealing hidden truths and impending consequences.

Ayelalá's Sacred Oath
A Prayer and Poem
Verse 1:1

Ayelalá, spirit strong and wise,
You see the truth and hear all cries.
We call your name with respect and care,
Knowing your justice is always fair.

With water pure and a knife held high,
We speak our oath beneath the sky.
We promise truth in all we do,
And pray you help us stay strong and true.

You see through lies and every trick,

Your judgment comes both fast and quick.
If someone cheats or breaks a vow,
You bring them justice here and now.

A snake might bite, or storms may roar,
If someone lies, they'll feel much more.
Illness or trouble may appear,
A sign your power is always near.

But if we speak with honest heart,
Your blessings come and never part.
You keep us safe, you help us grow,
And guide us when we need to know.

In dreams you speak, in signs you show
The truth we need, the path to go.
So, Ayelalá, hear our prayer:
Help us be truthful everywhere.

* * *

A PRAYER TO AYELALÁ, GUARDIAN OF TRUTH AND JUSTICE
VERSE 1:2

Ayelalá, fierce and divine,
Guardian of truth, your light will shine.
With your righteous wrath, you right the wrong,
Your justice is swift, your spirit strong.

We call to you with hearts so true,
To honor the word and be just too.
Guide us in fairness, show us the way,
That we may walk in truth each day.

Strike down deceit, expose the lies,
With your wisdom, make justice rise.
Protect the innocent, and avenge the wronged,
Your power is mighty, your justice long.

In your name, we stand with grace,
Seeking fairness, in every place.
Ayelalá, we honor you,
With truth in our hearts, and justice too.
So be it now, so it shall be,
With Ayelalá's justice, we are free.
Ase!

* * *

SACRED STORIES / LEGENDS
SECTION 2

THE RISE OF AYELALÁ
STORY 2:1

Ayelalá was born into slavery, her freedom taken from her the moment she entered the world. She lived in a place where cruelty was common, and her life was controlled by those who saw her as nothing more than property. Though she was kind and strong, the world around her was unfair, treating her as if she had no voice or worth. Despite her hardships, Ayelalá remained devoted to truth and the divine. She lived with honesty and faith, never straying from her path. But one day, people began to whisper lies about her. She was accused of a terrible crime she did not commit. Because she was a slave, no one cared to listen to her side of the story. There was no trial, no chance for her to prove her innocence. The people had already decided her fate.

Without mercy, they sentenced her to death. As she was dragged to her execution, tears streamed down her face. "This world is unjust!" she cried, her voice filled with pain. They buried her alive, and though her body grew still, her cry for justice did not fade. Soon, the truth came to light. The people realized they had been wrong. Ayelalá had been innocent all along, and their guilt weighed heavily on them. To make amends, they built a shrine in her honor, hoping to ease the pain of their mistake. But Ayelalá's story did not end with her death. At a crossroads, her spirit awakened, rising beyond the suffering she had endured. No longer a slave, she became a goddess of justice, powerful and unchained. Those who lie and do wrong now fear her name, for Ayelalá ensures that truth will always come to light. Her story teaches an important lesson: justice may be delayed, but it will never be denied. Truth will always shine through, and those who act unfairly will one day face the consequences of their actions.

REFLECTION & WISDOM

Ayelalá's story teaches that truth has a power that cannot be destroyed. Born into slavery and treated with cruelty, she remained devoted to honesty and faith. Even when she was falsely accused and buried alive without a fair trial, her spirit did not fade. After her death, the truth was revealed, and those who wronged her built a shrine to honor her memory. Rising beyond her suffering, Ayelalá became a powerful goddess of justice. Today, she stands as a symbol of truth, punishing lies and protecting the innocent. Her story reminds us that while injustice may prevail for a time, it cannot last forever, truth and justice will always rise.

* * *

INSIGHTS, OFFERINGS, RITUALS AND SPIRITUAL SIGNIFICANCE
SECTION 3

OFFERINGS TO AYELALÁ

To honor Ayelalá, offerings are made at sunrise, symbolizing devotion and respect. Common offerings include kola nut (Obi), palm wine, and cowrie shells. A goat or hen may also be offered as a symbol of reverence. Red feathers, white cloths, and palm fronds represent strength, purity, and respect. Fragrant flowers, such as roses and hibiscus, and fruits like bananas and pineapples symbolize beauty, growth, and abundance. Fresh water is offered for cleansing and renewal, often placed in a sacred vessel. Candles and lanterns are lit to represent light, clarity, and guidance, honoring Ayelalá as the bringer of truth and justice. Other offerings may include gin, palm oil, honey, and white animals, all symbolizing purity and sustenance. Each offering is a heartfelt expression of devotion, seeking Ayelalá's guidance, protection, and justice.

* * *

9. BABALÚ-AYÉ, SOPONA
ORISHA OF DISEASE, HEALING AND COMPASSION

A CLOSER LOOK AT BABALU-AYE

BABALÚ-AYÉ IS a powerful Orisha who embodies the dual nature of illness and healing, representing the balance between life and death. He walks the path between suffering and restoration, deeply connected to diseases like smallpox and leprosy, yet his touch also brings relief and cures. Known for his limping steps and the marks of illness on his body, Babalú-Ayé symbolizes the strength gained through hardship and the resilience required to overcome it. Though often feared for his ability to bring sickness, Babalú-Ayé is equally revered for his healing powers. He is a guardian of the body and a protector of life, offering not only physical healing but also spiritual guidance. His wisdom is found through suffering, teaching us the importance of balance, grace, and endurance in the face of adversity. Babalú-Ayé's connection to the Earth is profound, symbolizing the soil that nurtures life and the dust to which all life returns. His teachings show that sickness can be both a challenge and an opportunity for growth, resilience, and transformation. Adorned with cowrie shells and white garments, he reflects both the darkness of illness and the light of healing, emphasizing the interconnectedness of life's cycles. He is a healer of both body and mind, offering lessons in endurance, rebirth, and the need to face life's difficulties with strength and compassion. Babalú-Ayé's limping steps serve as a reminder of the power of renewal and the importance of rising with courage each new day. His presence teaches that true wealth is found in the wisdom gained from enduring and overcoming life's struggles.

BABALÚ-AYÉ: HEALER AND GUARDIAN
A Poem and Prayer
VERSE I:I

Babalú-Ayé walks the land,
With healing power in his hand.
Where sickness starts, he's near that place,
Bringing health and showing grace.

He comes from God with strength so wide,
To heal the pain, we feel inside.
Though people fear the things he brings,
He also heals all kinds of things.

When fevers rise and skin feels sore,
He helps us feel strong once more.
Even though he walks with pain,
He gives us hope and health again.

He guards us from bad diseases,
From things that hurt and make us sad.
With gifts of grain, we ask today:
Please help us, kind Babalú-Ayé.
Ase.

* * *

BABALÚ-AYÉ: THE CYCLE OF LIFE AND HEALING
VERSE 1:2

Babalú-Ayé, the Earth's own breath,
He walks between the realms of life and death.
From soil and stone, his power grows,
In illness and suffering, his wisdom flows.

He guards the body, both strong and frail,
The god of smallpox, who makes us wail.
Through pain and change, his path we trace,
In sickness and healing, we find our place.

With vessels full of holes, he stands,
A symbol of life's shifting hands.
The sores that pock his sacred skin,

Reflect the battle fought within.

In secrecy, his power lies,
Hidden beneath the darkened skies.
Some truths must wait to be revealed,
In silence, his strength is sealed.

Once exiled, limping in his pain,
He walks alone yet breaks the chain.
Through movement, exile turns to light,
From darkness' depths, he takes his flight.

He heals with herbs, both.
Poison and cure, through roads
And forests, his steps endure.
He moves between worlds, both dead and alive,
In his cycles, all beings survive. From
Death to resurrection, his path unfolds,
A story of life that forever holds.
Babalú-Ayé, in pain and grace,
A guide through time, in every place.

* * *

STRAW OF STRENGTH
VERSE 1:3

Babalú-Ayé, strong and tall,
Wrapped in straw, he walks by all.
His body marked with pox so deep,
A secret pain must keep.

With staff in hand, he moves with care,
Bringing sickness or healing air.
Feared by many, yet respected too,

He can heal or harm, depending on you.
No one dares to cross his might,
For Babalú-Ayé holds both dark and light.

* * *

SACRED STORIES / LEGENDS
SECTION 2

BABALU AYE'S SACRED LESSON
STORY 2:1

A long time ago, when the world was new and full of blessings from Olodumare, each Orisha was given a special gift. Oshun was given the power to rule over rivers. Yemaya was put in charge of the oceans. Shango was given control over thunder and storms. Babalu Aye also wanted a gift. He asked Olodumare for the ability to love all women. Olodumare said yes but gave him an important rule: on one special day, Babalu Aye must control himself and not give in to temptation. If he broke this rule, he would face serious punishment. At first, everything went well. But when the sacred day came, Babalu Aye gave in to his desire and broke the rule. Because of this, he was cursed. His body became covered in sores, and he got very sick. He lost his health, his money, and his happiness. After a long time of suffering, Babalu Aye realized his mistake. He learned that true strength means being able to control yourself, even when it's hard. He also learned that respecting divine rules is very important. Babalu Aye changed his ways and became a symbol of healing and hope for others.

REFLECTION & WISDOM

Babalu Aye's story teaches us that having special gifts comes with responsibility. He shows us that self-control and following important rules help us avoid trouble. Even if we make mistakes, we can always learn, change, and grow stronger.

* * *

THE STORY OF BABALÚ-AYÉ AND OYA
STORY 2 2

Babalú-Ayé was once powerful, but he became very sick, covered in painful sores. Ashamed of his condition, he isolated himself, fearing rejection by people and the other Orishas. One day, Ogun, the Orisha of strength, found Babalú-Ayé and urged him not to hide. "You belong with us," Ogun said. Though embarrassed, Babalú-Ayé followed Ogun, but when he approached the other Orishas, they turned away in fear when they saw his sores. Feeling even worse, he was about to leave when Oya, the Orisha of wind and change, saw his pain. She sent a gentle breeze to surround him. As the wind touched Babalú-Ayé, his sores healed, and his skin became smooth and healthy again. Everyone, amazed by the miracle, no longer feared him and respected his strength. With Oya by his side, Babalú-Ayé felt whole again. Together, they helped guide spirits and brought peace.

REFLECTION & WISDOM

This story teaches that even in our hardest and most painful times, when we feel lost, weak, or abandoned, hope, healing, and strength can still emerge. Babalú-Ayé's journey shows that no matter how broken or ashamed we feel, there is always the possibility for change. It was through the support of Ogun's encouragement and Oya's healing winds that Babalú-Ayé was able to overcome his illness and isolation. Just like Babalú-Ayé, when we feel rejected or misunderstood, we may find the strength to heal and transform with the right guidance and support from others.

FROM SICKNESS TO STRENGTH
STORY 2:3

Babalú-Ayé was once a powerful king, respected for his strength and authority. But one night, he broke a sacred taboo by sleeping during a holy observance. Soon after, illness struck him suddenly and severely. His body became covered with leprosy, and the king who once inspired fear and respect was now weakened and suffering.

When his people saw what had happened, fear took hold of them. Believing his condition to be a curse or danger, they cast him out of the village. Babalú-Ayé was left alone, isolated from the world he once ruled, carrying both physical pain and deep emotional sorrow. In his distress, his brother Esu Elegba found him. Unlike the others, Elegba did not turn away. He listened and then urged Babalú-Ayé to seek guidance from Orunmila, the wise oracle who understands the paths of destiny. Babalú-Ayé followed this advice.

When he reached Orunmila, he was told that healing would require patience, humility, and obedience. Orunmila instructed him to take offerings of grain and to work with dogs as part of his cleansing and healing path, and to follow the guidance of Ifá with faith and discipline. Though the journey was difficult, Babalú-Ayé committed himself fully to the process. He endured hardship, exposure to the elements, and the pain of his condition. Over time, something began to change. Rain fell upon him, dogs approached and tended to his wounds, and slowly his body began to heal. As his health returned, so did his strength and dignity. The man who had once been cast out was restored, transformed not only in body but also in spirit. His story became a lesson for others: even in the deepest suffering and isolation, healing is possible. With patience, humility, and perseverance, restoration can come after great trials.

REFLECTION & WISDOM

This poem recounts the story of Babalú-Ayé, a once-mighty king who fell ill with leprosy after dishonoring a sacred day. Rejected by his people, he was guided by his brother Elegba to seek wisdom from Orunmila, who revealed that healing would come through faith, dogs, and offerings of grain. Enduring hardship and aided by divine forces, Babalú-Ayé overcame his suffering and regained his strength. His journey became a lesson in perseverance, reminding all that even in times of pain and isolation, faith, resilience, and love can lead to healing and renewal.

* * *

BABALÚ-AYÉ'S DOGS
STORY 2:4

Babalú-Ayé was once strong, but he became very sick. His body was covered with painful sores, and he was in a lot of suffering. When the people in his village saw him, they became afraid. Instead of helping him, they turned away and cast him out. Babalú-Ayé was left completely alone. He wandered through fields and forests with no home and no one to care for him. He was hurt, tired, and lonely. Each day was harder than the last, and he felt like he had been forgotten by everyone. One day, while he was walking, dogs began to follow him. At first, he did not understand why they were there. But the dogs did not harm him or leave him. They stayed close to him wherever he went. The dogs became his companions. They licked his wounds and helped ease his pain. They stayed with him in the heat and in the cold, giving him comfort when no one else would. Slowly, Babalú-Ayé began to feel less alone. He was deeply moved by their loyalty and kindness. He blessed the dogs and showed them gratitude. From that time on, he said that wherever dogs are, his healing presence would also be there. Over time, the story of Babalú-Ayé and the dogs became well known. It became a lesson about kindness, healing, and how even in the worst suffering, help and compassion can appear in unexpected ways.

* * *

REFLECTION & WISDOM

This poem tells the story of Babalú-Ayé, the Orisha of healing and disease, who was abandoned by people due to his illness and suffering. Wandering alone, he found comfort in the loyalty of dogs, who tended to his wounds and stayed by his side through hardship. Moved by their kindness, Babalú-Ayé blessed them, declaring that wherever dogs are found, his healing spirit will be near. From that day on, dogs became sacred symbols of compassion and protection, representing the divine love and mercy of Babalú-Ayé.

* * *

INSIGHTS, OFFERINGS, RITUALS AND SPIRITUAL SIGNIFICANCE
SECTION 3

OFFERINGS TO BABALÚ-AYÉ

Babalú-Ayé, the Orisha of disease, healing, and resilience, is honored with offerings such as palm oil, roasted corn, black-eyed peas, grains, beans, coffee, and wine. Ritual sacrifices of goats and roosters are also part of his veneration. Peanuts and sesame seeds are strictly avoided due to his sacred taboos. In Santería, he is linked with Saint Lazarus, and his power is represented by sacred items like coral, clay, onyx, lead, and cat's eye stones. His sacred colors, brown, black, and deep purple, symbolize mystery, transformation, and resilience. As a healer and protector, he is honored with myrrh, clove, and rosemary, guiding his followers toward physical and spiritual healing.

THE SACRED TOOLS OF BABALÚ-AYÉ

Babalú-Ayé is also honored with specific tools that represent his journey and powers. These include crutches or a walking stick, symbolizing his own journey through suffering, a broom for purification, an earthen pot representing his connection to the earth, and a beaded gourd used in rituals to invoke his energy. His offerings often include cowrie shells, dry corn, and black-eyed peas, symbols of survival and sustenance. His sacred colors carry deep meaning: brown represents the earth and endurance; black stands for suffering and transformation; purple signifies healing and wisdom; and white, used occasionally, symbolizes purity and cleansing. These colors reflect his dual nature as both a bringer of affliction and a powerful healer. Animals such as dogs, vultures, and goats are sacred to him, and rituals often involve herbs like ewe tete and moringa. Together, these elements embody his role in guiding followers toward healing, protection, and spiritual growth.

A BATH FOR SPIRITUAL HEALING

To cleanse the spirit and help drive away illness, gather the following herbs:

- *Bay leaves for wisdom*
- *Clove for strength*
- *Rosemary for purification*
- *Rue to banish sickness*
- *Coffee for grounding*
- *Purple onions to draw out illness*
- *Sage for wisdom and clearing the darkness*

In a pot of water, combine these sacred gifts and bring them to a boil, then reduce the heat to release their healing essence. Strain the liquid and prepare a bath for spiritual renewal. While preparing the bath, say a prayer:

"Babalú-Ayé, hear me today, Healer of body, spirit, and soul, Grant me your blessing to make me whole. Cleanse me of sickness, restore my breath, Guard me in life and shield me from death."

Light a purple candle to accompany the ritual. Let it burn until it extinguishes, keeping its glow near the bath to guard and bless the space. As the candle flickers, let your heart be still. Feel the healing energies, the calm, and the will. Immerse yourself fully in the cleansing brew and let it wash over you, renewing you. Ase!

10. DADA
ORISHA OF INFANTS, FERTILITY, AND VEGETATION

A CLOSER LOOK AT DADA

DADA, also known as Ibani or Obanene, is a gentle yet powerful Orisha who protects babies and newborns. She is deeply connected to the beginning of life and is honored as a guardian of innocence, growth, and new beginnings. In addition to caring for children, Dada governs over plants, herbs, and everything that grows from the earth. Her deep connection to nature, life, and the rhythms of creation make her widely known as the Orisha of nurturing. In Yoruba culture, children born with naturally locked or coiled hair are believed to be specially blessed by Dada. These children are considered sacred and thought to carry strong spiritual energy. Because of this, Dada is deeply respected in communities that honor traditional Yoruba beliefs. Her presence is felt both in the home and in nature. She protects not only infants but also baby animals, young plants, and the entire cycle of reproduction and growth. Dada sustains the earth's ability to support life. Mothers often call on her for protection over their children, while farmers and healers seek her blessings during planting, harvesting, and times of healing. Dada's origins vary across Yoruba stories. In some traditions, she is said to be the daughter of Obatala, the wise and pure Orisha of creation. In others, she is considered the sister of Shango, the powerful Orisha of thunder and lightning. Regardless of her lineage, Dada is known as a protector, healer, and mother to all. Her spirit lives on in the cry, laughter, and playfulness of infants and in the thriving growth of crops, constant reminders of life's ability to renew, flourish, and thrive.

DADA, THE SISTER OF SHANGO
VERSE 1:1

51

Dada, the sister, fierce and strong,
Raised Shango, helped him along.
With wisdom deep, she leads the path,
Guiding Shango through storm and wrath.

A mother, a protector, powerful and wise,
She sees the world through knowing eyes.
Her hands, like the earth, steady and true,
Nurturing life as it begins anew.

She raised her brother, taught him to stand,
A warrior of the heavens, with a guiding hand.
Dada, the Orisha, with power untold,
Her heart like fire, her spirit bold.

Through all of life, she stands as a guide,
A protector, a healer, always by our side.
From the heavens to the earth, her influence wide,
Dada's strength is in all things, far and wide.

The sister of Shango, with love and grace,
Her power endures in time and space.

* * *

SACRED STORIES / LEGENDS
SECTION 2

DADA, PROTECTOR OF INFANTS
STORY 2:1

A long time ago, in a land full of fear and danger, a cruel king made a terrible rule: all newborn babies had to be killed. He was afraid that one of them might grow up and take away his power. Dada, a strong and loving mother, refused to let that happen. She promised to protect the babies, no matter what. She knew she couldn't fight the king's army alone, so she needed help. Dada prayed to Elegua, the Orisha who controls roads, paths, and choices. "Please, show me how to keep the babies safe," she begged. Elegua heard her and appeared at the crossroads. He told her, "Follow the secret paths that no one else can see. They will lead you to safety." Moving quickly, Dada carried as many babies as she could. She traveled through dark forests, across rivers, and over rocky hills. Sometimes she could hear the king's soldiers nearby, searching for her. She hid behind trees and under bushes, holding the babies close and whispering to keep them quiet.

Finally, after a long journey, Dada found a hidden grove filled with tall, strong Ceiba trees. These trees were sacred and powerful. They created a shield that kept out evil and danger. Under the wide branches of the Ceiba trees, Dada placed the babies. They slept peacefully for the first time in days. Dada cried not from sadness, but from happiness and relief. She stayed in the grove, guarding the children day and night. She made sure they had food, sang them songs, and told them stories to keep them brave. As they grew, the babies learned about kindness, courage, and the power of love. Over time, Dada's bravery became a legend. People said you could still hear her songs if you sat quietly under a Ceiba tree. The trees became a symbol of safety and hope, standing tall to remind everyone that even in the darkest times, love and courage can win.

REFLECTION & WISDOM

Dada's story shows that love and courage can overcome even the greatest dangers. Guided by Elegua, she risked everything to protect innocent lives, finding safety beneath the sacred Ceiba trees. Her bravery reminds us that true strength means trusting in guidance and acting with love, even in fear. When we stand for others, we plant seeds of hope that can last for generations.

* * *

INSIGHTS, OFFERINGS, RITUALS AND SPIRITUAL SIGNIFICANCE
SECTION 3

OFFERINGS TO DADA AT THE CEIBA TREE

Offerings are typically placed near a Ceiba tree, but if one is not available, they can be left at a large tree in the woods to honor Dada. Common offerings include fruits, vegetables, flowers, incense, grains, candles, and female animals such as goats, hens, and pigeons. These offerings seek her protection, help with fertility, and assistance in times of danger. Parents may offer these gifts to ask for blessings related to fertility, health, or the protection of their infants and newborns. Stones associated with Dada include Agate, Jasper, and Garnet.

PRAYER TO DADA

Dada, mother of all life, divine and true,
With your love, the world is made anew.
From the earth below to the skies above,
In every seed, we feel your love.
You shield the innocent with your gentle care,
Guiding us through darkness, through every prayer.

Protector of infants, nurturer of all,
We answer your call; we heed your call.
Grant strength to the newborn, love to the weak,
In your embrace, we find all we seek.
From the Ceiba's shade, your spirit flows,
In your wisdom, life forever grows.

Dada, with heart both fierce and kind,
Bless our hearts, our souls, and our minds.
We offer these gifts with reverence and grace,
May your blessings shine upon this sacred space.
So be it now, so it shall be,
With Dada's love, we are set free.
Ase!

* * *

11. Egbe-Orun
Our Heavenly Mates

A Closer Look at Egbe

In the Yoruba tradition, *Egbe Orun* refers to a group of spiritual companions linked to an individual's soul before birth. The term *"Egbe"* means "group" or "society," and *"Orun"* translates to "heaven" or "spiritual world." These companions are like close allies in the spirit realm. Some individuals may make promises with their Egbe before they are born. They might forget these commitments after birth, which could lead to certain challenges or obstacles in their lives. Even though they are often unseen, our Egbe remain with us, offering guidance through dreams, feelings, signs, and divination.

Maintaining a strong relationship with your Egbe Orun is crucial for your spiritual journey. These companions oversee and guide you throughout your life on Earth. Neglecting this connection can manifest as emotional difficulties, relationship issues, or financial problems. Such challenges might be signs that your Egbe are trying to get your attention, or that pre-birth commitments need to be fulfilled. To honor and appease the Egbe Orun, practitioners engage in rituals and offerings. These may include specific prayers, sacrifices and rituals that are done to help rebuild or strengthen one's connection to their Egbe. Regular engagement with one's Egbe Orun is believed to restore harmony and ensure a prosperous and balanced life. As children, we are often closely connected to the spiritual realm and surrounded by many unseen beings. But as we grow older and become more focused on the material world, this spiritual awareness tends to fade. Feelings of sadness, confusion, or not belonging may arise when a person becomes disconnected from their Egbe. In such cases, it may be necessary to rekindle this spiritual bond. Through the practices of Ifa and

Orisha traditions, special ceremonies can help restore the connection to one's Egbe, bringing peace, inner strength, and a renewed sense of purpose.

EGBE ORUN: THE SACRED BOND
A Prayer and Poem
VERSE I:I

Egbe Orun, my soul's true kin,
You knew me well before life did begin.
In Heaven's light, we danced as one,
Before my journey had begun.

There in Orun, so pure, so bright,
You helped me choose my path of light.
With love you watched me cross the gate,
To Earth below, to meet my fate.

You stayed behind, but never far,
Your whispers reach me where you are.
Though I forget, you still remain,
A voice that calls through joy and pain.

In lonely hours or restless dreams,
You stir the soul beneath the seams.
You guide my steps, you guard my way,
Though I may wander, still you stay.

Forgive me when I lose the thread,
When I forget the words we said.
I bring you offerings from the heart,
To mend the ties that drift apart.

Oh sacred bond that time can't break,
I call you now, for memory's sake.
Be near me in both night and day,
And light my spirit when I pray.

Egbe Orun, my closest guides,

You are my strength where love resides.
Until I rise and soar above,
Keep me safe with your endless love.
Ase.

* * *

HEAVENLY COMPANIONS
VERSE 1:2

Before we came to earth to live,
We had a place where love could give,
A special group we called our own,
In heaven's realm, we were not alone.

Egbe is the name for a group or clan,
In the heavens, we made our plan,
To come to earth, to live and grow,
But we forgot, as we didn't know.

Our Egbe Orun, our spirit friends,
Were with us then and still transcend,
They play with us, they laugh and sing,
And guide us through this earthly thing.

When we choose to live below,
We leave behind what we used to know,
Our Egbe stays to watch and guide,
Even though we may forget and hide.

Sometimes life can make us stray,
And Egbe calls to show the way,
Through dreams or signs, they try to show,
The promises we made long ago.

If you seek to learn more true,
Your Egbe can help, and guide you too,
Through prayers, offerings, and love,
We connect with them from up above.

Egbe Orun, our family bright,
Helps us find peace and set things right.
They're always near, they always care,
A bond of love beyond compare.

* * *

SACRED STORIES / LEGENDS
SECTION 2

THE PROMISE TO THE EGBE ORUN
STORY 2:1

In the Odu Ose Ogunda, a powerful story is told about three children who made a sacred promise before leaving heaven. In the land of spirits, known as Egbe Orun, they vowed that if they ever forgot their spiritual duties, they would return after seven years. This promise was bound to their destiny and could not be ignored. When these children were born into the earthly world, their mothers sought guidance. On the eighth day, following tradition, they visited a Babalawo to learn about their children's fate. The Babalawo listened carefully and then shared his wisdom: "These children made a promise before they were born.

They have forgotten their duties from heaven and now sacrifices must be made. If you do not honor their spiritual bond, they will return to Egbe Orun after seven years. But be wise do not waste your money on celebrations. Instead, focus on the offerings that truly matter." Each mother then made a choice. The first two ignored the Babalawo's warning. Instead of making the proper sacrifices, they spent their money on grand celebrations, throwing feasts and enjoying music. Their children grew up happily, but as the seventh year approached, an unseen force loomed over them. When the time came, both children fell ill. No remedy could save them, for their promise had been broken. As foretold, their spirits returned to Egbe Orun, leaving their mothers in sorrow.

But the third mother was different. She listened carefully and followed the instructions. With faith and humility, she made the necessary sacrifices, honoring her child's spiritual bond. When the seventh year arrived, her child remained strong and healthy. The spirits of Egbe Orun were pleased, and the child's life continued, their connection to both worlds now in balance. This story teaches an important lesson: our choices have consequences, and honoring spiritual obligations is essential. The unseen world influences the physical world, and when we respect our divine connections, we receive protection and guidance. The lesson of Ose Ogunda reminds us to remain faithful to our promises, for small actions can shape our destiny in ways we may not see.

REFLECTION & WISDOM

The story from the Odu Ose Ogunda tells of three children who, before their birth, made a sacred promise to the Egbe Orun, vowing to return to heaven after seven years if they forgot the sacrifices owed to their celestial family. Upon their birth, their mothers sought guidance from a Babalawo, who advised them to make offerings to honor the Egbe and ensure their children's well-being. Two of the mothers ignored the advice, spending their wealth on celebrations instead of fulfilling the spiritual obligations, leading to the death of their children when the seventh year arrived. The third mother, however, honored the pact with humble offerings, and her child thrived, teaching a lesson about the importance of honoring spiritual promises and the power of small, meaningful choices.

* * *

INSIGHTS, OFFERINGS, RITUALS AND SPIRITUAL SIGNIFICANCE
SECTION 3

HONORING EGBE

Egbe are the spiritual companions we left behind in the celestial realm before coming to Earth. Though they exist beyond our physical world, they continue to influence and support us, offering guidance and protection. Their presence is often felt through intuition, dreams, or an inner calling, reminding us of the bond we share with them. In the teachings of Ifá, maintaining a strong connection with Egbe requires reciprocity. Just as they watch over us, we must acknowledge them through offerings as a gesture of gratitude and respect. These offerings may include a variety of fruits, prepared foods, roosters, hens, guinea fowl, a glass of water, candles, incense, cowrie shells, or coins. Such gifts help strengthen our spiritual alignment and invite their continued blessings into our lives. Offerings are often placed in sacred locations where spiritual energy is strong. These include rivers, under trees, in caves, on rocks, hills, mountains, as well as at a corner of a home and also at the crossroads.

Sometimes, the need to honor Egbe arises naturally not from a vision or sign, but simply from love and devotion. Other times, they may reach out through subtle messages a persistent thought, a dream, or an unshakable feeling urging us to fulfill our part in this sacred relationship. When members of an Egbe group come together in unity, their collective offerings radiate spiritual power, fostering harmony, protection, and prosperity. Honoring Egbe keeps us connected to our higher purpose, ensuring that our journey aligns with divine order and that blessings continue to flow into our lives.

SOME COMMON EGBE COMMUNITIES

There are many different Egbe communities, each with its own unique characteristics, some of which are unknown to us. To determine which community you belong to, you would need to consult a Babalawo (Diviner). Some of the known Egbe communities include:

- **Egbe Iyalaje:** Connected to business, trade, and the marketplace, this group helps those they guide to attract wealth, prosperity, and success in financial matters.
- **Egbe Baale:** Associated with leadership, rulership, and authority, members of this group support and guide others toward positions of power and influence.
- **Egbe Jagunjagun or (Egbe Jagun)**: Known for their warrior spirit, strength, and protective nature, this group helps people overcome obstacles, conflicts, and challenges in life.
- **Egbe Emere:** These are spirits who move between heaven (*Orun*) and earth (*Aye*). They are often linked to children who are born but pass away at a young age, carrying a special spiritual destiny.
- **Egbe Ajoyo:** A group of spirits connected to joy, happiness, and celebration. They bring a spirit of lightness, festivities, and emotional uplifting to those connected with them.
- **Egbe Ara Orun:** Spirits who remain permanently in the heavenly

realm. They serve as guardians and watchers from the spirit world, maintaining a constant presence in Ọ̀run.

In conclusion, consulting a Babalawo to discover your Egbe community can help you spiritually align with and better serve your Egbe.

SPIRITUAL HERBS FOR
DREAMING AND ASTRAL WORK

MUGWORT
Spiritually used to protect against nightmares and ward off negative spirits during sleep. It is also believed to enhance dreams, visions, astral travel, and psychic awareness. For best results, place a small sachet of mugwort under your pillow. To specifically protect against nightmares, it is more effective to hang mugwort beside your bed.

ROSEMARY
Traditionally known for clearing mental fog, rosemary is believed to sharpen intuition and enhance psychic perception.

DANDELION ROOT
Commonly used in teas or incense, dandelion root is thought to promote psychic dreams and aid in spirit communication during sleep.

CHAMOMILE
Spiritually used to encourage peaceful sleep and gentle dreams. It also helps relax the mind and body before bed.

LAVENDER
Spiritually used to cleanse a space of negative energy. Lavender flowers are often mixed with water and sprinkled around the space for purification. Lavender oil can also be used for similar spiritual cleansing purposes.

* * *

DISCLAIMER

These herbs are meant to support spiritual practices like enhancing dreams, intuition, and astral travel. The information shared here is

for educational use only. Use these herbs at your own risk. They are not intended to diagnose, treat, or cure any medical conditions. Always talk to a healthcare professional before using any herbs, especially if you are pregnant, nursing, taking medications, or have allergies.

* * *

How to Create a Simple Dream Sachet

To create a dream sachet, take a small bag and mix one part of each herb listed above (mugwort, rosemary, dandelion root, chamomile, and lavender). Place the bag under your pillow or wear it around your neck to encourage peaceful sleep, enhance dreams, and promote spiritual protection while you rest.

* * *

Dream Journal Activity: Connecting to Your Egbe Through Dreams

Purpose

To deepen your connection with your Egbe and receive guidance or messages through dreams.

Materials Needed

- A journal or notebook
- A pen or pencil
- A quiet, comfortable space

Step 1: Set an Intention to Connect with Your Egbe Before Sleep

- Before bed, set a clear intention to connect with your Egbe. You can say a simple prayer or statement asking for guidance or communication through your dreams.

- *Example: "I ask my Egbe to guide me and share their wisdom with me through my dreams tonight."*

STEP 2: WRITE YOUR INTENTION IN YOUR DREAM JOURNAL

- Write down your intention in your journal before going to sleep. This helps focus your mind on receiving the messages you seek. You may also include any specific questions or concerns you'd like your Egbe to help with.
- *Example: "Please show me the path forward in my spiritual practice" or "Help me understand the challenges I am facing."*

STEP 3: RECORD YOUR DREAM AS SOON AS YOU WAKE UP

- As soon as you wake up, grab your journal and write down everything you remember from your dream. Pay attention to any interactions, symbols, or feelings that stood out. Look for any figures that might represent your Egbe, as they may appear directly or symbolically.
- *Example: "I dreamed of an elder who spoke in riddles and gave me a key" or "I saw a group of people in a circle, and one gave me a blessing."*

STEP 4: LOOK FOR PATTERNS OR SYMBOLS RELATED TO YOUR DREAMS

- Over time, look for recurring symbols or themes in your dreams that could be connected to your Egbe. Your Egbe may communicate using familiar symbols or experiences.
- In addition to writing down your dream details, jot down any insights or feelings that come to mind regarding the meaning or interpretation of the dream. For example, you may note if the dream could be related to stress or emotional baggage from the previous day.
- With practice, you'll begin to distinguish between regular dreams and true messages or insights from the spirit world.

* * *

12. EGUN
THE SPIRITS OF THE ANCESTORS

A CLOSER LOOK AT THE EGUN

IN YORUBA SPIRITUALITY, *Egun* (also spelled *Eggun*) refers to the spirits of the dead, especially one's ancestors. These ancestral spirits are deeply revered and are believed to advocate for the living on the other side in the spirit world. Their veneration forms a core aspect of the Yoruba spiritual tradition. The saying *"Egun before Orisha"* captures the belief that one must first honor the ancestors before engaging with the Orishas, highlighting the importance of ancestral connection as the foundation of spiritual practice.

The relationship with Egun is sustained through rituals and offerings that express love, respect, and devotion. A common form of ancestor veneration is the creation of a *bóveda*, or ancestral altar. These sacred spaces are typically adorned with water, coffee, rum, flowers, candles, and sometimes photographs or personal items of the deceased. The bóveda serves as a spiritual portal, a place where the living can communicate with the dead, offer prayers, ask for guidance, and receive blessings. Through consistent offerings and intentional connection, the bond between ancestor and descendant remains active and alive. Egun are also honored collectively in the traditional Yoruba *Egungun* masquerade, a vibrant and sacred public celebration in which masked dancers embody the spirits of the ancestors. These ceremonies are more than artistic displays; they are powerful communal rites that affirm cultural values, call in ancestral presence, and reinforce the moral and spiritual foundations of society. In some lineages, *Egungun* is also recognized as a collective Orisha: a spiritual embodiment of all ancestors unified as one.

The word *Egun* translates from Yoruba to English as "bone," symbolizing the lasting connection between the living and the dead, our bond with those whose physical bodies have passed but whose presence continues to guide and support us. This meaning emphasizes how the ancestors form the foundational "structure" of our spiritual and communal life, much like bones support and give shape to the body. Through honoring the *Egun*, we acknowledge that although their bodies are no longer visible, their strength and wisdom remain essential to our existence and well-being. The Egun are believed to be active participants in our lives, offering protection, wisdom, courage, and healing. They often communicate through dreams, inner sensations, signs, and divination. Maintaining a strong and respectful relationship with one's ancestors is considered essential to spiritual balance and personal growth. It helps us stay aligned with our *Ori,* our inner destiny and higher self.

When the Egun are neglected, individuals may experience spiritual confusion or challenges. But when they are honored, their support brings clarity, strength, and a deeper sense of rootedness. To work with Egun is to remember that we are never alone; we walk with the power, love, and knowledge of those who came before us, carrying their legacy as we shape our path forward.

A Prayer to Egun, Ancestors of Wisdom and Guidance
Verse 1:1

Egun, spirits of the past,
Your wisdom and love forever last.
From bones beneath to skies above,
You guide us with eternal love.

We honor you, with hearts so true,
In every step, we feel you too.
Through dance and prayer, we call your name,
A link in the chain, forever the same.

Ancestors dear, with power so bright,
Bless us with strength, through day and night.
Your voices echo in the rhythm's beat,
In every prayer, your presence we greet.

Guide us forward, as you've done before,
In your wisdom, we seek to soar.
With offerings humble, and hearts full of grace,
We honor you in this sacred space.
Eggun, your love lights the way,
In your hands, we find our stay.

May your blessings never fade,
And may our bond with you always be made.
So be it now, so it shall be,
With Eggun's love, we are set free.
Ase.

* * *

THE MASQUERADE OF LIFE
VERSE 1:2

Egungun comes in a dancing crowd,
Bright costumes shining, drums so loud.
They move with grace, they twist and sway,
A celebration of the past's display.

They're not just dancers, not just play,
They're the spirits of those who passed away.
They bring the strength, the wisdom, too.
The legacy of ancestors, pure and true.

Through every beat, through every sound,
Their energy fills the sacred ground.
They guard our town, protect the weak,
Their blessings are the gifts we seek.

With every step, they share their might,
To keep us safe both day and night.
Their spirits walk with us, side by side,
In their love and power, we take pride.

So when the drums begin to sound,
Our ancestors' love is all around.
Their voices echo in the rhythm's beat,
A connection felt in every street.

Their dance is more than just a show,
It's a bond that continues to grow.
For when the Egungun appear in the crowd,
We feel their presence, strong and proud.

They remind us of the ties that bind,
The strength of the past, the peace we find.
Through dance and song, we honor them,
Our ancestors' spirits, now and then.

* * *

BONES BENEATH, SPIRITS ABOVE
VERSE 1:3

Egun are spirits, wise and true,
Ancestors watching over you.
They lived before, they walked this land,
And now they guide with loving hands.

From "bone," the word Egun takes its name,
A sacred tie to whence we came.
The earth we walk on is not just ground,
It holds their bones, their love profound.

They hear our prayers, they see our tears,
They calm our doubts, they ease our fears.
To honor them is to remember,
Their strength burns like a glowing ember.
The soil beneath is not just dirt,
It's a sacred space, where spirits work.

Our ancestors lie in the earth below,
Their wisdom roots where life will grow.

Through songs and gifts, we show our care,
We honor the earth; they're always there.

For every step upon this land,
It is held by their eternal hands.
One day, our bones will rest the same,
Returned to earth, to hearth, to name.

Joined with the ancestors, we'll remain,
A link in the unbroken chain.
And when they're reborn, the cycle runs,
We'll watch and guide as they've done.

From life to spirit, the wheel will turn,
As those we protect will one day learn.

* * *

SACRED STORIES / LEGENDS
SECTION 2

THE HUNTER'S SON
STORY 2:1

Once, a hunter's son suffered a great loss. One tragic day, his father fell and died while hunting in the forest. Overcome with grief and fear, the boy could not bring himself to bury his father or bid him farewell. Instead, he turned away and left the place where his father had fallen. But as the years passed, hardship followed him. No matter how hard he tried, his life was filled with struggle and misfortune. Desperate for answers, he sought the wisdom of a Babalawo, a priest who could speak to the spirits and reveal hidden truths. The Babalawo consulted the Oracle, and the Odu *Oyeku Meji* was revealed. With a solemn voice, he said, "*You must return to the place where your father died. Honor him properly, and balance will be restored.*"

Determined to set things right, the son traveled back through the forest, searching for the place where his father had fallen. When he arrived, he saw that time and nature had scattered his father's remains. Yet, with great care, he gathered the bones and wrapped them in some of the red cloth that was a part of the garments his father had once worn. He returned to the priest, who performed the sacred burial rites. Together, they laid the hunter's bones to rest beneath a strong and ancient tree. Then, the Babalawo handed the young man a special staff adorned with nine brightly colored cloths.

"Each day," the priest instructed, *"tap the ground nine times with this staff. Your ancestors will hear you and guide your steps. Build a shrine to honor your father, and in return, blessings will come to you."*

The son followed these instructions with deep reverence. He built a shrine for his father and honored him with prayers and offerings. Over time, his life transformed. Prosperity and wisdom came to him, and he became a respected leader known for his kindness and knowledge. His family name carried honor for nine generations, remembered for their strength and devotion. This story teaches an important lesson: *honoring our ancestors is the key to a strong and blessed future.* By showing respect for those who came before us, we invite their guidance and protection into our lives.

REFLECTION & WISDOM

This story highlights the importance of honoring our ancestors for a balanced and prosperous life. The young man's failure to properly bury his father caused a disconnection that led to years of struggle. It wasn't until he sought guidance from the Babalawo and returned to honor his father that his life began to transform. The lesson here is that neglecting our ancestors can lead to imbalance, while honoring them invites their wisdom and protection. This story teaches us that by respecting those who came before us, we invite blessings and guidance into our own lives, ensuring our path is aligned with wisdom and strength.

* * *

THE BIRTH OF THE EGUN TRADITION
STORY 2:2

In the kingdom of Òyó, there was a wise and respected chief named Alaroye, who had three sons. Before leaving for a nearby village, he warned his sons about a dangerous flower that grew by the river. He told them that the flower's root was cursed and could only be handled by those with the proper training.

He advised them not to touch it, as doing so would lead to death, no matter how tempting its bright glow seemed. The youngest son heeded his father's warning, but the two older sons ignored it, believing they could handle the root's power. They took the root and drank from the river, but soon found themselves suffering from an unbearable thirst that no water could quench. Their condition worsened until they died. The youngest son, horrified, returned to find his brothers dead. He rushed to his father, who was devastated by the loss. In his grief, Alaroye consulted a Babalawo, a wise spiritual leader, who advised him on how to bring his sons back. The Babalawo told Alaroye to bury his sons under a sacred tree in the grove where spirits are known to roam, and on the ninth day, to strike the ground with a sacred staff while chanting for their spirits.

Alaroye followed the instructions carefully. On the ninth day, as the sun rose, his sons were brought back to life, their forms glowing with a new light. The elders of the village suggested that they cover their glowing forms with robes and masks to preserve their dignity. At the village feast, the sons, now transformed, healed the people with their touch. The grove where they were buried became a sacred place, known as the Egun Grove, honoring the ancestors and the bond between the living and the spirits. From then on, the Egun Rite was practiced to maintain a connection with the ancestral spirits and to invite their blessings.

REFLECTION & WISDOM

This story highlights the importance of respecting wisdom and guidance, especially from those with experience. The elder sons ignored their father's warning about the cursed root and suffered the consequences. In contrast, the youngest son showed humility by seeking help and following the right rituals, ultimately bringing healing to his brothers. The transformation of the sons symbolizes growth through honoring our ancestors. The story teaches that respecting their wisdom and following sacred traditions can lead to protection, healing, and spiritual renewal. By honoring the past, we create a strong connection to the wisdom and guidance that can shape our future.

* * *

INSIGHTS, OFFERINGS, RITUALS AND SPIRITUAL SIGNIFICANCE
SECTION 3

OFFERINGS TO EGUN

We honor Egun with offerings of fresh water, wine, coffee, tea, alcohol, fruits, vegetables, fish, beans, roosters, honey sweets, and candles, depending on their preference. Salt is avoided, following tradition. Egungun communicate through visions and intuition, offering us guidance and support throughout our lives.

* * *

ACTIVITY: SETTING UP AN ANCESTOR SHRINE

PURPOSE
The purpose of this activity is to create a sacred space where you can honor your ancestors, establish a stronger connection with them, and invite their wisdom and support into your life.

INSTRUCTIONS

Choose a location in your home that doesn't have a lot of foot traffic ideally a quiet corner of a room or a closed-off space. You can use either a small table or a clean spot on the floor for your shrine.

ITEMS YOU WILL NEED

- 2 glasses of clear water
- 1 white candle
- Photos of deceased family members (optional)
- A small plant or white flowers (optional)
- An offering of their favorite food or drink (optional)
- A table
- A note book and pen

* * *

Place one glass of water on the **left side** of the shrine (for ancestors from your **mother's side**) and the other on the **right side** (for ancestors from your **father's side**). Pour clear water into both glasses. Bubbles in the water often indicate spiritual receptivity. If the water becomes cloudy or dirty, replace it with fresh water the water is used for cleansing and clarity.

Light the white candle as a symbol of spiritual light and connection. You can add photos of your deceased relatives to the shrine. I personally only use photos of people who have already passed and avoid placing photos that include living individuals. You may also place a small plant, white flowers, or an offering of food or drink that your ancestors loved. I usually leave offerings on the shrine for a day or two, then place them outside so animals can enjoy them, but discarding them respectfully is also fine. Feel free to be creative setting up your shrine is about building a personal connection with your ancestors, giving thanks, and asking for their continued support.

WEEKLY PRACTICE

I personally spend about fifteen minutes each week at my shrine, meditating and talking to my ancestors. I usually begin this time with a short prayer, then sit quietly with a notebook in hand. During these moments, I write down any ideas, feelings, or inspirations that arise. After maintaining this practice consistently for six weeks, I noticed an increase in intuition, inspiration, and a deeper sense of connection with my ancestors. Keeping a pen and notebook at my shrine allows me to capture any thoughts, emotions, or messages that come up during these sessions. Writing them down helps me stay connected and reflect on the guidance my ancestors may offer. Over time, this simple habit has significantly deepened my relationship with them.

* * *

13. Eshu, Esu & Elegua
The Divine Messenger and Guardian of the Crossroads

A Closer Look at Esu & Elegua

Eshu, also known as Èṣù, Elegba, or Elegua, is one of the most frequently honored Orishas. He is best known for his complex and contradictory nature. As the guardian of the crossroads, Eshu symbolizes choice, opportunity, and the unpredictable turns of life. Often portrayed as a trickster, he uses cleverness, mischief, and unexpected challenges to teach lessons, test integrity, and uphold divine justice. Eshu stands at the threshold between worlds, serving as the messenger who connects humans with the other Orishas. He sees the past, present, and future, influencing the direction of our lives and the paths we choose. Though he is associated with chaos and uncertainty, Eshu is not a harmful force. Instead, he represents the balance between order and disorder, reminding us of life's complexity and the importance of making conscious, intentional decisions. Eshu is a shapeshifter sometimes appearing as a playful child, other times as a wise elder. He moves freely between the spiritual and physical realms, maintaining harmony between them. In every ritual, Eshu is honored first, as he opens the way for communication with the divine. He governs the gateways to the spirit world, ensuring that offerings and prayers are received. As one of the oldest Orishas, an Irunmole Eshu is the guardian of natural laws and the enforcer of destiny. Without his presence, no journey or ceremony can begin or succeed.

ESHU, KEEPER OF THE CROSSROADS
A Prayer and Poem
VERSE I:I

Eshu, wise one, trickster, guide,
You walk with us, side by side.
You open doors we cannot see,
And help us be who we should be.

You laugh like a child, think like a sage,
You carry the truth from age to age.
You live between the earth and sky,
You help our prayers and hopes fly high.

Before all others, we call your name,
Without your help, life's not the same.
Speak for us where we cannot go,
Clear the path and let it flow.

Eshu, we thank you for your grace,
For guiding us from place to place.
Stand with us as we begin,
With your blessing, we will win.
Ase.

* * *

ESU: THE DIVINE TRICKSTER
VERSE I:2

Esu, the trickster, with many a guise,
A child, an elder, with secrets to prize.
He moves through the realms, both hidden and clear,
Opening doors for those who draw near.

The messenger to God, the divine courier,
He speaks in riddles, and visions are clearer.
With keys in his hands, he unlocks the way,
Guiding us forward to the break of day.

He's the one who balances fate and design,
Turning the wheel in a grand cosmic line.
In his role, he opens and shuts the door,
To the spirit world, where mysteries soar.

Esu's path is long, with twists and turns,
A guide through the unknown, where wisdom burns.
He sees the future, the present, the past,
Every moment and memory, perfectly cast.

A trickster, a guardian, both wise and sly,
Esu watches the world through a knowing eye.
He teaches the lesson of life's ebb and flow,
That to understand all paths, we must first know.

So honor Esu before all you do,
For without him, the path would be few.
He is the key, the one who unlocks,
The doors to the divine, where wisdom knocks.

* * *

SACRED STORIES / LEGENDS
SECTION 2

ELEGUA AND THE HEALING OF OLOFI
STORY 2:1

A long time ago, in the heavens and on Earth, the great Creator, Olódùmarè, grew very tired. He had spent so much time creating life and giving power to the world that he became weak. The Orishas, powerful spirits who helped take care of the world, were called to his grand hall. Their job was to find a way to heal him. One by one, the Orishas tried their best. Obatalá, the Orisha of wisdom and purity, brought a white cloth, hoping it would bring peace to Olódùmarè. But Olódùmarè stayed weak, his eyes dull and tired. Orunmila, the Orisha of wisdom, mixed a special drink filled with sacred knowledge, but it didn't help. Ozain, the Orisha of herbs, brought powerful plants from the forest, but nothing changed.

The Orishas had no idea what else to do. Then, little Elegua, the youngest of them all, stepped forward. "Can I try?" he asked. The older Orishas laughed. "This is a serious matter! Go play somewhere else," they told him. But Elegua didn't give up. "Why can't I try?" he asked again. Obatalá, who was kind and fair, said, "Let him try. Maybe he will surprise us." Elegua stepped up to Olódùmarè's throne. He reached into his small bag and took out three tiny leaves. Gently, he placed them where no one else had thought to look. Then, he carefully moved Olódùmarè's lips and waved a feather through the air. The Orishas whispered to each other, thinking it wouldn't work.

But suddenly, a bright light began to shine from Olódùmarè. The light grew stronger and stronger until Olódùmarè stood tall again, his strength fully restored. The Orishas gasped in amazement. Olódùmarè smiled at Elegua and asked, "How did you know what to do?" Elegua grinned and said, "I watched and learned from all of you." Olódùmarè was pleased with Elegua's cleverness and gave him a special key. "With this key, you will open all doors and guide travelers on their paths. From now on, nothing will begin without your blessing." Elegua skipped away happily, knowing that even though he was the youngest, he had an important role. The Orishas, who once doubted him, now understood his wisdom. This story teaches us that no one should be underestimated. Even the smallest and youngest person can have great wisdom and make a big difference.

REFLECTION & WISDOM

In this story, the Orishas are called upon to heal Olofi, the Creator, who is weakened from his tireless work. Despite their efforts, none of them can restore his strength. However, Elegua, the youngest and often overlooked Orisha, steps forward with a simple yet profound solution. Using three small leaves and a feather, Elegua miraculously revives Olofi, earning his respect and a key to guide both Earth and time. This tale highlights the power of humility, creativity, and the wisdom that can come from even the most unexpected places.

* * *

ESHU AND THE TWO FRIENDS
STORY 2:2

Two friends began their journey one day,
To seek wisdom from the elder, far away.
Along the road, they met Eshu's disguise,
He tricked them both with clever lies.

The farmer went right, the hunter went left,
Each thinking their way was the best.
When they reached the elder, confused and lost,
They realized Eshu had tricked them at a cost.

The elder smiled, for he knew the truth,
Eshu's tricks help to guide our youth.
"Life is full of choices, paths unseen,
And it's not just the end, but the journey between."

* * *

REFLECTION & WISDOM

This story reminds us that Eshu, though tricky, teaches important lessons through his mischief. His actions show that life is full of different paths, and what matters most is not always who is right, but what we learn along the way.

* * *

ESHU AND THE SACRIFICE
STORY 2:3

The village prayed for rain to fall,
They gathered round, one and all.
They made their offerings, strong and true,
But Eshu was left out of the view.
The clouds gathered, but rain was scarce,
The villagers puzzled, their hope did impair.

Eshu appeared, and with a laugh,
Said, "Without me, your prayers won't last."
They called to him, their hearts now clear,
And soon the rain began to appear.
For Eshu opens paths, both wide and tall,
Without his blessing, none would fall.

Reflection & Wisdom

This story reminds us that no matter how sincere our efforts are, we must honor all the forces that open the way. Eshu teaches that nothing moves forward without his blessing, and when we forget him, even our strongest prayers may be delayed.

* * *

INSIGHTS, OFFERINGS, RITUALS AND SPIRITUAL SIGNIFICANCE
Section 3

Key Facts About Esu/ Elegua

- **Orisha of Communication and Messenger:** Esù is the Orisha of communication, often acting as a messenger between humans and the other Orishas. He is known for his ability to speak and translate messages, ensuring that important communications reach their intended destinations.
- **Trickster and Protector:** Esù is often seen as a trickster, using cleverness and wit to outsmart others. Despite his mischievous nature, he is also a protector, ensuring the smooth flow of communication and events, especially in spiritual and ritual contexts.
- **Sacred Role in Rituals:** Esù is an essential part of Yoruba rituals and ceremonies. He is often the first Orisha invoked in any spiritual offering or prayer, as his approval is required to ensure that messages and requests reach the divine.
- **Mischievous Nature:** Known for his playful and unpredictable behavior, Esù challenges people to think critically, face their fears, and embrace the complexity of life's decisions. His actions are

often designed to teach lessons about cause and effect, and the consequences of one's choices.

* * *

OFFERINGS TO ESU AT THE CROSSROADS
VERSE 3:1

Elegua is the Orisha who stands at the crossroads, where paths meet. He is both a trickster and a messenger, holding great power and guarding the gates to new beginnings. He plays an important role in guiding people on their journeys and shaping their paths. To honor Elegua, offerings are made, including male goats, roosters, cornmeal, cigars, toasted corn, and candies. Other gifts may include coconuts, palm oil, kola nuts, pigeons, strong alcohol, coffee, and candles. Incense is often burned in his honor, and tobacco smoke may be offered as well. Natural stones like jasper, garnet, black onyx, and yangi stones are also considered powerful gifts for Elegua. However, there are rules to follow. For example, a whistle near him can lead you astray, and certain offerings, like Adi Eyan (black palm kernel oil) and two-eye ikins, are said to protect you from his wrath. Elegua is a gatekeeper who opens paths for those who seek his help, but he also tests the hearts of those who approach. Offering gifts with respect and care is important, as Elegua holds the key to new beginnings and determines which paths are open. Honor him with love and respect, and he will guide you on your journey. Ase.

THE MANY FACES OF ESU

Eshu is a powerful Orisha with many different forms, called caminos or paths. Each path shows a different part of his personality, role, and influence in the world. Some of Eshu's paths are playful and fun, others are wise and serious, while some are protectors or tricky tricksters. In the Yoruba tradition, people believe Eshu has over 201 paths, showing that he can be present in all situations and challenges. Some of the most common paths of Eshu include:

- **Eshu Añanki:** *A female path of Eshu, she resides in the forest and* works alongside the Orisha Oya. She has the power to heal using ewé (sacred herbs).

- **Eshu Agbanuke**: Known as the Eshu of clairvoyance, he protects Babalawos from those who come with bad intentions. He works closely with the Orisha Orunmila.
- **Eshu Ala Lu Ban**: He is the one who opens roads and helps people obtain a better life.
- **Eshu Abaile**: One of the Eshus who receives ebbós, interprets their purpose, and helps ensure they are delivered to the correct spiritual destination.
- **Eshu Odara**: His name means "the one who brings goodness" or "the one who makes things better." He works closely with Babalawos and the Orisha Orunmila to ensure that ebbós are properly delivered and transformed into blessings.
- **Eshu Alaguana**: A fierce warrior known for his quick action and sharp decision-making.
- **Eshu Elegba**: The guardian of crossroads and divine messenger who opens and closes all paths. He is sometimes referred to as Eleguá.
- **Eshu Aje**: The bringer of wealth and prosperity, guiding success in business and the flow of material blessings.
- **Eshu Laroye**: The playful child full of laughter, who teaches through joy, humor, and clever mischief.
- **Eshu Onibara**: The trader and negotiator, skilled in speech, bargaining, and exchange.

* * *

14. THE IBEJIS
THE ORISHA OF DIVINE TWINS AND JOY

A CLOSER LOOK AT THE IBEJI

IN YORUBA CULTURE, the birth of twins is considered very special and powerful. The Yoruba people of Nigeria have more twins than any other group in the world. Twins are respected not just as siblings, but as spiritual beings. When twins are born, it's common for the parents to visit a Babalawo, a spiritual priest, who helps explain the meaning of their birth and what the spirits want for their future.

The first twin to be born is named *Taiwo*, which means "the first to taste the world." Taiwo is thought to be the one who checks if the world is ready. The second twin, *Kehinde*, means "the one who comes after," but is actually seen as the older one. Kehinde is believed to send Taiwo out first and waits for the result. Sometimes, the child born after twins is called Idowu. This child is believed to be spiritually special and may bring both blessings and challenges. Idowu children are often seen as mysterious because they come after such a powerful event. In Yoruba religion, twins are not just regular children, they are seen as divine. They are linked to the Orisha called Ibeji, the twin spirits known for being playful but also powerful. Ibeji bring joy, protection, healing, and good luck. Even though they can be full of energy and a little mischievous, they are strong spiritual protectors. Today, twins are celebrated and loved, but in the past, some people were afraid of them or didn't understand their power. Sadly, twins are more likely to have health problems at birth, and sometimes one may pass away early. When that happens, a Babalawo makes a special wooden figure called an ere Ibeji to represent the twin who died. This figure is cared for like a real child; it is bathed, dressed, and even given food. People believe the spirit of the lost twin lives inside the figure.

The Ibeji remind us that life is full of opposites, joy and sadness, life and death, what we see and what we don't. Honoring twins helps keep the values of love, unity, and spiritual balance strong. Through the Ibeji, the Yoruba teach us that every soul, especially those born together, has a divine purpose.

THE SPIRIT OF TWINS
A Prayer and Poem
VERSE I:I

Ibeji, twins of sky and earth,
We thank you for your special birth.
You bring us joy and make us strong,
You help us find where we belong.

Taiwo comes first to lead the way,
Kehinde watches, wise each day.
Together you protect and guide,
With playful hearts and love inside.

Stay with us both night and day,
And bless our steps along the way.
Ase.

* * *

SACRED LIGHT OF IBEJI
VERSE I:2

Born from Chango's might,
And Oshun's radiant light,
The Ibeji spread joy and cheer,
Protecting twins, both far and near.

Two hearts beat as one, shining bright,
Their laughter brings joy, their presence calms fright.
In red and blue, they dance and play,
Bringing magic in every way.

They heal with joy, guide with grace,
A divine reflection in their embrace.
Ibeji, hearts so pure,
Filling the world with love, secure.
In their balance, strength is found,
Peace and love in every sound.
We honor you in all we do,
Celebrating the magic of you.

* * *

SACRED STORIES / LEGENDS
SECTION 2

THE SACRED TWINS
STORY 2:1

A long time ago, Oshun, the Orisha of love and beauty, gave birth to twin babies Taiwo and Kehinde. They were bright and full of life, but the people of the village were afraid. They believed that only animals had twins, so they saw them as something strange and unnatural. Instead of celebrating, they called Oshun a witch and cast her out of the village. Heartbroken and filled with shame, Oshun had nowhere to turn. With tears in her eyes, she made a painful decision she left her babies by the ocean, hoping her sorrow would disappear with the waves. But the ocean was home to Yemaya, the great mother of all. She saw the abandoned twins and, filled with love, took them into her care. She raised them with kindness, protecting them under the sun and moon. Though she knew they truly belonged to Oshun, she loved them as her own.

As time passed, the twins continued their journey and eventually came to Oya, the powerful Orisha of wind and storms. Oya had longed for children, but she had suffered great loss. When she found the twins, she welcomed them with open arms, filling their lives with love and warmth. Under Oya's care, Taiwo and Kehinde grew into strong and wise beings. They became known as the first twins on Earth, carrying the strength of their father, Shango, and the grace of their mother, Oshun. With their presence, they brought joy, healing, and balance to the world. Their laughter and energy lifted spirits, and their sacred drums were said to drive away misfortune. The story of the Ibeji teaches us that even when life begins with hardship, love can heal and bring new beginnings. It reminds us that those who are rejected can still rise, and through kindness, we can turn sorrow into joy.

REFLECTION & WISDOM

The story of the Ibeji reminds us that even in times of rejection and pain, love can bring healing and new beginnings. Oshun's twins, once feared and cast aside, were saved by the love of Yemaya and Oya, showing that care and compassion can come from unexpected places. Though born into hardship, Taiwo and Kehinde grew into symbols of joy, strength, and balance. Their story teaches that what is misunderstood today may be celebrated tomorrow. It reminds us to embrace difference, offer kindness, and trust that love can transform sorrow into light.

* * *

THE TWINS WHO CHASED AWAY THE DEVIL
STORY 2:3

A village once was filled with fear,
A devil's curse had lingered near.
It brought them sickness, hunger, pain,
And left them crying in the rain.

The people prayed, but all seemed lost,
The devil stayed at every cost.
Until one day, the twins appeared,
With laughter bright, the darkness cleared.

They danced and drummed a sacred beat,
A rhythm pure, so strong, so sweet.
The devil shook, it couldn't stay,
Its power started fading away.

Their hearts were pure, their souls were kind,
They showed the strength of two combined.
The Orishas blessed their plan,
And gave them tools to take a stand.

With unity, the twins stood tall,
Their love and balance broke the wall.
The devil fled, its grip undone,
The village cheered, new life begun.

The Ibeji saved them all that day,
Their joy and light had paved the way.
Now they are hailed for what they give,
Protectors of the lives we live.

REFLECTION & WISDOM

In this story, a village plagued by a devil's curse experiences sickness, hunger, and despair. Despite their prayers, the devil's presence remains unshaken, until the twins, Taiwo and Kehinde, appear. With their joyful laughter and sacred drumming, they bring a powerful rhythm that weakens the devil's hold. The Orishas bless the twins, giving them the strength and tools to break the curse. Through their unity, love, and balance, the twins banish the devil, bringing new life to the village. Celebrated for their power to restore peace, the Ibeji (twins) are revered as protectors, embodying the strength and light that guide and safeguard the community.

* * *

THE IBEJI TWINS AND THE HEALING WATERS
STORY 2:4

A long time ago, a village suffered under a terrible drought. The sun burned hot, the rivers dried up, and the land cracked from thirst. No matter how hard the people prayed, no rain came to save their dying crops. The Ibeji twins, Taiwo and Kehinde, heard the cries of the suffering villagers. Their hearts filled with compassion, and they knew they had to help. They set out on a journey to find the sacred river, the only place where water still flowed. When they reached the river, they called upon Oya, the powerful Orisha of storms, asking her to bring the rain. They also prayed to Oshun, the Orisha of fresh waters, to bless the land with life once more. Moved by the twins' pure hearts and determination, the Orishas answered their call. Dark clouds gathered in the sky, and soon, gentle raindrops began to fall. The earth drank deeply, and the river swelled with fresh, flowing water. The villagers rejoiced as their fields turned green again, and their wells filled with cool, clean water. The twins did not leave right away. They stayed by the river, making sure the water continued to flow. For many weeks, they watched over the land, ensuring that life remained strong. Because of the Ibeji's kindness and courage, the village thrived once more. Their story reminds us that even the smallest among us can bring great change, and that with love, determination, and faith, we can heal the world around us.

REFLECTION & WISDOM

In this story, a village suffering from a severe drought prays desperately for rain, but their pleas go unanswered. Hearing the village's cries, the Ibeji twins, filled with purity and light, travel to a sacred stream where they call upon Oya, the powerful Orisha of winds and storms, and Oshun, the goddess of rivers and streams, to bring forth the rain. Their combined efforts restore balance, and rain falls gently, bringing life back to the land. Crops begin to grow, and the village rejoices. The twins remain by the river, ensuring its continued flow, as the village flourishes once more. Their work marks the beginning of a divine renewal, showing how love, unity, and divine intervention can heal even the harshest of droughts.

* * *

INSIGHTS, OFFERINGS, RITUALS AND SPIRITUAL SIGNIFICANCE
SECTION 3

TRADITIONAL OFFERINGS FOR THE IBEJI

Offerings to the Ibeji often include sweet fruits like oranges, apples, and bananas, which symbolize life, abundance, and joy. Candies and chocolates are given to reflect their childlike spirit and love of sweetness. Grains such as rice and corn are offered to encourage prosperity and growth. Bright or golden flowers are used to honor their beauty and divine balance. Palm oil, sacred and nourishing, represents blessings and spiritual strength. Toys are included to celebrate their playful energy, and a glass of fresh water is offered for purification, peace, and to welcome their calming presence.

* * *

Interesting Facts About the Ibeji

- **Protectors of Families and Children:** *Ibeji are known to protect families, help with fertility, and look after children, especially twins.*
- **Celebrated with Sweet Treats and Music:** *People honor Ibeji with gifts like candy, fruit, toys, and music, celebrating their fun and joyful nature.*
- **Their Sacred Colors: Red and Blue:** *Red and blue represent the balance of their energies, fire and water, strength and peace.*
- **Bring Harmony to the Home:** *Offering devotion to Ibeji can bring peace, protect children, and heal family conflicts.*
- **Ibeji Represent Youthful Energy:** *Ibeji are a symbol of the fun, playful energy of youth. Their laughter and carefree spirit remind us to enjoy life with enthusiasm and innocence.*
- **Ibeji Are Associated with Healing:** *Ibeji not only bring joy but also have the power to heal. They are believed to help with emotional and spiritual healing, especially for children and families.*
- **Ibeji's Influence Extends Beyond Twins:** *While Ibeji are linked to twins, their blessings and protection go to all children and families, helping bring good health and prosperity.*
- **Ibeji's Energy Brings Fertility:** *People call on Ibeji for help with fertility and to bless couples who want children, especially twins, as they are seen as a sign of good fortune.*

* * *

In conclusion, the Ibeji represent the dual nature of life combining the joyful innocence of childhood with powerful energies of protection and healing. Their story reminds us that even in difficult times, love and compassion have the power to bring about transformation. By embodying the balance of opposites, the Ibeji teach us the value of unity, harmony, and the divine purpose within each of us. Honoring them is a way of embracing life's sacred rhythm, learning to face both joy and sorrow with grace, strength, and an open heart.

* * *

15. INLE, ERINLE
ORISHA OF MEDICINE, HUNTING AND BALANCE

A CLOSER LOOK AT ERINLE, INLE

INLÉ IS the Orisha who rules the estuary, where the river meets the sea. He represents balance and harmony between opposites, like fresh water and salt water, land and sea, and strength and healing. Inlé is a skilled healer and hunter. He knows how to use plants and natural remedies to help both people and other Orishas. He is also a great fisherman, often seen with a staff and fishing hook. Inlé's tools show that he provides and protects. He was once a great hunter who became an Orisha after he passed away. Inlé has a special bond with his best friend, Ochósí. They spend time by the water, hunting and fishing together. Inlé is connected to nature and teaches us how to find balance in both our physical and spiritual lives. He also protects people who are often overlooked, such as those individuals within the LGBT (*Lesbian, Gay, Bisexual and Transgender*) communities. Inlé teaches love, compassion, and the importance of accepting everyone regardless of gender, sexual orientation, race or ethnic background. Even though Inlé cannot speak because of a sacrifice he made to save the waters, his presence is felt in the flow of the tides and the sounds of nature. He reminds us to embrace change, find balance, and be strong in difficult times. Inlé is a guide who helps those who seek harmony in their lives.

A PRAYER TO INLE
VERSE I:I

Inlé, guardian of rivers and sea,
We call to you with hearts humble and free.
Where fresh waters meet the salty embrace,
Guide us with balance, in your sacred space.

We offer you fish, fresh from the stream,
Pigeons and fowl, as our spirits redeem.
Candles and wine, with hearts full of grace,
May your healing touch be found in this place.

Sweet plantains, oranges, and yams,
Blessings we offer with open palms.
Mangrove leaves and basil, we bring,
In your presence, our voices sing.

Healer of land, of water, of soul,
Guide us to balance and make us whole.
Inlé, protector, we honor your name,
Through your wisdom, we find peace again.
Ase!

* * *

THE ESTUARY SPIRIT
VERSE 1:2

Inlé, guardian where river meets sea,
A healer and hunter, wise and free.
He rules the estuary, where waters blend,
Ensuring life thrives, from start to end.

With cowries, coral, and a staff in hand,
He guides and protects the water and land.
Silent from sacrifice, his voice now gone,
His presence speaks in tides and dawn.

Master of herbs, he heals and protects,
Loving all beings, with no regrets.
Inlé teaches balance, in life and tide,
A guide through change, with wisdom as a guide.

* * *

89

The Hunter and Healer
Verse 1:3

Inle is a hunter, strong and fast,
In forests and rivers, he makes life last.
With bow and arrow, or herbs in hand,
Inle brings abundance to the land.

He hunts for food, but heals with care,
A spirit of strength who's always fair.
Inle is both hunter and guide,
In his wisdom, we all can rely.

* * *

SACRED STORIES / LEGENDS
Section 2

The Story of Yemaya, Inlé, and Abbata
Story 2:1

A long time ago, near the great ocean, lived Yemanjá, the powerful Orisha of the sea. She loved her children deeply, but one day her son Shango betrayed her trust. His lies broke her heart, leaving her hurt and angry. In her sorrow, Yemanjá made a painful decision, she cast her children away into the ocean. As punishment, she took Inlé's voice, leaving him unable to speak. His brother Abbata became deaf and weak, unable to hear the world around him. The two brothers drifted together in the vast waters, unable to communicate in the usual ways. But over time, their love and under-standing grew. Through glances and gestures, they found comfort in each other and created a bond stronger than words. They stayed together in the ocean's embrace, silent but never alone. Their story teaches us that even when life is painful and confusing, love can still thrive in unexpected ways. Change may come, but connection can remain even in silence.

Reflection & Wisdom

This tale of Yemayá, Inlé, and Abbata speaks to themes of deception, exile, and forbidden love, illustrating how silence and suffering can forge unbreak-

able bonds. Yemayá, shamed by Shango's trickery, cast Inlé and Abbata into the depths of the sea, stripping them of their voices and leaving them isolated in the ocean's embrace. Yet, in their solitude, they found solace in each other, forming a bond that transcended words. This legend explains the origins of their silence and reflects the profound mysteries of fate, transformation, and the hidden truths within the Orisha tradition.

* * *

INLÉ, THE PROVIDER
STORY 2:2

A long time ago, the land was in bad shape. The rivers had dried up, the forests were empty, and the people were hungry and scared. In their desperation, they called on Inlé, the Orisha they believed could help. Inlé was a skilled fisherman and hunter, closely connected to both the land and water. Seeing the people's suffering, he prayed to Olodumare for wisdom to save them. Olodumare answered, giving him the knowledge to speak to the rivers and the land. Inlé went to the dry riverbed and began to dig. Guided by hope, he soon uncovered a hidden spring, and fresh water began to flow, bringing life back to the land. The river returned, bringing fish with it, and the people celebrated as the land healed. But Inlé didn't stop there, he planted seeds in the forest, which grew into trees that provided food and shelter for all. Inlé also taught the people how to fish, hunt, and grow food, ensuring they would never go hungry again. He showed them how to care for the land and water. Thanks to Inlé's wisdom and actions, the people were saved. They no longer lived in fear and were filled with gratitude. Inlé showed them how one person's wisdom and care for the earth could make a big difference. His story reminds us that sharing knowledge, helping others, and protecting nature are the keys to creating a better world.

REFLECTION & WISDOM

This story of Inlé highlights his role as a provider and guardian of balance, demonstrating his deep connection to both land and water. When famine struck and the rivers dried, he sought wisdom from Olodumare and uncovered a hidden spring, restoring life to the waters and forests. Through his knowledge, he not only saved his people but also empowered them to sustain themselves, teaching them to fish, hunt, and cultivate the land. His actions embody the essence of wisdom, generosity, and resilience, showing that true abundance comes not just from provision, but from sharing knowledge and nurturing harmony with nature.

* * *

INSIGHTS, OFFERINGS, RITUALS AND SPIRITUAL SIGNIFICANCE
SECTION 3

KEY FACTS ABOUT INLÉ

- **Orisha of Balance and Harmony:** Inlé is known as the Orisha of balance, harmony, health, and medicine. He is associated with maintaining equilibrium in nature and in people's lives.
- **Healer and Physician:** Inlé is regarded as a healer, known for his knowledge of medicinal plants and natural remedies. He is often called upon to restore health to both humans and other Orishas.
- **Patron of Marginalized Communities**: In some traditions, Inlé is seen as a protector and patron of marginalized groups, especially homosexual and transgender people, symbolizing acceptance, balance, and inclusivity.
- **Connection to Estuaries**: Inlé is deeply connected to estuaries, the places where freshwater rivers meet the salty sea. These environments symbolize his ability to bring together different forces and create balance.
- **Syncretization with Archangel Raphael**: Inlé is often syncretized with the Archangel Raphael in Christian tradition. Raphael is the angel of healing, and like Inlé, he is seen as a divine healer, often depicted with fish and wearing blue and pink.

Inlé's tools reflect his roles as a healer, hunter, and protector. His bow and arrows symbolize his hunting skills, both on land and sea, while his fishing net represents his ability to provide and maintain balance in aquatic environments. As the Orisha of health, Inlé uses herbs, plants, and other natural remedies to heal physically and spiritually. Cowrie shells, associated with wealth and protection, highlight his connection to the ocean and are often used in healing rituals. Feathers and coral further represent his bond

92

with the sea, emphasizing his role as both a protector and healer of land and water.

OFFERINGS FOR INLÉ

We offer these gifts to Inlé with deep respect and love. Our offerings include fresh fish, white pigeons, guinea fowl, a glass of clear water, and lit candles to welcome his presence. We also present sweet wine, plantains, lettuce, basil, watercress, and fruits like oranges, guava, and avocado. Herbs such as mangrove leaves, purslane, and bitter vine, along with flowers, are included as sacred plants. A ram, a rooster, and pigeons are also offered in gratitude for Inlé's healing power and guidance.

* * *

16. The Iroko Tree
An Ancient Sacred Tree
Stands Tall in the Forest

A Closer Look at the Iroko

In Yoruba tradition, the Iroko tree (*Milicia excelsa*) is seen as sacred and powerful, believed to be home to spirits and ancestral forces. It is thought to have strong mystical energy, connecting the physical world with the spiritual one. The Iroko represents time, wisdom, and destiny, quietly witnessing history and human events. People make offerings and perform rituals at its base to seek guidance, protection, and blessings. It is believed that disturbing the tree without proper rituals can lead to misfortune, as it is closely linked to the Orisha and other spiritual beings who protect its secrets. Cutting down an Iroko tree is believed to bring serious bad luck to the person and their family.

The Wise Old Iroko Spirit
Verse 1:1

The wise old Iroko stands so still,
A spirit that time cannot kill.
Its roots are deep, its branches wide,
A keeper of secrets, where spirits hide.
Through countless seasons, it has seen,
The rise and fall of lands once green.

Its bark is etched with stories old,
Of wisdom passed and truths untold.
The winds that rustle through its leaves,

Carry whispers of those who grieve.

Yet in its shade, there's peace to find,
A refuge for the heart and mind.
The Iroko knows the earth's true song,
A melody where all belong.

With age comes sight, both clear and deep,
A guardian of dreams we keep.

* * *

SACRED STORIES / LEGENDS
SECTION 2

ESHU'S CLEVER TRICK
STORY 2:1

Oshun, the Orisha of love and rivers, longed for a child of her own. She prayed beneath the sacred Iroko tree, pouring out her heart and begging for a baby. One night, as she sat beneath its branches, the tree spoke to her. "I am Iroko," it said. "I can give you a child, but you must keep your promise to me when the time comes."

Desperate to become a mother, Oshun agreed. Soon after, she gave birth to a beautiful baby boy. Her sorrow turned to joy as she raised her son, watching him grow strong and happy. However, she never forgot the deal she had made with Iroko. As the years passed, Oshun tried to keep her son far away from the sacred tree, hoping to protect him. But on his seventh birthday, something strange happened. While she was at the market, her son wandered off. When Oshun realized he was missing, she searched frantically until she saw him standing near the massive Iroko tree. Her heart pounded in fear. The ground beneath the tree began to shake and open, ready to take the child as payment for Oshun's wish.

Just as it seemed there was no hope, Eshu, the trickster Orisha, appeared with a mischievous grin. Eshu quickly came up with a plan. He found a strong goat and disguised it, leading it toward the tree. Iroko, believing the goat was the promised child, swallowed it whole. The earth closed, and the danger passed. Oshun ran to her son and held him tightly, overwhelmed with relief. She thanked Eshu for his cleverness and celebrated with joy. From that day on, she danced in gratitude, knowing she had nearly lost what she loved most.

REFLECTION & WISDOM

This tale tells of Oshun's deep longing for a child and her desperate plea to the mystical Iroko tree, which grants her wish in exchange for an unspoken debt. As her son grows, Oshun tries to shield him from the tree's claim, but fate leads him back to its grasp on his seventh birthday. Just as the earth threatens to take the boy, the cunning trickster Eshu intervenes, using his wit to deceive Iroko with a disguised goat. With the boy's life spared and the debt cleverly paid, Oshun rejoices, dancing with gratitude, her heart finally at peace.

* * *

INSIGHTS, OFFERINGS, RITUALS AND SPIRITUAL SIGNIFICANCE
SECTION 3

THE IROKO AND CEIBA
VERSE 3:1

In Africa, the Iroko tree,
A spirit lives so wild and free.
Its branches stretch, its roots run deep,
A place where ancient secrets sleep.

Far across the ocean wide,
In the Caribbean's warm, bright tide,
The Ceiba tree stands tall and grand,
A sacred tree in this new land.

The Taíno people knew it well,
They believed spirits there did dwell,
Resting gently in the shade,
Where the roots and branches softly swayed.

When Africans came from distant shores,
They saw the Ceiba, and much more,
To them, it seemed the same to be,
A cousin of the Iroko tree.

But cutting down this mighty tree,
Brings sorrow to both land and sea.
It's said to bring great harm and pain,
A curse upon the sun and rain.

So let the Ceiba grow so tall,
A guardian spirit is watching all.
In its shade, both earth and sky,
The spirits rest, as time goes by.

* * *

THE CEIBA TREE

Ceiba pentandra, commonly known as the Ceiba tree, is a large tree native to Central and South America, as well as the Caribbean islands. This tree was considered sacred by the Indigenous peoples of the Caribbean, including the Taíno, who were the first inhabitants of these islands before European colonization. When enslaved Africans were brought to the Americas, they recognized the significance of the Ceiba tree, as its sacred nature resembled that of the Iroko tree, which only grows in Africa. As a result, the Ceiba came to be viewed with similar reverence. *In many Afro-Caribbean spiritual traditions, such as Santería, Candomblé, and Umbanda, the Ceiba tree holds a place of high esteem due to this cultural connection.* The tree is believed to house spirits, and various offerings are left at its base to honor and appease these spirits. Common offerings include incense, fruits, and a variety of foods.

* * *

17. Iyami Osoronga
The Ancient Witches and
The Owners of the Birds

A Closer Look at the Iyami Osoronga

The Iyami Osoronga, or Mothers of the Night, are powerful and mysterious spirits in Yoruba tradition. "Iyami" means "mother of mine," while "Osoronga" refers to the screech or call of a flock of birds at night. They are often called the rulers of the birds. Though not considered Orishas, the Iyami Osoronga are primordial spirits that represent the deep forces of women, nature, and justice. While some may view them as diabolical, they are not evil. Instead, they protect the balance of the world and punish those who act unjustly or disrespectfully.

The Iyami Osoronga are typically depicted as a trio of spirit women: the White Witch, the Red Witch, and the Black Witch, each representing a different stage in a woman's life, youth, adulthood, and old age, along with the natural powers connected to those stages. They are closely associated with birds, particularly vultures, owls, and crows, and with women's blood and life force. Olodumare, the Supreme Creator, granted them the power to influence the fate of humans when they break their vows made in heaven or stray from the destiny they chose before coming to Earth. In the beginning of creation, the Iyami Osoronga were said to be the guardians of Olodumare. Some traditions believe they also hold authority over the Ajogun, spirits that cause illness, conflict, and chaos. Because of this, the Iyami must be approached with great caution and respect.

The Iyami have the power to bring Osogbo or spiritual problems like illness, confusion, infertility, and mental distress. They can also send the Ajogun to carry out tasks. If disrespected or ignored, the Iyami may curse or draw energy from the body, leading to serious conditions like cancer, blood disorders, or emotional imbalance. This emphasizes the importance of honoring them properly. As guardians of the sacred mysteries of women, the Iyami are deeply connected to menstruation, childbirth, and the cycles of life and death. They remind us to honor and respect women, the feminine, and the sacred vows we make.

* * *

SACRED STORIES / LEGENDS
SECTION 2

A TALE OF BROKEN VOWS
STORY 2:1

In the early days of the world, humans were struggling to survive. The Earth had plenty of land, but people didn't yet know how to find or grow enough food. Many went hungry and didn't understand how to live well. The birds in the sky saw what was happening. They could see far across the land, and they felt sorry for the humans. They decided to help. They showed the people where food could be found and taught them how to live more safely and successfully. Before helping, the birds made a request. They asked the humans not to harm or kill them in return. The humans agreed and promised to protect the birds.

For a long time, the promise was kept. Life improved, and the birds continued to guide and help the humans. But over time, humans started to become greedy and as a result things became harder again. Food became scarce, and people became desperate and afraid. Esu, the trickster, saw their struggle and gave them a bad idea. He suggested that the birds could be used as food. Some humans, driven by hunger, broke their promise and began hunting the birds. The Iyámì, the spiritual Mothers connected to the birds, were angry and hurt by this betrayal. They went to Olodumare, the highest power, to report what had happened.

Olodumare said the balance had been broken. Because the humans broke their promise, there would be consequences. He gave the Iyámì the power to bring either blessings or problems, depending on how they were respected. From that time on, people learned an important lesson. If they respect the Iyámì and the natural world, they receive blessings. But if they show disrespect, they may face hardship. The story teaches that promises should be kept and that humans must respect the natural world and the help they are given.

REFLECTION & WISDOM

This story teaches that promises must be kept, even when times are hard. When the humans broke their vow to the birds, they upset the balance of nature and faced serious consequences. It reminds us that trust is sacred, and breaking it brings harm to both people and the world.

* * *

INSIGHTS, OFFERINGS, RITUALS AND SPIRITUAL SIGNIFICANCE
SECTION 3

WORSHIP AND OFFERINGS TO THE IYAMI OSORONGA

The proper way to make offerings to the Iyami Osoronga is through a sacred ritual known as Ìpèsè (*ee-PEH-sheh*), which only trained Babalawos are authorized to perform. This practice originates from an ancient pact made with Orunmila during a time when the Iyami sought to destroy the Orishas. In response, Orunmila and Eshu devised a plan to trap and kill the birds representing the Iyami using glue and a machete. However, some of the birds pleaded for mercy, and a new agreement was formed. Through this covenant, the Ìpèsè ceremony became the only acceptable and effective way to make offerings to the Iyami. The ritual is performed to nourish their energy and prevent them from drawing power or life force from the person to whom they are spiritually connected. Offerings in the Ìpèsè ritual often include items such as boiled eggs, red palm oil, pork, rats, mice, rabbits, and other small animals. Each item is chosen carefully based on guidance from an Ifa divination.

CREATING A BIRD FEEDER TO HONOR THE IYAMI AJE

While only a trained Babalawo can carry out direct sacrifices or rituals for the Iyami, anyone can show them reverence by honoring their sacred symbol, the bird. Placing a bird feeder in your yard is a respectful and symbolic way to connect with the natural world and acknowledge the presence of the Iyami. Below is a simple guide for making a bird feeder from a recycled milk jug. This small act honors nature and the sacred role of birds in the spiritual ecosystem.

MATERIALS

- One empty plastic milk jug (clean and dry)
- Scissors or a utility knife
- String or twine
- A stick or wooden spoon (for a perch)
- Birdseed

STEP 1: CUT THE OPENINGS
Cut two openings on opposite sides of the jug, about 2–3 inches wide and 3–4 inches tall, halfway up the jug. These allow the birds to reach the seed.

STEP 2: INSERT A PERCH
Just below each opening, poke small holes and insert a stick or wooden spoon through the jug so it sticks out both sides. This gives birds a place to perch.

STEP 3: ATTACH HANGING STRING
Tie a piece of string or twine securely around the jug's handle to make a loop for hanging.

STEP 4: FILL WITH BIRDSEED
Add birdseed to the jug, keeping the level below the openings.

STEP 5: HANG IN A TREE
Hang the feeder from a tree branch where birds can easily find it. Choose a quiet, shaded spot if possible.

STEP 6: ENJOY!
Watch the birds come and feed, knowing that your small act is part of a larger honoring of life and spirit.

* * *

18. Nana Buruku
Orisha of Creation and Ancient Power

A Closer Look at Nana Buruku

Nana Buruku is deeply respected among some Yoruba communities in Benin and in the diaspora. She is honored as the grandmother of the Orishas and the guardian of life, death, and rebirth. Nana Buruku embodies the ancient wisdom of the earth and oversees the natural cycles of existence and transformation. She is closely associated with swamps and deep waters, where she serves as a healer and protector, guiding souls through the mysteries of death and reincarnation. With a firm yet nurturing presence, Nana upholds justice, brings spiritual cleansing, and offers renewal. In Vodun, Nana Buruku is seen as the great mother and the original creator behind the universe. She is honored as the supreme mother who gave birth to the first divine beings, Mawu and Lisa, who then shaped the world.

Nana, The Grandmother of the Orishas
Verse 1:1

In the swamp where the water flows slowly,
Nana Buruku walks, and all will know.
She is the grandmother of the Orishas,
wise and grand, with power that comes
From the earth and the land.

Her skin is dark, and her presence is strong,
When Nana enters, you feel she belongs.
With ancient knowledge, she heals the ill,
Her hands work magic; her heart is still.

She loves the children, keeps them near,
Her care and wisdom are always clear.
If you seek healing or need help to cope,
She will guide you with love and hope.

She can heal wounds of the spirit and soul,
Bringing you peace, making you whole.
Life, death, karma, she understands it all,
She is the wise woman who answers the call.

Her wisdom is deep, her presence is pure,
With Nana, you'll always feel secure.
She lives by the swamp, near the ocean's tide,
Where nature and spirits walk by her side.

She cares for the earth and feels its pain,
She fights for the planet, for the world to sustain.
Her judgment is firm, her will unyielding,
She stands for justice and spiritual healing.

If you wish for her help,
show respect in kind,
For Nana's power is not blind.
Treat her with care, and you will see,
That Nana will guide you to where you need to be.

* * *

THE GUARDIAN OF REBIRTH
VERSE 1:2

Nana: Keeper of Life and Death
Nana, goddess of life and death,
Guides the spirits with every breath.

Her symbol, a bundle of palm fronds and cowries,
Holds the wisdom of ancient stories.
She is the soft earth, warm and deep,
Cradling the dead in an eternal sleep.

Like a womb that protects and shields,
Her mystery is what she yields.
Through death, Nana creates rebirth,
A new beginning, a new place on Earth.

She transforms the dead, erasing the past,
Preparing them for a vast future.
Austere and just, she stands alone,
Her power felt in every stone.

Her word is law, a solemn vow,
A promise that cannot be broken now.
With each reincarnation,
she clears the mind,
Dissolving memories, leaving none behind.

Old age and senility, in her hand,
Make way for souls to take a stand.
From Yemanjá's motherhood, she stands apart,
Ending fertility with a steady heart.

Her role is vital, yet full of grace,
She guides souls to a peaceful place.
Both mother and grandmother, she protects the old,
Oversees the family, so strong and bold.

She governs floods, rain, and mud,
Her power flows like an endless flood.
When Nana dances, slow and deep,
Her movements cradle, the spirits keep.

In her dance, there's peace and care,
A nurturing presence beyond compare.

* * *

SACRED STORIES / LEGENDS
SECTION 2

HOW NANA HELPED CREATE HUMANITY
STORY 2:1

Nana's Gift of Sacred Clay
Olorun called Obatala near,
"Create the world, make life appear."
Obatala tried with all his might,
But his first attempts didn't turn out right.

He shaped a figure from the air,
But it vanished, wasn't there.
He carved from wood, but it was too stiff,
And the stone was worse; it couldn't be lifted.

From fire, the form was burned away,
Oil and water, too, wouldn't stay.
Palm wine failed; all seemed lost,
Creation came with such a cost.

Then Nana saw Obatala's plight,
And offered her a gift to make things right.
"Take my clay from the lagoon's deep bed,
The sacred earth where life is fed."
With care, Obatala shaped the clay,
And humans began to take their way.

Olorun breathed life, gave them souls,
And soon humanity was whole.
The orishas helped them thrive and grow,
But Nana's balance, they must know:
She gave the clay to form their start,
And takes it back when they depart.

From earth to life and life to ground,
In Nana's clay, all is bound.

This story tells of Obatala's struggle to create humanity, as his early attempts with various materials all failed. Seeing his plight, Nana, the wise and ancient orisha, offered her sacred clay from the depths of the lagoon. With this gift, Obatala shaped the first humans, and Olorun breathed life into them, completing the creation. The tale reminds us of the cycle of existence, Nana's clay not only gives form to life but also reclaims it in the end, binding all to the balance of nature.

INSIGHTS, OFFERINGS, RITUALS AND SPIRITUAL SIGNIFICANCE
SECTION 3

NANA BURUKU'S OFFERINGS

Nana Buruku is honored with natural and simple offerings that reflect her deep connection to the earth and the mysteries of life and death. Traditional offerings include rum, tobacco, coffee, white cloth, soil, clean water, cooked foods, shrimp, coconut, tomatoes, fresh fruits, grains, and flowers. Sacred plants like cypress, garlic, juniper, mint, and marshmallow root are also commonly presented to her. Her associated colors are white and earth tones, symbolizing purity, wisdom, and her bond with the natural world. Offerings are made with deep respect to seek her blessings for protection, healing, wisdom, and spiritual guidance. They may be given near swamps, marshes, rivers, under large trees, or placed in earthen pots or clay vessels, sometimes buried or poured directly onto the ground.

* * *

19. OBA
ORISHA OF MARRIAGE, DEVOTION AND COMMITMENT

A CLOSER LOOK AT OBA

OBA IS the Orisha of marriage, devotion, and commitment, revered for her strength, wisdom, and unwavering loyalty. As the eldest wife of Shango, her story is one of love, sacrifice, and the pain of betrayal, yet she remains a guardian of enduring relationships. She oversees the sacred bonds of marriage, guiding couples through challenges and renewal. Despite the sorrow in her tale, Oba embodies resilience, offering protection and wisdom in matters of the heart. Her presence ensures that love, trust, and commitment remain steadfast, making her a powerful force in maintaining harmony within unions.

OBA: QUEEN OF LOVE AND STRENGTH
VERSE 1:1

In marriage, she reigns with a regal grace,
Her wisdom and strength, no one can replace.
Though her tale is tinged with sorrow and strife,
Oba embodies the power of life.

The eldest wife, with heart so true,
Her love, a gift both old and new.
Yet jealousy's sting, sharp as a knife,
Tore at her heart, disrupting her life.

But still, she rules over bonds that bind,

A queen of relationships, strong and kind.
For in the trials of love and pain,
Oba remains, in heart, unchained.

* * *

THE QUEEN OF COMMITMENT
VERSE 1:2

Oh, queen of commitment and bond,
Oba rules where hearts connect and respond.
In relationships, she holds the key,
Guiding us toward harmony.

She governs the vows we make so true,
Helping connections grow and renew.
In unions, her wisdom shows,
Bringing peace where discord flows.

She watches over the ties that bind,
In moments of joy or when we're blind.
Oba's strength leads through the pain,
Helping us to love again.

Through trials and storms, she stands near,
Offering guidance, wiping the tear.
Oba reigns over bonds and trust,
In her care, our hearts adjust.

* * *

SACRED STORIES / LEGENDS
SECTION 2

THE STORY OF OBA'S SACRIFICE
STORY 2:1

Oba was loyal, Shango's first bride,
She stood by his side with devotion and pride.

But Shango, the king of thunder and might,
Loved Oshun's beauty, her charm, and her light.

Oba grew sad, feeling left all alone,
Her heart ached for Shango, her love's only throne.
She went to Oshun, seeking her way,
To win Shango's heart and make him stay.

Oshun, so cunning, with a sly little grin,
Spoke words to Oba that burned deep within:
"Do something bold, something no one would dare,
And Shango will love you beyond all compare.

"Cook him his meal, his favorite stew,
Add a part of yourself to prove your love true."
Believing the lie, Oba obeyed,
Her love was pure, but her trust was betrayed.

She cut off her ear, her heart full of cheer,
Thinking, "Shango will see my devotion so clear!"
The stew was prepared, and with pride in her soul,
She served it to Shango, her love her sole goal.

But Shango grew angry, his face filled with rage,
"This act isn't love, it's foolish!" he raged.
He pushed her away, his words harsh and cold,
And Oba's heart shattered, her spirit turned old.

With tears on her cheeks, she ran far and wide,
To the river she fled, with no place to hide.
Her grief took her over, she dove deep below,
And the waters embraced her, soft in their flow.

Oba transformed to the river's pure grace,
Her sorrow now flowing in each gentle trace.
Her story remains, of loyalty's cost,
Of love that is true, but too often gets lost.

Now Oba's a river, her spirit runs deep,

A lesson for hearts and the promises we keep.
She teaches us all, through the waters that flow,
That love should be gentle, not born out of woe.

This tale recounts the tragic story of Oba, Shango's first wife, whose deep devotion led her to a heartbreaking fate. Feeling neglected as Shango favored Oshun, Oba sought advice to regain his love, only to be deceived into a desperate act of sacrifice, cutting off her own ear to prove her devotion. Instead of earning his affection, her action provoked Shango's anger, leading to her rejection and despair. Overcome with sorrow, she fled to the waters, where she transformed into the Oba River. Her story serves as a timeless lesson on the dangers of blind sacrifice in love and the importance of self-worth.

* * *

INSIGHTS, OFFERINGS, RITUALS AND SPIRITUAL SIGNIFICANCE
SECTION 3

OBA'S SACRED OFFERINGS
VERSE 3:1

To Oba, queen of love and grace,
We offer gifts in sacred space.
Pigeons, goats, and chickens, too,
With hearts of respect, we give to you.

Guinea fowl and ducks we bring,
In honor of the queen, our offering.
A glass of water, crystal clear,
Symbolizing peace, we hold dear.

Specific plants and foods so pure,
Her blessings on them will endure.
In reverence, we bow and pray,
For Oba's guidance every day.

Through these offerings, we seek her aid,
In bonds of love, where hearts are laid.
Oba's favor, we hope to gain,
With every gift, her peace we claim.
Ase.

20. OBATALA
ORISHA OF PEACE, PURITY AND THE FATHER OF ALL HUMANITY

A CLOSER LOOK AT OBATALA

OBATALA IS one of the oldest and most revered Orishas in Yoruba tradition, embodying purity, truth, white light, and justice. Known as the Orisha of wisdom, clarity, creativity, and peace, he is often seen as a fatherly figure who nurtures, guides, and protects humanity with grace and moral strength. Cloaked in pure white light, Obatala symbolizes light itself radiant, pure, and transcending all colors. As the divine creator of humanity, Obatala governs all aspects of the human body, particularly the head and mind, overseeing thoughts, intelligence, and some aspects of human consciousness. While he is most associated with peace and serenity, Obatala also possesses a fierce warrior aspect, enforcing justice and defending the vulnerable with unwavering strength. His connection to purity and strength is reflected in his association with silver and all white metals.

In nature, Obatala is symbolized by mountains powerful, steadfast, and always reaching toward the heavens. Unlike other Orishas, Obatala has both male and female manifestations, symbolizing divine completeness and perfect balance. Obatala's primary color is white, though his path may be accented with red, purple, or other hues depending on the aspect he represents. His sacred number is 8 and its multiples, representing his infinite connection to creation and cosmic order. When a person's tutelary Orisha cannot be determined, they are often consecrated to Obatala, trusting in his role as a universal father and protector. Above all, Obatala teaches that peace, honesty, humility, and compassion are the highest virtues, guiding humanity toward wisdom and spiritual fulfillment.

PRAYER TO OBATALA, SPIRIT OF PEACE AND LIGHT
VERSE 1:1

Obatala, Father so bright,
You shine with love, wrapped in white.
You made our bodies, mind, and soul,
You help us grow and make us whole.

You teach us peace and how to be kind,
You guide our hearts and calm our mind.
Like a mountain, strong and tall,
You help us rise when we might fall.

You stand for truth, and what is fair,
You show us how to love and care.
When we are lost or feeling low,
You lead us where the good paths go.

Obatala, please hear our prayer,
Protect us with your gentle care.
Bring us peace, and help us see
The best of who we all can be.
Ase.

* * *

OBATALA: THE WISE AND JUST
VERSE 1:2

Obatala, wise and kind,
A father figure, gentle and refined.
Dressed in white, with staff in hand,
He guides with wisdom, across the land.

But sometimes, He's young, bold, and bright,
Holding a torch or sword of light.
He seeks the truth, He fights for right,
Bringing justice into the night.

King of Kings, with mind so clear,
Intelligent, wise, without fear.
He shows sobriety, strength, and grace,
Moral energy lights His face.

A creator at heart, He loves to see,
Creativity in all that can be.
Big or small, in any form,
Obatala values art, the calm, the storm.

* * *

THE LIGHT OF WISDOM AND PEACE
VERSE 1:3

Obatala, the Orisha of light,
Shining brightly, pure and white.
With wisdom deep and heart so kind,
He guides us all, both heart and mind.

In white he shines, so full of grace,
A father's love, a warm embrace.
He watches over, calm and true,
Helping us all in all we do.

The head and mind, he rules with care,
Our thoughts, our dreams, he helps us share.
A peaceful soul, so full of might,
He stands for justice, for what's right.

Silver and white, his colors gleam,
Like mountains high, a steady beam.
Obatala, so strong and wise,
With strength that reaches to the skies.

In balance, he is both male and queen,
A perfect mix, a sight unseen.
His number eight shows endless ties,
To all creation, reaching skies.

When lost or unsure, we call his name,
Obatala, always the same.
He teaches love, compassion, peace,
And guides us to a life's release.

* * *

SACRED STORIES / LEGENDS
SECTION 2

THE CREATION OF HUMANITY AND THE GIFT OF COMPASSION
STORY 2:1

In the beginning, when Olodumare, the supreme creator, decided to shape the world, he entrusted Obatala with an important task. He gave Obatala a sacred bag, filled with everything needed to create the earth, the seas, the trees, and the animals. Obatala, chosen for his wisdom and grace, was to bring the world into existence.

Before beginning his work, Olodumare reminded Obatala of one important thing: he must first offer palm wine to Esu, the divine messenger, as a sign of respect. This offering was not just a ritual; it was meant to ensure success in his task. But Obatala, filled with pride and confidence, decided he didn't need to make the offering. Instead of honoring Esu, he drank the palm wine himself. He drank too much, letting the effects take over, and soon he fell into a deep, uncontrollable sleep, leaving his task unfinished. While Obatala slept, another divine being, Odudua, saw the opportunity to step in. Odudua took the sacred bag and completed the work Obatala had started. Odudua shaped the land, planted the trees, and created the seas and the winds. When Obatala awoke, he found the world already made, but it wasn't by his hands. He was filled with sorrow and shame.

Realizing his mistake, Obatala went to Olodumare and confessed everything. Olodumare, seeing the genuine remorse in Obatala's heart, forgave him and gave him another task: to create human beings. This time, Obatala worked with great care, molding the first humans from earth and sand. Olodumare breathed life into them, bringing them into existence. But Obatala, still struggling with his pride, drank too much palm wine again. As a result, some of the humans he created came out imperfect, missing limbs or with other unique features. When Olodumare saw the differences among the people, he asked Obatala what had happened. Ashamed, Obatala admitted his mistake once more and promised never to drink again. Olodumare, once again filled with compassion, forgave him and gave him a new role: to become the father of all humanity. Obatala declared that those born with differences, those who were seen as imperfect, would be his closest and most beloved children. From that day forward, Obatala became the Orisha of purity and the protector of people with physical or mental disabilities. His story serves as a reminder that every person, no matter their appearance or abilities, has sacred value and deserves to be treated with love, respect, and kindness.

REFLECTION & WISDOM

This story of Obatala teaches us about the importance of responsibility, humility, and compassion. Despite his initial pride and mistake, Obatala's journey shows that even the greatest among us can falter. However, his genuine remorse and willingness to correct his wrongs led to a greater understanding of love and care for all people, especially those who are different. His story reminds us that perfection is not the goal, kindness, empathy, and acceptance of others, regardless of their differences, are what truly make us whole.

* * *

OBATALA'S JOURNEY
STORY 2:2

A long time ago, it was believed that the Orishas including, Obatala, walked the earth and lived side by side with humanity. One day, he decided to travel to the city of Oyó to honor Shango, the mighty king. Before beginning his journey, a wise babalawo gave him some important advice: "Wear three sets of white clothes to stay pure and bright, and no matter what challenges you face along the way, do not complain."

Obatala, known for his wisdom and patience, took the advice to heart. He dressed in pure white and set off on his journey. As he traveled, he encountered Esu, the trickster, who made it his mission to make Obatala's journey as difficult as possible. Esu spilled palm oil, charcoal, and syrup on Obatala's clothes, making a mess wherever he went. But Obatala refused to let Esu's mischief get the best of him. He calmly bathed and changed into a fresh set of clothes each time, continuing his journey with patience and grace. After some time, Obatala finally reached Oyó. However, his journey took an unexpected turn. He was wrongfully accused of a crime he did not commit and was thrown into jail. As he sat in the dark prison, the kingdom around him began to suffer. The crops dried up, the land grew barren, and the people grew anxious. Shango, desperate to restore balance, set out to uncover the truth. After much searching, he discovered that Obatala had been falsely accused and quickly worked to free him.

Once Obatala was released, the Orishas gathered around him, cleaning him with great care and respect. The kingdom began to heal, the crops flourished once again, and the people showed their deep gratitude and respect by offering prayers for Obatala's well-being. Obatala's journey teaches powerful lessons about patience, humility, and perseverance. Despite the many trials he faced, Obatala remained true to his values, maintaining his purity of heart and calm demeanor. His story reminds us that no matter how difficult life's challenges may be, staying grounded in our values and maintaining a peaceful spirit can help us overcome anything.

REFLECTION & WISDOM

The story of Obatala offers valuable lessons on resilience, humility, and the importance of maintaining integrity. It teaches us that no matter how difficult the journey or how many obstacles we face, we should remain calm and avoid letting frustration control us. By persevering through hardships and staying true to our values, we can overcome challenges with grace. It also emphasizes the power of patience and the need for justice, reminding us that even when things seem unfair, the truth will eventually prevail, and balance will be restored.

* * *

INSIGHTS, OFFERINGS, RITUALS AND SPIRITUAL SIGNIFICANCE
SECTION 3

OFFERINGS TO OBATALA

- **Stones associated with Obatala**: Moonstone, Quartz, Silver.

- **Offerings to Obatala include:** Rice, Eggs, Coconut, Yams, White Hens, Doves, Cotton, Milk, Cocoa Butter, White Flowers, White Cloth, Candles, Pears, Snails, Silver Coins.
- **Taboos include:** Alcoholic Beverages, Beans in some lineages.
- **Plants associated with Obatala:** Sage, Cotton, Mugwort, Clover, Mint, Peace Lilies, White Flowers.
- **Sacred Places/ Locations to this Orisha:** Obatala is linked to high mountains and the sky, symbolizing his association with purity, wisdom, and fairness. These elevated places are considered his domain, where offerings are often made in honor to his divine presence.

* * *

THE MANY FACES OF OBATALA

Obatala is a revered Orisha with many different forms, known as *caminos* or paths. Each of Obatala's paths reflects a unique aspect of his nature, character, and influence in the world. Some paths are nurturing and compassionate, while others are strict and wise. Obatala's many forms help guide, protect, and bring balance to different situations. In the Yoruba tradition, it is believed that Obatala has numerous paths, each showcasing his versatility in addressing life's challenges. Some of the most well-known paths of Obatala include:

- **Obatala Ayaguna (Obatalá Ayagguna):** A warrior-like aspect of Obatalá, known for being bold and fiery.
- **Obatalá Ibaibo:** A mysterious form of Obatalá symbolizing deep wisdom and the "all-seeing eye."
- **Obatala Okeilu:** Obatalá's aspect that lives in high places, like mountaintops.
- Obatala Obalufón: Represents the sun and is connected to Christ in Christian tradition.
- **Obatala Yeku Yeku:** Protector of health.
- **Obatala Alaguema/Agemo:** The chameleon who helped defeat Olokun and played a role in the creation of the world.
- **Obatala Oshanla:** A female form of Obatalá, known as the mother of white light and the bride of Olofin.

- **Obatala Ogan:** Another female aspect of Obatalá, believed to have captured death and stolen its scythe. Protects against injustice and greed.

* * *

A Simple Obatala Tranquility Bath

The purpose of this ritual is to honor Obatala and invite peace, calm, and tranquility into your life.

Items Needed (choose a few or all):

- White flower petals
- Herbs like basil, mint, lavender, or cotton (whatever you have)
- A little coconut milk, regular milk, cr rice water
- Crushed eggshell powder (if you have it)
- A clear quartz crystal or a piece of silver (optional)
- A white candle (offering for Obatala)
- Do not use salt or alcohol in the bath (they are considered taboos for Obatala).
- Be creative! Add what feels right to you. Let your inner self guide you.

* * *

Step 1: Make an Herbal Water (Omiero)
Boil the herbs, petals, and other ingredients together in water then strain out the herbs, keeping only the water.

Step 2: Take Ycur Bath
Use the strained herbal water in your bath, and as you bathe, focus your mind on calmness and inner peace.

Step 3: Offer a Candle to Obatala
Light a small white candle, dedicate it to Obatala, and ask Obatala to bring peace, healing, and tranquility into your life.

Optional Step: Save some of the herbal water for future baths, keep the bottle near the candle, and pray over it daily for several days, then use the remaining liquid for a future bath.

STEP 4: RECITE A SIMPLE PRAYER
Simple Prayer Example: *"Obatala, please bring peace and calm into my life. Surround me with your healing light. Ase."* Alternatively, you can use the prayer that feels right to you or the one above:

STEP 6: CLOSURE & FINAL THOUGHTS
Thank Obatala for his presence and guidance. You can say something like: *"Thank you, Obatala, for your strength, wisdom, and peace of mind."*

* * *

21. OCHOSI
ORISHA OF HUNTING AND JUSTICE

A CLOSER LOOK AT OCHOSI

OCHOSI, also spelled Oshosi or Oxóssi, is an important Orisha in the Yoruba pantheon. He is known as a divine hunter and protector who represents justice, focus, and fairness. He is often depicted with a bow and arrow, symbols of his sharp aim and ability to seek the truth. These tools also highlight his deep connection to nature and the wild. Ochosi typically wears clothing made from animal skins and feathers. His main colors are blue and yellow. Blue stands for calmness, clarity, and truth, reflecting Ochosi's peaceful yet focused nature and his link to the sky and spiritual wisdom. Yellow represents energy, optimism, and strength, showing his vibrant spirit and the powerful drive he gives to those pursuing justice and guidance. Together, these colors symbolize the balance Ochosi maintains between calm patience and active determination.

In Yoruba stories, Ochosi is closely tied to the forest and hunting. He helps keep balance in the world and protects innocent people or those treated unfairly. People turn to him for guidance when facing challenges related to justice and fairness. Ochosi works alongside Ogun, the Orisha of iron and war. While Ogun focuses on building and creating, Ochosi ensures that justice is served. He uses his skills to find wrongdoers and restore fairness. As the guardian of hunters, trackers, and all who spend time in nature, Ochosi teaches that hunting should be done respectfully and only to meet basic needs, not for sport. To Ochosi, every animal's life is a sacred gift that helps keep the balance of nature, highlighting the need to honor and respect all living creatures. Ochosi also teaches people to care for the environment and live in harmony with the earth. Beyond guiding hunters, he watches over the wilderness and its creatures, making sure forests remain healthy and sacred. He reminds people of their responsibility to protect nature and honor the sacred places of the Orishas. In addition, Ochosi is connected to healing through his close relationship with Osain, the Orisha of herbs. He has deep knowledge of medicinal plants and encourages the careful, respectful use of nature's resources for healing rather than harm. Finally, Ochosi helps people stay focused and determined as they work toward their goals. He offers protection and strength to those who seek to do what is right and fair.

PRAYER TO OCHOSI, ORISHA OF JUSTICE
VERSE I:I

O Ochosi, hunter so true,
With eyes sharp and wisdom too,
Guide our hearts through paths unknown,
Bring us justice, make it shown.

With arrows swift and steady hand,
You hunt for truth across the land.
Clear our minds, dispel the lies,
Let fairness rule beneath your skies.

O protector, wise and just,
In your strength, we place our trust.
Guide our steps, lead us right,
O Oshosi, bless our fight.

May your arrows of justice fly,
To heal the wounds that never die.
O Ochosi, we call to thee,
Bring us truth and set us free.
Ase!

* * *

OCHOSI, HUNTER OF TRUTH
VERSE 1:2

Deep in the forest, wild and free,
Ochosi roams where none can see.
With bow in hand and arrow strong,
He hunts for truth and rights the wrong.
The Orisha of justice, sharp and wise,
He sees through secrets, tricks, and lies.

If someone suffers, lost and unheard,
Ochosi strikes with truth like a word.
His arrows fly, so fast, so true,
They never miss, they find their due.

He walks with Ogun, side by side,
Through shadowed trees, their spirits guide.
For those who seek what's fair and right,
Ochosi shines, a steady light.
In courts, in hearts, in times of need,
He fights for justice with skill and speed.

So call his name when wrong is near,
He'll bring the truth, so strong, so clear.
Through forests deep and skies above,
Ochosi rules with strength and love.

* * *

OCHOSI, HUNTER OF WISDOM
VERSE 1:3

Through forests deep and rivers wide,
Ochosi walks with silent stride.
The hunter keen, so sharp and fast,
His arrows fly, they hold steadfast.

He tracks the deer, the birds, the beast,
Providing meals, a mighty feast.

With wisdom bright and aim so true,
He brings the gifts that help us through.

A spirit wise, both light and strong,
He loves the arts, the dance, the song.
He sees the beauty, deep and bright,
In nature's grace and morning light.

With careful thought and hunter's mind,
He waits, he plans, he moves like wind.
Both craft and cunning guide his way,
A master of the hunt each day.

Ochosi, bring your gifts so fair,
Your truth, your strength, your endless care.
With wisdom deep and hunter's might,
You lead us through both dark and light.

* * *

SACRED STORIES / LEGENDS
SECTION 2

THE ARROW OF JUSTICE
STORY 2:1

Ochosi was a skilled and dedicated hunter, known for his sharp aim and strong sense of justice. One day, Elegua gave him an important task: to find a rare bird as a gift for Orula. Determined to complete his mission, Ochosi set out into the wilderness. Using his expert tracking skills, he quickly found the bird and carefully captured it. He placed it in a cage and hurried home, eager to deliver it to Orula.

However, while Ochosi was away, his mother returned home and saw the bird. Thinking it was meant for a meal, she killed, prepared, and cooked it, then left for the market without knowing its true purpose. When Ochosi returned and saw what had happened, he was devastated. The bird he had worked so hard to capture was gone. Filled with anger and disappointment, he knew he had no choice but to go back and find another one. Wasting no time, he went hunting again. With great skill and patience, he caught another rare bird and delivered it to Orula and then to Olodumare. Impressed by his determination and hunting ability, Olodumare granted him the honor of becoming an Orisha. But even after his success, Ochosi could not let go of his anger. He wanted justice for what had happened, so he asked Olodumare for a special request: "Let me punish the one who destroyed my work." Olodumare granted his wish. Ochosi took his bow and arrow, aimed high, and released a powerful shot. But as the arrow flew, he suddenly heard a painful cry, his own mother's voice. At that moment, he realized the terrible mistake he had made. His own mother was the one he had struck down. Filled with grief and regret, Ochosi accepted the weight of his actions. From that day on, he became the Orisha of justice, truth, and consequences. He hunts not for food, but for fairness, ensuring that all wrongdoing is met with the right judgment. To this day, Ochosi is known as the divine hunter, using his skills to guide justice and protect those who seek the truth.

REFLECTION & WISDOM

This story follows Ochosi, a skilled hunter tasked with capturing a rare bird for Orula. After successfully trapping it, he left it at home, unaware that his mother, thinking it was food, had unknowingly prepared and sold it. Upon discovering the loss, Ochosi, filled with anger and urgency, caught another bird and presented it to Olofi, who rewarded him by making him an Orisha. When granted a wish, Ochosi, seeking justice, chose to punish the one responsible, only to realize too late that it was his own mother. Overcome with grief, he accepted his fate as the Orisha of justice, forever ensuring truth and fairness prevail.

* * *

THE HUNTER'S TRUTH
STORY 2:2

A kingdom once was filled with fear,
A wild beast caused danger near.
It killed the cows and ruined crops,
And none could make the creature stop.

The king declared a mighty prize,

To anyone who'd end the beast's rise.
Many tried, but none could win,
Until Ochosi, the hunter, stepped in.

With bow in hand and arrows true,
He tracked the beast, as hunters do.
Through forest deep, for days he went,
Until the beast's dark home was spent.

With one great shot, he took it down,
And brought the beast to the king's crown.
But jealous men, with hearts of spite,
Framed Ochosi in the dead of night.

They claimed he stole the royal gold,
And left him locked in prison cold.
Ochosi called to Eshu's might,
To help him find the truth's true light.

The very next day, a bird did sing,
Of lies and plots within the king.
The truth was clear, the king did see,
The court had framed him unfairly.

The king then freed him, and all was right,
He punished those who caused the fight.
From that day on, Ochosi's name,
Was known for justice and fair fame.

* * *

REFLECTION & WISDOM

This story tells of Ochosi, a skilled hunter who saved a kingdom from a deadly beast, earning the king's favor. However, envious courtiers falsely accused him of stealing royal gold, leading to his unjust imprisonment. Calling upon Eshu, Ochosi sought the truth, and the next day, a bird exposed the conspirators' lies. The king, realizing the deception, freed Ochosi and punished those responsible. From that day forward, Ochosi became known as the Orisha of justice, ensuring fairness and truth prevailed.

* * *

INSIGHTS, OFFERINGS, RITUALS AND SPIRITUAL SIGNIFICANCE
Section 3

Offerings to Ochosi

Offerings to Ochosi often include game animals like rabbits, goats, pigs, guinea fowl, and pigeons, along with foods such as eko (corn pudding), plantains, mangoes, pears, papayas, and other fruits. People also offer items like gin, rum, honey, yams, and arrows, which symbolize the call for justice. These offerings are typically placed in forests and natural settings, where Ochosi's energy is believed to be strongest.

* * *

The Many Faces of Ochosi

Ochosi is a skilled and focused Orisha with many different forms, known as caminos. Some paths show him as a patient hunter, others as a fierce protector of justice and freedom. As a master tracker who never misses his target, Ochosi's many paths reflect his ability to guide, protect, and overcome obstacles. Some of the most well-known paths of Ochosi include:

- **Ochosi Móta:** Oshosi Móta defends the land, hunting both physical and spiritual enemies.
- **Ochosi Ibualámo:** A skilled hunter and fisherman, Ochosi Ibualámo resides in the river's depths, armed with a bow, arrows, and a whip.
- **Ochosi Alé:** Oshosi Alé hunts evil spirits and malevolent individuals by night, shielding the area from their influence.
- **Ochosi Marundé:** A warrior and skilled healer, Ochosi Marundé uses plants for healing.
- **Ochosi Otín:** The female aspect of Ochosi, often seen as his twin and constant companion during hunts.

- **Ochosi Kayoshosi:** A path of Ochosi known for hunting down thieves and wrongdoers, as well as helping resolve conflicts and disputes.

In conclusion, the offerings and various paths of Ochosi reveal his strength as a hunter, protector, and spiritual guide. He teaches us to pursue justice, act with integrity, and live in harmony with both nature and the divine.

* * *

22. ODUDUWA
ANCESTRAL KING AND FATHER
OF THE YORUBA PEOPLE

A CLOSER LOOK AT ODUDUWA

ODUDUWA IS one of the most important figures in the Yoruba religion. He is known as the first ancestor and founder of the Yoruba people. Many stories say he came down from the sky to bring order to the world. According to legend, he worked with Obatala to create the world. Oduduwa dropped some earth onto the water, and a rooster spread it out to form land. This land became *Ile-Ife*, the sacred city of the Yoruba. Oduduwa became the first king of Ile-Ife and helped unite different groups of people. He started the first Yoruba kingdom and is seen as the beginning of the Yoruba royal family. Today, many Yoruba kings believe they are his descendants. Oduduwa is remembered as more than just a king; he is also seen as a divine ancestor of the Yoruba people, a leader, and an Orisha. He helped shape Yoruba life by starting important systems of leadership, religion, and culture. Many Yoruba people proudly call themselves *"Omo Oduduwa,"* which means "children of Oduduwa." Different places tell different stories about him. Some say he was an Orisha from the start, while others say he became divine after his great deeds. But in every story, Oduduwa is honored as the one who began the journey of the Yoruba people. He stands as a symbol of wisdom, leadership, and unity. Through his story, the Yoruba people remember where they come from and the values that matter most.

ODUDUWA: THE FIRST KING
A Prayer and Poem
VERSE I:I

Oduduwa, first of kings,
From you, our sacred spirit springs.
You breathed the world from dust and flame,
And gave the Yoruba a holy name.

O father wise, O source of might,
You turned the chaos into light.
With hands that shaped both land and law,
You built the world with silent awe.

Guardian of earth, so rich, so wide,
In you, the deepest truths abide.
The soil you bless, the fields you tend,
Bring forth the life that has no end.

You stand where justice finds its voice,
Where culture lives, and hearts rejoice.
Protector of the sacred lore,
You open ancient wisdom's door.

O keeper of our roots so deep,
In dreams and stories that we keep,
You walk with kings, with chiefs, with seers,
And whisper guidance through the years.

Oduduwa, great and high,
Your name shall never fade or die.
When storms arise or paths grow dim,
We look to you we call to him.

Shine through our joy, stand in our pain,
Let your strong spirit still remain.
And as we rise, and as we lead,
Let your great light fulfill our need.

O father, founder, flame and guide,
In you, our faith shall still abide.
Oduduwa, hear this humble cry:
Lift our spirits, draw us high.

* * *

THE ONE WHO BROUGHT US TOGETHER
A Prayer and Poem
VERSE 1:2

Oduduwa, father of the Yoruba people,
Ancestor of kings, source of our strength,
We honor you, the great unifier,
The one who brought harmony to the land.

From Oke Ora, your journey began,
To Ile-Ife, where you shaped our clan.
You built a legacy, strong and true,
A foundation of wisdom for all to pursue.

Father of nations, protector of peace,
Your spirit guides us and will never cease.
Teach us to walk in unity and pride,
With the strength of our ancestors by our side.

Oduduwa, hero of our story,
May we reflect your eternal glory.
Bless your children, now and forever,
As we honor you, always together.
Ase.

* * *

SACRED STORIES / LEGENDS
SECTION 2

THE STORY OF ODUDUWA
STORY 2:1

In Ile-Ife, the first city of light,
Oduduwa ruled with wisdom and might.
He built a place where peace could grow,
Where the Orishas' wisdom would always show.

131

The Orishas, spirits of sky and land,
Guided the people with a gentle hand.
Oduduwa taught them how to pray,
To honor the Orishas in every way.

He was the father of kings, strong and wise,
Teaching his people to rise and to rise.
Justice and peace were his guiding rule,
And harmony was his golden tool.

His legacy lives on, strong and true,
In every king, in all they do.
Oduduwa's name will never fade,
For the Yoruba people, his light will never trade.

From Ile-Ife, where the world began,
Oduduwa led with a divine plan.
He showed the way to honor the earth,
And his story reminds us of our worth.

REFLECTION & WISDOM

This story honors Oduduwa, the revered founder of Ile-Ife and the first king of the Yoruba people. With wisdom and strength, he established a land of peace, where the Orishas guided humanity and spiritual devotion flourished. As the father of kings, he instilled justice, harmony, and reverence for tradition, ensuring that his legacy endured through generations. His teachings shaped the foundation of Yoruba culture, reminding his people of their divine heritage and the sacred connection between the earth and the heavens.

* * *

INSIGHTS, OFFERINGS, RITUALS AND SPIRITUAL SIGNIFICANCE
SECTION 3

HISTORICAL FACTS ABOUT ODUDUWA

- ***Founder of Ile-Ife***: *Oduduwa is believed to be the legendary founder of Ile-Ife, the spiritual heart of the Yoruba people. He descended from the heavens to create the first humans and establish Yoruba civilization.*
- ***Ancestor of Yoruba Kings***: *Many Yoruba kings trace their lineage back to Oduduwa. His descendants founded powerful kingdoms such as Oyo, Ijebu, Ekiti, and Ondo.*
- ***First King (Oba)***: *Oduduwa is regarded as the first Oba (king) in Yoruba history. His leadership is seen as divinely chosen, linking him to the Orishas and ancestral spirits.*
- ***Various Stories of His Origin***: *Some stories say Oduduwa came from heaven, while others say he traveled from the East on a divine mission sent by Olodumare, the supreme God.*
- ***Ile-Ife: The Sacred City***: *Ile-Ife, where Oduduwa first ruled, is considered the birthplace of the Yoruba people and their cultural and spiritual center.*
- ***Influence on Other African Kingdoms***: *Oduduwa's descendants spread Yoruba culture beyond Yorubaland, influencing kingdoms like Benin and other parts of West Africa.*
- ***Oduduwa's Legacy***: *Today, Oduduwa is honored in Yoruba culture through festivals and ceremonies, with his name and influence central to many Yoruba kings.*

23. Ogun

Orisha of iron, war, and craftsmanship

A Closer Look at Ogun

OGUN IS a powerful and ancient Orisha in the Yoruba tradition, revered as the spirit of iron, labor, war, and technology. As both a divine blacksmith and an unstoppable warrior, Ogun holds a unique place in the pantheon of Orishas. He is credited with teaching humanity how to forge and use metal tools, revolutionizing the way people build homes, cultivate land, and protect their communities. His influence extends to all who rely on tools: blacksmiths, hunters, engineers, mechanics, surgeons, and soldiers, making him a vital guardian of progress and productivity. In myth, Ogun is the one who forged a path through the dense wilderness with his iron tools, allowing the Orishas to descend from the heavens to Earth, symbolizing his role as a trailblazer and problem-solver. He is also remembered as one of the earliest kings of the sacred city of Ife, whose reign was marked by justice and innovation.

After disappearing into the forest, he vowed to continue supporting those who honor him and call on his name with sincerity and purpose.Ogun's presence is felt wherever there is determination, struggle, and transformation. He represents the energy that overcomes obstacles, whether they be physical, emotional, or spiritual. His character teaches that real power comes not just from brute force, but from discipline, skill, and integrity. As the Orisha of iron and industry, Ogun stands at the crossroads of tradition and modernity, reminding us that all advancements are rooted in the sacred forces of nature, hard work, and the courage to face life's challenges head-on.

OGUN, THE BRAVE AND STRONG
VERSE 1:1

Ogun, the warrior, so strong and wise,
With iron and fire, you light up the skies.
You rule over hunting, farming, and war,
Your power and courage we all adore.

A machete you carry, shining and bright,
It clears the path, bringing the light.
You taught us to build, to shape and create,
With tools and knowledge, you opened the gate.

Iron is sacred, and strength is your way,
Through struggles and battles, you help us each day.
At the railroad tracks, we leave you gifts,
Hoping for strength as your spirit lifts.

Ogun, the fearless, with power so true,
We honor and thank you in all that we do.

* * *

OGUN'S KNIFE
VERSE 1:2

Ogun's knife, sharp and true,
Used in sacrifice, a sacred hue.
Not the Orisha Priests, but Ogun's might,
Takes life with his guiding light.

Before the offering, the words are said,
"Ogun shoro shoro, Ogun shoro shoro," we tread.
Ogun is fierce, his power is clear,
Eyebale Kuwo, blood offering here.

We invoke Ogun, his strength we seek,
Sacrifice protects us, bold and unique.
Against death's reach, we stand tall,

135

Ogun's protection guards us all.

Ogun speaks loudly, his voice is strong,
In the rhythm of life, we all belong.

* * *

SACRED STORIES / LEGENDS
SECTION 2

OGUN, THE PROTECTOR OF IRE
STORY 2:1

Long ago, Ogun, the Orisha of iron, war, and labor, was known for his great strength and skill. As a powerful warrior and blacksmith, he carried sharp iron tools and weapons, forging paths and clearing the way for civilization. However, despite his many achievements, Ogun often felt unappreciated and alone. One day, after a long and exhausting hunt, he returned home feeling disheartened. His frustration grew, and he climbed a hill to be alone. In his anger, he slashed at the air with his blade, spilling his own blood as a sign of his power and dedication. In that moment, he vowed to protect those who respected his strength and contributions. Ogun traveled far and wide, using his abilities to help people. He provided them with iron tools, weapons, and knowledge of metalworking, shaping the future of many civilizations. Eventually, his journey led him to the town of Ire, where the people had heard of his great power. Though they feared his legendary rage, they wished to honor him rather than face his wrath. The priests and townspeople gathered and prepared offerings to welcome Ogun. They sang songs, danced, and brought gifts of palm wine and food, hoping to show their respect. When Ogun arrived, he was met with cheers and celebration, and for the first time in a long while, he felt appreciated. His anger subsided, and he accepted their tribute with gratitude. However, the king of Ire did not share in the people's reverence. He refused to offer gifts or acknowledge Ogun's power. Seeing this disrespect, Ogun's fury reignited, and with a swift strike, he punished the arrogant king. The people of Ire quickly realized the importance of honoring Ogun, and they humbled themselves, bringing even greater offerings to appease him.

Moved by their sincerity, Ogun forgave the town and chose to stay. He became the ruler of Ire, teaching its people how to forge iron and build weapons, tools, and structures. Under his leadership, the kingdom flourished, becoming strong and prosperous. Though Ogun eventually left to continue his battles, his legacy remained in Ire. The people never forgot the lessons he taught them strength, respect, and the value of hard work. Even today, his followers honor him with songs, offerings, and ceremonies, remembering the Orisha who protected them and brought them the power of iron.

REFLECTION & WISDOM

This story tells of Ogun, the powerful Orisha of iron and war, who, after a day of hunting, felt isolated and unappreciated. His anger led him to the hills, where he swore to protect and forge new weapons for humanity. As he traveled, he came to the town of Ire, where the people honored him with respect and gifts, calming his anger. However, the proud king of Ire refused to show respect, angering Ogun once more. After striking down the king, Ogun taught the people the importance of respect and humility, becoming their king and protector. His legacy lives on as a symbol of strength, peace, and justice.

* * *

OGUN, THE MASTER OF IRON
STORY 2:2

Long ago in Ife's wide land,
People worked with tools so bland,
Made of wood and stone so weak,
Hard the labor, futures bleak.

The fields were small, the trees stood high,
They needed more land beneath the sky.
In sorrow, they called with hearts full of care,
"Orishas, please help us, hear our prayer!"

"Clear the forest, give us space to grow,
So we may feed all, and watch our crops glow.
With your guidance, we'll till the land,
Help us, Orishas, with your mighty hand!"

Oko, Orisha of farmers, gave all his might,
But his wood and stone tools just weren't right.
Then Obatala stepped forth with silver in hand,

His machete gleaming but soon couldn't stand.
It bent and broke, no longer strong,
For the task was greater than they'd thought all along.
One by one, the other Orishas tried,
But the trees stood tall, thick and wide.

None could win, though their strength was true,
The mighty forest remained, as it grew.
Then Ogun, Orisha fierce and bold,
Stepped forward, his presence uncontrolled.

Without a word, his blade did gleam,
An iron machete, sharp and keen.
He chopped the trees with speed and ease,
The people and Orishas watched with glee.

"Where did this tool come from, so strong?"
They asked in wonder, amazed all along.
"My machete is made from iron,"
Ogun smiled, his heart now shining.

The people begged him, "Teach us too,
We need your strength to help us through."
At first, Ogun was quiet and still,
But then he said, "If you make me king, I will."
The people agreed, they made him rule,
and Ogun taught them to use iron as a tool.

They forged new spears and sturdy hoes,
The fields they plowed began to grow.
Under Ogun's steady hand,
Ife thrived across the land.

But hunting called him more than rule,
And some said, "Ogun's acting a fool."

So banished far, with heavy sigh,
He left Ife, voice a quiet cry.
Without Ogun, tools fell apart,
The iron lost its beating heart.

Crops failed under sun's harsh eye,
The land grew dry, and threats drew near.
Remembering his strength and might,
They sent a call deep through the night:
"Return and lead us once again,
We'll honor you through loss and gain."
Though hurt, Ogun understood,
Ife needed his strong might.

He came back brave to lead the fight,
Restoring peace, reclaiming light.
Ife flourished, hearts aflame,
Ogun's name forever came.

Each year they sing his praise aloud,
Master of iron, strong and proud.
Protector, hero, by their side,
In every tool his strength resides.

* * *

REFLECTION & WISDOM

This story recounts the tale of Ogun, the Orisha of iron and strength, who helped the people of Ife clear a mighty forest that obstructed their growth. When the Orishas' wood and stone tools failed, Ogun stepped forward with his powerful iron machete, effortlessly chopping through the trees. The people, amazed by his strength, made him their king, and he taught them to forge iron tools, which helped Ife thrive. However, Ogun's love for hunting led to his banishment, and without him, Ife faltered. Realizing they needed him, the people begged Ogun to return, and once again, he led them to victory and prosperity. His legacy, as the master of iron, lives on in every tool and in the hearts of the people he protected.

OGUN AND THE POOR MAN'S CRAFT
STORY 2:3

A poor man struggled, day by day,
Laboring hard in the sun's hot ray.
He worked the fields, with little pay,
But misfortune came and took it away.

Frustrated, tired, with hope gone thin,
The man sought help, to begin again.
He went to the Babalawo, wise and old,
To find a way from the life so cold.

The Babalawo listened, then said with care,
"Offer to Ogun and ask for help there.
Go to the forest, with a humble heart,
He'll show you the way, a brand new start."
With few belongings, the man set out,
Fruits, herbs, and palm wine, no doubt.

Through the forest, he walked with hope,
Following the Babalawo's rope.
In the forest, he called with plea,
"Ogun, help me, set me free!"
Ogun, passing by, heard the cry,
And approached the man, standing nearby.

The man knelt down, with respect so true,
Offering all he had, through and through.
Ogun stepped forward, his eyes did gleam,
Seeing the man's heart, pure as a dream.

"What troubles you, dear one?" Ogun asked,
The man shared his story, long and vast.
Of landowners who kept him poor,
Despite his work, he couldn't do more.

Ogun listened, then spoke with might,

"I will not give you riches or light.
But I will show you how to create,
Your own power, your own fate."
He led the man to iron ore,
And taught him how to craft and more.

With iron tools, he showed the way,
To build his future, day by day.
Weeks went by, the man worked hard,
Shaping the ore with each sharp shard.
His spirit grew, his patience, too,
Learning that persistence was true.

At last, the spear was sharp and bright,
Ogun said, "Now, take this sight,
And go to the king, with tools in hand,
Show him the work, and you will stand."
The man did as Ogun told,
The king was amazed at the tools so bold.

He hired the man, to craft with skill,
And rewarded him with land and will.
The man's life changed, from poor to grand,
With wealth and power, he took a stand.

He returned to Ogun, with gratitude deep,
Thanking Orisha, for the promise to keep.
Ogun smiled, proud of the man,
For he had learned to build his plan.

True power, Ogun had shown him well,
Comes from within, where strength does dwell.
From that day on, the man did live,
In peace and joy, with much to give.

He helped others with his strength and craft,
And honored Ogun with each year's draft.

* * *

This story follows a poor man who, struggling to survive, seeks help from a wise Babalawo. The Babalawo directs him to Ogun, the Orisha of iron, who teaches the man how to create his own future by crafting iron tools. Through persistence and hard work, the man learns to shape his destiny and earns the respect of a king, who hires him and rewards him with land. Grateful for Ogun's guidance, the man returns to honor the Orisha, now thriving and helping others with his newfound strength and craft. The tale highlights that true power comes from within and the ability to create one's own fate through perseverance.

INSIGHTS, OFFERINGS, RITUALS AND SPIRITUAL SIGNIFICANCE
SECTION 3

- **Some offerings to Ogun include:** Iron tools, Male animals such as goats, roosters, pigeons, and cobras, Peppers, Palm oil, Alcohol, particularly gin or rum, Watermelon, Yams, Plantains, Cool water, Metal trinkets, Steel tools, Tobacco, especially cigars, Candles, Incense, Various fruits, Kola nuts.

- **Plants and Stones Associated with Ogun:** Ogun is linked to various plants and stones that represent his strength and power. Red pepper and black pepper are commonly associated with him, symbolizing his fiery and intense nature. Iron-rich stones, as well as meteorites, are connected to Ogun's energy, holding the force of his desire and power. Specific stones like hematite, magnetite, and pyrite are also associated with Ogun. Hematite shines with a metallic gleam, magnetite has a magnetic pull, and pyrite reflects golden light, all embodying Ogun's strength and resilience. Black stones, steadfast and enduring, are considered to carry Ogun's essence.

- **Sacred Locations Associated with Ogun:** Offerings to Ogun are placed in locations where his energies are strongest, such as railroad tracks, metalworking areas, sites with iron deposits, forests, and construction sites, reflecting his connection to tools, building, and nature.

* * *

The Many Faces of Ogun

Ogun is a powerful and fearless Orisha with many different forms, known as caminos or paths. Each path reflects a unique part of his character, strength, and influence in the world. Some paths show Ogun as a fierce warrior and protector, while others highlight his role as a builder, creator, and bringer of civilization. In the Yoruba tradition, Ogun is the master of iron, tools, and technology, and his many forms show how he helps open roads, overcome obstacles, and build the foundations for progress. His different paths reveal the ways he fights for justice, provides strength, and supports human growth. Some of the most well-known paths of Ogun include:

- **Ogun Onile:** Ruler of uninhabited lands and the first to cultivate the earth.
- **Ogun Alagbede:** Blacksmith and protector of metalworkers.
- **Oggun Meyi:** Dual-natured: one face is hardworking and kind, the other violent and destructive.
- **Ogun Arere**: Butcher path, tied to cutting, sacrifice, and mastery over flesh.
- **Ogun Shibiriki:** Wild and fierce, forges weapons and battles Shango over Yemoja.
- **Ogun Adeola:** A royal Ogun who ruled wisely, bringing strength and peace.

* * *

WALKING WITH OGUN RITUAL

PURPOSE:

This ritual is designed to help you connect with the powerful energy of Ogun. It invites his strength, protection, and guidance into your life, supporting you as you move forward with courage and determination.

ITEMS NEEDED:

- An offering: gin, palm oil, pepper, or a piece of candy
- Comfortable shoes for walking

Step 1: Find a Sacred Place

It is recommended to visit a train track or the woods, where Ogun's energy is especially strong.

Step 2: Make an Offering

Find a quiet place and respectfully place your offering (gin, palm oil, pepper, or candy) on the ground. As you present the offering, say: *"Ogun, mighty warrior and opener of roads, accept this gift. Walk with me, bless my path, and give me strength. Ase."*

Step 3: Walk with Ogun

Start walking along the train tracks or forest path, moving slowly and mindfully. As you walk, speak openly to Ogun. You can: thank him for his presence and support, ask for his protection, strength, and guidance, and share any challenges you're facing, asking him to clear your path.

Step 4: Receive Ogun's Blessing

If you find a railroad spike, a sturdy stick, or another meaningful object during your walk, pick it up respectfully, accepting it as a gift from Ogun. If you don't find anything, trust that Ogun has heard your request and blessed you. If you do find something, like a walking stick or railroad spike, honor it with gratitude, recognizing it as a symbol of Ogun.

Step 5: Thank Ogun

Before closing, thank Ogun for his presence and guidance. You can say something like: "Thank you, Ogun, for your strength, wisdom, and protection. I am grateful for your energy." Optional: You may also leave an offering near a strong tree outdoors as a sign of gratitude.

Step 6: Record insights

Keep pen and paper nearby to jot down any thoughts, ideas, or intuitions you receive during your meditation.

* * *

PRAYER TO OGUN, MASTER OF IRON AND STRENGTH
VERSE 3:3

O Ogun, warrior of iron and might,
With blade so sharp, you bring the light.
Through toil and struggle, you lead our way,
Grant us your strength with each new day.

From iron tools to fire's glow,
You show us how to build and grow.
In your honor, we offer with grace,
Goats, roosters, and foods to embrace.

O Ogun, we seek your fierce protection,
Guide us through challenges, give us direction.
May your strength in our hearts reside,
As we walk with courage, with you by our side.

We offer you gifts, humble and true,
With love and respect, we honor you.
O Ogun, the mighty, the brave, the wise,
Bless us now, as we lift our eyes.
Ase!

* * *

24. Oko
Orisha of Agriculture and Farming

A Closer Look at Oko

Orisha Oko is the Orisha of farming, the earth, and fertility. He is the guardian of the land and helps crops grow by blessing the soil, bringing rain, and keeping the earth healthy. Farmers and people who work with the land pray to him for good harvests and food to feed their families and communities. He is especially known for helping important crops like yams, corn, and grains grow strong. During planting and harvest seasons, people honor him with offerings and prayers, asking for his guidance and giving thanks for his blessings. Orisha Oko also supports fertility, helping people who want to have children. Because he brings life to both the land and people, he is seen as a symbol of growth, peace, and abundance. He is known for being honest and fair. People turn to him when there are disagreements over land or when they seek the truth. As a protector of nature, he teaches us to respect the earth and to care for it. He reminds us that with patience, hard work, and respect for the natural world, we can live well. In Yoruba tradition, Orisha Oko is also seen as a brave and noble hunter who defends against evil and stands for what is right. He is often shown holding a hoe or a staff, standing tall in the open fields as a strong and wise guardian of nature, truth, and life itself.

Prayer to Orisha Oko
Verse 1:1

Oko, Orisha of soil and seed,
We honor you in word and deed.

Bless our fields, our work, our land,

Guide us with your steady hand.

With roosters, grains, and heartfelt praise,
We thank you for your giving ways.

Protector, guardian, strong and true,
May your blessings see us through.
Ase!

* * *

OKO'S BLESSINGS
VERSE 1:2

Oko, the Orisha, strong and wise,
Calls to farmers under open skies.
He helps them plant, grow, and reap,
A bountiful harvest for all to keep.

Associated with farming, land, and more,
He guides those who work and adore
The earth's great gifts, the seeds we sow,
Bringing prosperity as they grow.

Oko, Orisha of harvest and soil,
You bless the hands that work and toil.
Fertility flows where your spirit treads,
Bringing life to the seeds in farmers' beds.

When worshippers call with earnest plea,
You appear with wisdom, wild and free.
An old man, humble, with staff held tight,
Guiding the crops with sacred might.

But when the work is complete and done,
You vanish with the setting sun.
Only your staff, left firm in place,
Holds the power of your grace.

147

In every village, near and wide,
Your shrines stand tall with farmer's pride.
Oko, Orisha, ancient and true,
The fields forever owe their thanks to you.

* * *

SACRED STORIES / LEGENDS
SECTION 2

THE MAKING OF THE GRASS MAN
STORY 2:1

In ancient times, in Yoruba land,
The crops were ripe, the fields so grand.
But birds came swarming, dark and bold,
Devouring harvests, young and old.

No matter how the villagers tried,
The birds would come; none could hide.
Their numbers vast, their hunger great,
The crops were ruined, sealing famine and fate.

Despair took root where hope once grew,
The people faced a famine's hue.
In desperate need, with hearts so weak,
They called for help, their voices meek.

In their time of need, with hearts laid bare,
The villagers called to Oko, in prayer.
The Orisha of crops, strong and wise,
Heard their cries from the endless skies.

With gentle grace, he answered their plea,
And appeared before them, full of decree.
"Build an image of me, tall and true,
Place it in the fields, where the crops grew."
He left his staff, a gift so bright,
To guide their hands through day and night.

"Let it stand, a protector, bold,
And your harvest will no longer be sold."
Following Oko's words, they worked as one,
With poles and grass beneath the sun.

They shaped the figure, tall and grand,
A man of grass to guard the land.
Dressed in clothes, with palm fronds filled,
A figure strong, their hearts were thrilled.

When the birds returned, their wings so wide,
They saw a grass man on a pole and turned in fright.
Afraid to face what seemed unknown,
They fled the fields, leaving seeds unsown.

The crops stood safe, the land was clear,
The villagers cheered, their hearts sincere.
Grateful for Oko's guiding hand,
They left their gifts upon the land.

At the feet of the image, offerings lay,
Honoring Oko, who saved the day.

REFLECTION & WISDOM

In this Yoruba tale, the villagers face a devastating famine as swarms of birds destroy their crops. In their desperation, they call upon Oko, the Orisha of agriculture, who answers their plea by instructing them to build a tall image of him in the fields. With faith and unity, they craft the figure, and when the birds return, they are frightened by the mysterious sight and flee. The crops are saved, and the villagers, grateful for Oko's protection, honor him with offerings, ensuring prosperity and peace for their land.

* * *

THE HARVEST AND SACRIFICE
STORY 2:2

In a time when the earth was green,
Orisha Oko worked, unseen.
The fields were vast, the crops did grow,
But Oko's labor, it did show.

From dawn to dusk, Oko would toil,
Turning the earth, planting the soil.
The crops grew tall, the harvest near,
But Oko's heart was filled with fear.

"I work so hard, yet none can see,
The weight of this task burdening me.
Why must I alone, day and night,
Keep the earth alive and bright?"
Olofi heard Oko's plea,
And appeared in the sky, for all to see.

"Oko," said Olofi, wise and true,
"Your work is sacred, and it's all for you.
Each Orisha has a role to play,
And yours brings life in its own way.
Though your labor seems endless, it's true,
It keeps the world balanced and new.

When life ends, it returns to the ground,
Nourishing the earth where life is found.
Your work, though tiring, makes it clear,
The circle of life is why you're here."
Oko listened, his heart now bright,
With understanding, he saw the light.

The work he did, though hard to bear,
Was needed for life to be fair.
In ancient times, to keep death at bay,
People would offer food and pray.

They'd feed the earth and Oko, too,
To ensure the crops would thrive and renew.
Now Oko worked with joy once more,
Knowing his labor was at the core.
Of life and death, the cycle spun,
A dance of the earth, for everyone.

* * *

REFLECTION & WISDOM

This Yoruba story portrays Orisha Oko, the hardworking deity of agriculture, who toils tirelessly to nurture the earth and ensure crops grow. Despite his dedication, Oko feels unseen and burdened by the weight of his labor. When he expresses his frustration, Olofi, the supreme deity, reveals the sacred purpose behind Oko's work, his labor maintains the balance of life and death, nourishing the earth and fostering renewal. Reassured and filled with new understanding, Oko continues his work with joy, knowing that his efforts are vital to the cycle of life, death, and rebirth.

* * *

INSIGHTS, OFFERINGS, RITUALS AND SPIRITUAL SIGNIFICANCE
SECTION 3

HONORING ORISHA OKO

Offerings to Orisha Oko typically include root vegetables, harvest produce, pigeons, and roosters, all given as symbols of gratitude and respect. In some traditions, food is also shared with the poor to ask for his protection against hunger. These offerings seek his help in preventing crop loss, famine, drought, poor soil, and pests that threaten crops. Orisha Oko is especially honored during planting and harvest festivals, with shrines often built in rural or farmland areas. His worship is prominent in Yorubaland, as well as in Santería (Cuba), Candomblé (Brazil), and parts of the Caribbean.

Symbols and Sacred Items of Orisha Oko

Orisha Oko is deeply connected to farming and abundance. Tools like the hoe and machete, along with harvested crops, represent his blessings and strong bond with the earth. The mortar and pestle symbolize food preparation and nourishment, while earth or clay stands for the land he governs. In some traditions, bulls and oxen are sacred to him due to their vital role in agriculture. Orisha Oko is also seen as a force of fertility and prosperity, with people praying to him for help with infertility, both in the land and in themselves. He is believed to ensure rich harvests and fertile soil.

* * *

25. Olokun
Orisha of the Ocean's Depths, Mysteries, and Wealth

A Closer Look at Olokun

OLOKUN IS the Orisha who rules the ocean's deepest, most mysterious realms, places beyond sunlight, where immense spiritual forces lie hidden. While the surface of the sea is visible and familiar, Olokun governs what is concealed below: a powerful abyss symbolic of the unseen parts of reality and us that shape life in profound ways. In Yoruba tradition, Olokun is revered as the keeper of vast spiritual and material wealth. Represented by the cowrie shell, once used as currency, Olokun embodies prosperity, divine communication, and sacred hidden energy. These riches are not only material but also include ancestral wisdom and inner truth.

Olokun is also associated with deep emotional healing. Just as the ocean hides its secrets, we often bury pain and trauma within. Olokun teaches that healing requires us to confront these inner depths with courage, bringing the unconscious into light. This Orisha calls us to embrace introspection, shadow work, and emotional honesty. True transformation begins when we face what we've long ignored. As a spiritual guide, Olokun leads us toward self-awareness, balance, and growth. Olokun is closely linked to Aje, the Orisha of wealth and power. In some traditions, Aje is seen as an extension or child of Olokun, suggesting that all abundant material or spiritual resources originate from the ocean's depths. Olokun also shares a strong connection with Yemoja, the Orisha of the ocean's surface. While Yemoja nurtures life with gentle waves, Olokun holds ancient memory, raw power, and transformation. Together, they reflect the dual nature of existence, seen and unseen, surface and depth.

The Deep's Hidden Riches
Verse 1:1

In ocean's depths, Olokun's grace,
A wealth untold, a sacred place.
The colors swirl, the treasures gleam,
In depths unknown, where none may dream.

She guards the secrets, dark and bright,
A treasure trove, concealed from sight.
The ocean holds her power tight,
Her riches shine beneath the night.

* * *

SACRED STORIES / LEGENDS
Section 2

Olokun's Warning: The Flood of Change
Story 2:1

Long ago, in the world so wide,
Humans took from the earth and the tide.
They built their cities, they claimed the land,
But they didn't listen to nature's hand.

They forgot the Orishas, forgot to care,
Ignoring the balance, unaware.
The sea and earth, both strong and wise,
Were pushed aside, much to their surprise.

From the deep where the sun can't shine,
Olokun stirred, both fierce and fine.
"The sea is mine," Olokun said,
"No human will take what's beneath my bed."
The waters rumbled, the skies grew dark,
A mighty wave left its mark.

The rivers flooded, the towns were gone,
The land was swept, all life withdrawn.
The Orishas gathered, their hearts in pain,
Trying to calm the wild ocean's reign.

Orunmila spoke with wisdom clear,
"Olokun, please, let peace draw near.
The humans have erred, but they can learn,
If they honor the sea, the tide will turn.

If they respect what you've given, so vast,
The flood will end, and peace will last."
Olokun listened, the waters slowed,
The flood receded; the land was restored.

REFLECTION & WISDOM

This story teaches a powerful lesson about the dangers of ignoring nature and spiritual wisdom. In the tale, humans chase power and progress without respecting the Orishas, disturbing the balance between land and sea. In response, Olokun the mighty Orisha of the deep ocean, unleashes a great flood that destroys towns and villages. Orunmila, the Orisha of wisdom, steps in and pleads with Olokun to show mercy. He promises that if people learn to respect and care for the natural world, peace will be restored. Olokun agrees, and the floodwaters begin to recede. This reminds us that living in harmony with nature is essential to avoid disaster. In another version of the story, told in the diaspora, Orunmila and Obatala ask Ogun, the Orisha of iron, to forge a huge chain. Obatala uses it to descend into the ocean and bind Olokun, bringing the flood to an end and restoring balance to the world.

* * *

OLOKUN AND YEMAYA
STORY 2:2

Deep beneath the ocean, where no sunlight reaches, Olokun ruled over the vast and mysterious depths. Their kingdom was a place of silence and shadows, holding ancient secrets, lost treasures, and the wisdom of the deep. No one could measure Olokun's power, for the ocean's depths were endless and unknowable. Above, where the sun kissed the waves and life flourished, Yemayá reigned as the mother of the seas. She guided the currents, nurtured the fish, and cared for sailors who traveled across the waters. The tides moved at her command, bringing both calm and storm, yet always ensuring the ocean remained full of life. One day, a disagreement arose between the two Orishas. "My domain is the greatest!" Olokun declared. "The depths of the sea are immeasurable. No one can fathom the power I hold beneath the waves."

"But I bring life to the ocean!" Yemoja countered. "Without me, the waters above would be barren and empty. Fish swim, ships sail, and the world thrives because of the life I provide." Their voices echoed through the ocean, shaking the waters above and below. The balance of the sea trembled with their argument, and soon, Olodumare, the Supreme Being, intervened. "Enough," Olodumare's voice resounded like thunder across the waves. "Neither of you stands alone. The ocean is one, and both of you are essential to its balance." Turning to Yemoja, Olodumare spoke, "You are the nurturer of the waters. You bring life, movement, and breath to the sea.

The world above depends on you." Then, Olodumare addressed Olokun, "And you are the keeper of the deep, the guardian of mysteries, the holder of knowledge and power beyond human understanding. The foundation of the ocean rests with you." Hearing these words, Yemoja and Olokun understood their purpose. They saw that the sea was not divided, but whole, each of them playing a role in maintaining its harmony. Since that day, they have worked together, each fulfilling their sacred duty. Yemoja continues to bring life to the waters above, while Olokun guards the secrets below. The ocean flows in perfect balance, a reminder that power and nurture, depth and surface, must always exist together. And so, from the vast depths to the sparkling waves, the sea remains whole endless, mysterious, and full of life.

REFLECTION & WISDOM

This story highlights the essential balance between Yemoja, the Orisha of the surface of the ocean, and Olokun, the Orisha of the deep waters. When they argue over their respective powers Yemoja claiming to bring life and Olokun boasting of their vast and mysterious depths Olodumare intervenes, reminding them that both play vital roles in maintaining the harmony of the sea. Yemoja nurtures the ocean's life, while Olokun guards its hidden treasures and wisdom. The two Orishas come to understand that their complementary roles ensure the health and balance of the ocean, working together to maintain its harmony from the surface to the deepest depths.

* * *

OLOKUN AND ORUNMILA
STORY 2:3

When first the humans came to stay,
Olokun's anger filled the bay.
Her waters rose, the land was wet,
The earth, a place of deep regret.

She swirled in fury, full of might,
Making the earth a fearful sight.
The humans cried, with hope grown thin,
For the sea would not let peace begin.

Orunmila, wise and true,
Saw the storm that Olokun knew.
He offered her a gift so rare,
A chance to glimpse what's hidden there.

"I'll show you how to see ahead,
To read the future, where it's led."
Olokun thought, her heart torn tight,
But peace was something she sought that night.

She took the gift with careful grace,
And calmness took the sea's cold place.
Now the waters still and clear,
Olokun's wisdom drew her near.

The earth was safe, the humans free,
And peace now reigned upon the sea.
For with the gift, the future bright,
Olokun's heart embraced the light.

* * *

REFLECTION & WISDOM

This story portrays the powerful Olokun's wrath when humans first arrived, disturbing the balance of the sea. In her anger, the ocean swells and threatens the earth with destruction. However, Orunmila, ever wise, offers Olokun a rare gift a vision of the future, a chance to see beyond the present and find peace. Torn but intrigued, Olokun accepts the gift, allowing her heart to soften. The ocean calms, the humans are spared, and harmony is restored, as Olokun's newfound wisdom guides her toward a peaceful future, embracing the light of understanding.

* * *

INSIGHTS, OFFERINGS, RITUALS AND SPIRITUAL SIGNIFICANCE
SECTION 3

OLOKUN'S OFFERINGS
VERSE 3:1

Pigeons, roosters, and shells we bring,
Beads of color, their praises sing.
Ram and coconut, sweet syrup's flow,
Cornmeal and fruit where blessings grow.

Bananas, pineapples, mangoes too,
We offer these gifts, both old and new.
Olokun, hear our humble prayer,
Guide us through waters, always there.

* * *

PRAYER TO OLOKUN: KEEPER OF THE DEEP
VERSE 3:2

Olokun, mighty guardian of the ocean's depths,
We call upon you, keeper of hidden treasures and ancient wisdom.
With your power vast as the sea, we seek your guidance and grace.

Grant us the riches of your knowledge,
The strength to navigate the tides of life,
And the peace that flows from your deep waters.

May your healing touch soothe our spirits,
And may we honor the balance of all things,
From the surface to the deepest depths.

Olokun, in your wisdom, guide us,
In your mercy, protect us.
We offer our hearts, our prayers, and our gifts,
With respect and reverence.
Ase!

* * *

26. ORI
THE SPIRIT OF CONSCIOUSNESS, AND PERSONAL GROWTH

A CLOSER LOOK AT ORI

IN YORUBA SPIRITUALITY, ORI MEANS "HEAD," but it refers to much more than the physical head; it represents the inner self, consciousness, and spiritual essence that guides a person's destiny. It is believed that before birth, everyone chooses their Ori, selecting a life path or destiny (*ayanmo*) that they are meant to fulfill. Ori then serves as an inner compass, influencing thoughts, decisions, and actions to align with that path. Considered more important than even the Orisha, Ori is the force most directly responsible for a person's success, well-being, and spiritual fulfillment. It is closely linked to one's higher self and divine purpose. Honoring Ori is central in Yoruba practice and often includes morning prayers, spiritual cleansing rituals such as *itutu ori* (head washing), and consultations through Ifa divination to receive guidance and overcome obstacles. Developing a strong relationship with one's Ori is essential for living in alignment with one's true destiny.

ORI: THE KEEPER OF OUR DESTINY
VERSE I:I

Ori, the crown, our sacred head,
our higher consciousness.
The force where soul and fate are wed.
It is the mind, the heart, the guide,
A vessel where destiny and spirit reside.

More than the head that we see and feel,
Ori is the power that shapes what's real.
A fragment of truth, the self within,
The consciousness is deep where choices begin.

Our Ori walks with our soul from when we are born,
unseen, aware, The keeper of thoughts,
of dreams and prayer.
Chosen in heaven before the earth,
Ori holds the key to purpose and birth.

Ori-Inu, the silent voice inside,
Speaks of truth where mysteries hide.
A compass of wisdom, a throne of fate,
It leads us onward through every gate.

Before the Orisha, before the divine,
It is Ori who claims the path as mine.
No force is greater, no power more true,
For my Ori alone carries me through.

So we bow to the head, both body and mind,
To the consciousness vast, eternal, aligned.
Ori mi, my guide, my anchor, my light
You are the spark that gives my soul flight.

* * *

ORI: THE SEAT OF CONSCIOUSNESS
VERSE 1:2

Beneath the crown of flesh and bone,
Dwells Ori, the mind's sacred throne.
More than the head where thoughts reside,
Ori is the soul's eternal guide.

You are the spark that lights our way,
The unseen force in each word we say.
A fragment of destiny, divine and pure,

Ori shapes paths we cannot ignore.

Ori-Inu, the voice within, Whispering
truths where journeys begin. Consciousness
deep, both vast and wise,
A reflection of heaven behind mortal eyes.
When we choose, it is you who speaks,
Through silence profound or answers we seek.

Before the stars and worlds were spun,
Ori was bound to the soul as one.
A living compass of fate and thought,
Ori recalls what time has forgotten.

In dreams and reflection, in stillness or strife,
It carries the weight of our spirit's life.
No wind can sway it, no hand can mold,
For Ori holds destinies untold.

A piece of Olodumare's design,
The sacred consciousness, wholly divine.
So we honor the head, both seen and unseen,
The consciousness is vast, where truth lies serene.
Ori mi, I trust, I follow, I know
You are the root from which my being will grow.

* * *

SACRED STORIES / LEGENDS
SECTION 2

THE JOURNEY OF ORI
STORY 2:1

In the beginning, when the world was still new, Olodumare, the Supreme Creator, fashioned the souls of all beings, giving each a sacred gift Ori. More than just a presence, Ori was an inner guide, a divine spark of wisdom meant to shape each soul's destiny. To receive their Ori, the spirits traveled to the house of Ajala, the celestial potter. With skilled hands, Ajala crafted countless Ori, each unique in shape and essence. Some shone brightly like the stars, while others appeared simple and unremarkable. As the spirits arrived, Olodumare spoke: "Choose with wisdom, for your Ori is your fate. It will guide your steps and shape your journey."

But many spirits, eager and impatient, chose quickly drawn to the brightest and most beautiful Ori, believing that outward radiance promised a life of ease. Few stopped to ask if their Ori would truly walk with them on their path. Standing at the crossroads was Elegua, the clever Orisha of fate and decisions. He watched as spirits passed by, some seeking guidance, others rushing ahead. "Have you asked your Ori to walk with you?" Elegua asked. "Without its blessing, your journey may not go as planned." Some spirits, humble and thoughtful, knelt before their Ori and asked for guidance. In response, their Ori glowed with a steady light, promising wisdom and protection. Others, too proud to bow, ignored the warning and stepped forward into the unknown. When the spirits arrived on Earth, their chosen Ori began to shape their lives. Some found fortune and joy, their paths clear and purposeful. Others struggled with hardship crops failed, loved ones left, and misfortune followed their steps.

"Why is my life so difficult?" they cried. "Did I not choose my Ori wisely?" Then, in the stillness of their hearts, Ori spoke: "You chose me, but you did not honor me. You rushed forward without asking for my guidance. You must nourish our bond, for I am your greatest ally." Realizing their mistake, the people began to honor their Ori through prayers, offerings, and reflection. Slowly, their paths grew clearer, and their burdens lightened. Their lives, once filled with struggle, became meaningful journeys of growth and fulfillment. From that day forward, the wisdom of Ori was passed down through generations: "Your Ori is your truest guide, more valuable than gold. Honor it daily, trust its wisdom, and it will never lead you astray."

REFLECTION & WISDOM

This story speaks of the creation of the soul and the gift of Ori, a divine spark given to each spirit by Olodumare, the Creator. Ori serves as an inner guide, shaping one's path and destiny. The spirits, upon arriving at Ajala's house, must choose their Ori, with some rushing impulsively and others seeking guidance. Elegua, the Orisha of crossroads, advises the spirits to seek their Ori's blessing for a successful journey. Many spirits, however, neglect to honor their

Ori, leading to difficult lives. Eventually, they learn the importance of daily devotion and respect for their Ori, finding peace and guidance through prayer and offerings. The story teaches that Ori, when honored, leads one to their true path, shaping their destiny and life's purpose.

* * *

INSIGHTS, OFFERINGS, RITUALS AND SPIRITUAL SIGNIFICANCE
SECTION 3

OFFERINGS TO ORI
VERSE 3:1

My Sacred Song Ori, divine, my highest crown,
To you, I bow and lay gifts down.
With hands uplifted, I call your name,
Honoring the force that shapes my frame.

Cool water I pour, pure and clear,
To cleanse my path, to calm each fear.
It flows like wisdom, soothing my soul,
Bringing clarity and making me whole.

Omiero, sacred herbs and rain,
Mint and sage to ease my pain and cool my head.
Peppermint cools where heat has burned,
Restoring balance where chaos turned.

Fresh rose petals, beauty divine,
For love, for grace, in your light I shine.
Honey, sweet nectar, abundance to share,
A blessing of sweetness beyond all compare.

Eggshells, white as a morning sky,
For purity, growth, and spirits high.
Obi and bitter kola, sacred and true,
For health and insight that guide me through.

Coconut, strong, with its milk of light,
Breaking through darkness, revealing the bright.
Fruits of the earth, so vibrant and sweet,
Bring life's nourishment to lay at your feet.

Lavender's scent drives worry away,
Clearing my thoughts, inviting the day.
Gin or rum, with strength to endure,
Powerful, bold, and steadfastly pure.

Palm oil, red as the dawn's embrace,
For protection and purity, granting me grace.
Ori, my compass, my soul's sacred throne,
In these offerings, let your presence be known.
Guide my journey, align my fate,
With blessings of wisdom, forever great.

* * *

SIMPLE ORI OFFERING CEREMONY

PURPOSE
To connect with your inner self (Ori), align with your destiny, and invite
clarity, blessings, and inner peace.

ITEMS NEEDED FOR THIS MEDITATION

- Fresh water (cool or herbal mixture such as mint, sage, or basil)
- Honey (symbolizing sweetness and blessings)
- A small bowl (to hold offerings)
- Fresh flowers (e.g., rose petals)
- An offering of fruit or kola nut (optional)

* * *

STEP 1: CREATE A SACRED SPACE
Find a quiet, peaceful area where you can focus without distraction. Light a
candle or incense to set a calm, spiritual atmosphere.

STEP 2: CONNECT WITH YOUR ORI

Sit comfortably and close your eyes. Take slow, deep breaths. Focus inward on your higher self, your purpose, and your spiritual path. When ready, say: *"Ori, I honor you today. I ask for guidance, clarity, and alignment with my true path and purpose."*

STEP 3: OFFER TO ORI

Pour the honey, water, and flowers into the small bowl. As you do, say: *"I offer these gifts to my Ori, asking for clarity, peace, and alignment."* If using fruit or kola nut, place them beside the bowl as a symbol of abundance and gratitude.

STEP 4: PURIFY AND CLEANSE

Dip your fingers in the cool or herbal water. Gently sprinkle a bit over your head, forehead, hands, and chest. Say: *"I cleanse and refresh my Ori, opening the way to my highest potential."*

STEP 5: REFLECT AND LISTEN

Sit quietly for a few minutes. Meditate, pray, or simply reflect. Be open to any insight or feeling that may arise. If anything, meaningful comes through, write it down.

STEP 6: GIVE THANKS AND CLOSE

Thank your Ori for its presence, wisdom, and support. A simple statement is enough:
"Thank you, Ori, for your guidance and light."

STEP 7: (OPTIONAL): SPIRITUAL BATH

Use the remaining water and offerings from the bowl in a bath. As you bathe, imagine the energy of the offerings renewing and uplifting you. Visualize a bright, cleansing light flowing from head to toe, aligning you with your destiny.

STEP 8: (OPTIONAL): FINAL OFFERING TO NATURE

After your bath, you can leave any remaining offerings outside, near a natural element like the river, or in a place that feels sacred to you, to complete the offering.

* * *

PRAYER TO ORI
VERSE 3:2

Ori, my head, my sacred light,
I honor you with all my might.
You are the force that guides my soul,
The compass that makes me whole.

Through waters pure, I seek your grace,
Clear my mind, guide my pace.
With herbs and fruits, I lay before,
The gifts of life, I offer more.

In sweetness and in bitter ways,
I honor you through nights and days.
Strength like coconut, firm and true,
I trust in you to see me through.

May your wisdom lead my heart,
From every trial, never to part.
Ori mi, my fate, my destiny,
Bless me now, in unity.
Ase!

* * *

27. ORO
ORISHA OF JUSTICE, TRUTH, AND SACRED DECREES

A CLOSER LOOK AT ORO

ORO IS a powerful Orisha who represents justice, truth, and the enforcement of community laws. He acts as a spiritual enforcer, called upon when people break rules or disrupt the moral order. In the past, serious offenses committed in the community could result in punishment or banishment carried out in his name. Oro ensures that justice is served and wrongdoers are held accountable. Closely tied to sacred authority and leadership, Oro is often symbolized by a mask or experienced as a mysterious presence known only to high-ranking priests and elders. His presence inspires both fear and respect, reminding the community to live with integrity, honor, and respect for tradition. Beyond his role in law and order, Oro also provides spiritual guidance, helping communities stay rooted in their ancestral values.

The most important event honoring him is the Oro Festival, a traditional ceremony involving rituals, prayers, and spiritual cleansing. Its purpose is to purify the land, protect the people, and reinforce the authority of local leaders. Only initiated men may participate in the festival. During this time, women, children, and outsiders are required to stay indoors after sunset, and a strict curfew is enforced. Violating this curfew is believed to invite serious spiritual consequences. Oro's presence during the festival serves to renew the community's connection to justice, tradition, and sacred law.

THE SPIRIT OF ORO
VERSE 1.1

Oro, the king of wisdom and might,
Ruled with justice, fair and bright.
A kingdom vast, his reign was just,
His people loved him; in him they trust.

But one day, Oro vanished away,
Leaving his people to wonder and sway.
Where had he gone, none could tell,
Until they learned of his spirit's spell.

Transformed to spirit, no longer seen,
Oro left the world, but still he'd glean.
Watching over his people with care,
Protecting them from harm in the air.

In the forest, Oro's power grew,
Linked to justice, fierce and true.
His spirit now a force to fear,
While Egungun's ancestors drew near.

A cult emerged to honor the king,
Those who communed with him could sing.
With Oro's wisdom, they'd plead and pray,
For justice in the light of day.

But Oro and Egungun, not always kind,
A feud long held between the two aligned.
Oro, a hunter in the woods so deep,
Egungun's spirits, a bond to keep.

Yet Oro, the Orisha, bold and strong,
Brings justice where the wrongs belong.
In the name of ancestors, he stands tall,
A protector of all, in spirit's call.

In forests dark, and stars so bright,

Oro brings justice, fierce as night.
A king turned spirit, ever near,
Guiding the people, their souls to steer.

* * *

VOICE OF JUSTICE
VERSE 1:2

Oro is strong, both wise and bold,
A god of justice, as stories are told.
He stands for truth, with power and might,
Guiding us to what's good and right.

His voice is heard in a bullroarer's sound,
A sign that his spirit is all around.
Oro leads with strength and care,
In rituals and justice, he's always there.

* * *

SACRED STORIES / LEGENDS
SECTION 2

THE BROTHERS OF DAY AND NIGHT
STORY 2:1

Egungun and Oro
Two brothers lived in Orun above,
Egungun and Oro, bound by love.
They dreamed of wealth on Earth below,
And sought Ifa's wisdom to help them grow.

The Odu came, Ojuani Osa,
Orunmila's words, a guiding kasa:
"Share your blessings, be kind and true,
And earthly riches will come to you."

Egungun, eager, took the lead,

Descending to Earth with hope and speed.
Oro stayed back, his trust secure,
Believing his brother's word was pure.

On Earth, Egungun's heart did shine,
Helping the poor, his deeds divine.
His wealth grew vast, his fame spread wide,
With kings and villagers at his side.

But Oro watched from the heavens high,
His calls ignored, his patience dry.
Anger burned as his trust was betrayed,
And Oro descended as sunlight decayed.

The sky grew dark, the air turned cold,
As Oro's rage began to unfold.
He chased his brother through the night,
Filling the villagers' hearts with fright.

Elders gathered, wise and fair,
To mediate the brothers' despair.
Egungun admitted his broken vow,
Promising justice here and now.

"By day, I'll reign, my work I'll show,
But after sunset, you'll rule below."
Oro agreed, his anger ceased,
As night became his time of peace.

So, Oro claimed the dark as his own,
A patron of justice, deeply known.
Egungun thrived when the sun was high,
While Oro ruled the starry sky.

Thus, the brothers found their way,
One by night and one by day.
A lesson told through their dispute:
Honor your word or face the truth.

This story tells of two brothers, Egungun and Oro, who sought wealth on Earth and sought guidance from Ifa to achieve their dreams. Egungun, eager for success, descends to Earth, helps others, and gains wealth and fame. Oro, waiting patiently in the heavens, feels betrayed when his brother's actions seem to ignore their shared plan. Anger consumes Oro, and he descends to Earth, bringing fear with his fury. After a confrontation, the elders mediate, and Egungun admits to his broken vow, promising to give Oro his rightful place. From that moment, Egungun reigns by day, while Oro rules the night, each fulfilling their roles in harmony. The story emphasizes the importance of keeping one's promises, as failure to do so leads to consequences.

INSIGHTS, OFFERINGS, RITUALS AND SPIRITUAL SIGNIFICANCE
SECTION 3

COMMON OFFERINGS

- **Omi (Water):** *Known for its soothing and cleansing properties, it symbolizes the need for peace and harmony within the community.*
- **Oti (Sweetness/Honey):** *Represents joy, abundance, and the blessings bestowed by Oro.*
- **Obi (Kola Nuts):** *Used in divination to communicate with the spiritual realm, it serves as a conduit for receiving blessings and guidance.*
- **Epo (Palm Oil):** *Symbolizes wealth, prosperity, and sustainability, playing a vital role in daily life and in honoring this Orisha.*

* * *

PRAYER FOR JUSTICE
VERSE 3:1

Oro, mighty spirit of justice and truth, Guide me with your wisdom, show me the way. Protect me from wrong, and help me stand strong, In your light, let righteousness lead each day. Ase.

* * *

28. ORUNMILA
ORISHA OF WISDOM, DESTINY, AND DIVINATION

A CLOSER LOOK AT ORUNMILA

ORUNMILA IS a powerful Orisha (a spirit or deity) associated with wisdom, destiny, and divination. It's believed he was present when the world was created, holding deep spiritual knowledge. This knowledge is shared through the Ifa divination system, a sacred way to communicate with the divine using special signs called Odu Ifa.

Ifa divination helps people understand their life's spiritual purpose, which they chose before being born. It also helps them receive blessings and get rid of negative energy through sacrifices. This system guides people in making wise decisions and reveals answers to important questions, connecting humans to universal wisdom. In the Yoruba tradition, divination is a crucial gift that helps guide people through life Known as the "witness to fate," Orunmila understands each person's destiny and helps them follow their divine path. He is closely connected to Olodumare, the supreme being. Orunmila taught humans and his followers how to use the sacred opele chain and palm nuts to perform divination and understand the Odu Ifa. These Odu are stories and patterns full of spiritual wisdom about life, health, relationships, and more. Each Odu represents a unique cosmic energy pattern that provides insights into a person's challenges and opportunities. These patterns form a living cosmic language that connects the physical and spiritual worlds. By interpreting them, Orunmila and his priests uncover hidden truths and offer guidance on how to live in harmony with divine will.

Orunmila is also a healer who addresses the core reasons behind problems. He works closely with Eshu, who acts as a messenger between worlds. In Afro-Caribbean traditions, Orunmila is often linked to saints like Saint

Francis or Saint Anthony, showing how widely respected he is. His priests, called Babalawos, act as spiritual guides. They protect and share Orunmila's teachings through the Ifa tradition.

ORUNMILA, THE ORISHA OF WISDOM
VERSE 1:1

Orunmila, wise and full of grace,
The Orisha of wisdom, in a sacred place.
Guiding Babalawos and Iyanifas each day,
Through the path of IFA, he shows the way.

He walked the earth in human form,
Bringing knowledge to help transform.
The first Babalawo, his name shines bright,
A beacon of wisdom, a guiding light.

Priests and priestesses call his name,
For insight and answers, he's always the same.
With IFA divination, the future is clear,
Orunmila's wisdom brings hope and cheer.

All Orishas seek his guiding hand,
For he witnessed destinies and helped life expand.
A helper to Olodumare when the world was made,
His knowledge and insight will never fade.

To Orunmila, we give our respect,
For his wisdom and power, we always reflect.
A teacher, a guide, a shining star,
Orunmila, the wise, knows who we are.

* * *

ORUNMILA, SPIRIT OF DESTINY
VERSE 1:2

Orunmila, the wise and strong,
Keeper of secrets, where we belong.
The master of Ifa, the sacred art,
Guiding our minds, touching the heart.

A witness to creation's birth,
He saw the making of heaven and earth.
When Olorun shaped the skies so wide,
Orunmila stood faithfully by his side.

He reveals the Odus, the wisdom we seek,
Through proverbs and teachings, his voice will speak.
The mysteries of life, he helps us see,
Unlocking the doors of destiny.

Orunmila, prophet, priest, and guide,
In your knowledge, we all confide.
Spirit of wisdom, forever stay,
Leading us forward, lighting the way.

✳ ✳ ✳

SACRED STORIES / LEGENDS
SECTION 2

ORUNMILA'S PACT WITH DEATH
STORY 2:1

Long ago, Death, known as Iku, was taking the lives of many of Orunmila's children before their time. People were suffering, and no one was safe. In response, Orunmila, the Orisha of wisdom, wanted to protect his children. So, he sought the guidance of his divine friend, Eshu, the Orisha of crossroads. Through his divination, Orunmila saw that Iku was not only coming for his children but had even set its sights on him. He knew he had to act quickly. Eshu, always clever and quick-thinking, advised Orunmila to prepare a feast and welcome Death as if it were an honored guest. Eshu told

Orunmila that they would invite Iku in and create an opportunity for a deal.

So, Orunmila made a sacred meal with roasted yams, fruits, and honey, carefully preparing it with love and devotion. When Iku arrived, Eshu welcomed him warmly and invited him to sit and eat. Tempted by the delicious offerings, Iku ate until he was full and eventually fell into a deep sleep. While Iku slept, Eshu quietly took his scythe, the tool Iku used to take life, and hid it away. When Iku woke up and realized his scythe was missing, he was startled and upset. Eshu, with a knowing smile, asked, "Would you ever take the life of the one who prepared such a glorious feast for you?" Iku, now fully awake and content from the food, replied, *"No, of course not."* Eshu then revealed the truth: it was Orunmila who had prepared the feast. Iku, humbled, begged Eshu to return his scythe. But Eshu, ever wise, set a condition. "You must promise not to take the life of Orunmila's children before their time, unless Orunmila gives his consent."

Iku agreed, but there was one more question. *"How will I know who Orunmila's children are?"* he asked. Eshu answered, *"By the green and brown beads they wear on their wrists and necks."* From that day forward, Iku agreed to spare Orunmila's children, allowing them to live out their destinies. The beads became a sign of protection, ensuring that those who wore them were safe from untimely death unless it was truly their time to go. This story teaches us that through wisdom, faith, and the protection of Orunmila, we can find safety, even from Death itself.

REFLECTION & WISDOM

In the Yoruba tradition, the green and brown beads worn by Orunmila's followers symbolize protection and long life. These beads identify Orunmila's children and ensure that Iku (Death) will not take their lives before their time. In some communities outside of Africa, especially in the diaspora, the beads are often green and yellow instead of green and brown. This variation represents cultural adaptations, but the meaning remains the same: protection, a connection to Orunmila, and safety from premature death.

* * *

THE BOND BETWEEN ESHU AND ORUNMILA
STORY 2:2

Long ago, in the time of the Orishas, there were two powerful deities with very different roles. Orunmila was the Orisha of wisdom and divination, known for his deep understanding and calm nature. He guided people through Ifá, helping them find clarity in their lives. On the other hand, Eshu was the Orisha of mischief and change. He loved to create chaos, challenge people, and disrupt order to test their strength. Because of their differences, Orunmila and Eshu did not get along. Orunmila valued peace and order, while Eshu thrived in unpredictability and disruption. However, their destinies were intertwined in ways neither fully understood. One day, Eshu decided to test Orunmila. He disguised himself as a poor and hungry traveler and knocked on Orunmila's door, asking for food.

Even though Orunmila had little to offer, he generously shared what he had. But Eshu was not finished. He stayed longer than expected and began causing trouble, scattering Orunmila's sacred divination tools, confusing his clients, and disrupting his work. Over time, Orunmila's reputation began to suffer because people lost trust in his ability to guide them. Despite this, Orunmila remained patient. Using his wisdom and divination, he soon realized the troublesome guest was none other than Eshu in disguise. Instead of reacting with anger, Orunmila calmly restored order and solved each problem caused by Eshu's tricks.

Eshu, watching closely, was impressed. He had expected frustration and defeat, but instead, Orunmila's wisdom remain unshaken. "You have passed my test," Eshu admitted, smiling. "Your patience and intelligence are greater than I thought." "And you," Orunmila replied, "have shown me something important. Chaos and difficulty are not always bad. They challenge us to think, grow, and become wiser." At that moment, both Orishas understood something new: chaos and wisdom must exist together. Eshu's challenges made people stronger, and Orunmila's wisdom helped them navigate those challenges.

From that day on, their bond changed from rivalry to respect. Orunmila understood that wisdom is tested through hardship, and Eshu recognized that even chaos needs direction. That is why, before any divination begins, Eshu must be honored first, because he clears the way, allowing wisdom to shine through. Their story reminds us that life is a balance of order and disorder, struggle and growth, and both forces are needed to create harmony.

REFLECTION & WISDOM

Long ago, Orunmila, the wise Orisha of divination, and Eshu, the playful trickster, didn't get along because they were so different. One day, Eshu disguised himself as a poor traveler to test Orunmila's patience, causing trouble and making people doubt Orunmila's wisdom. Despite the chaos, Orunmila stayed calm and treated the traveler with kindness, eventually realizing it was Eshu in disguise. Impressed by Orunmila's wisdom and patience, Eshu admitted it was a test, and the two came to understand that chaos and wisdom are deeply connected. From then on, they formed a bond of respect, and every divination now begins by honoring Eshu, reminding us that challenges and wisdom go hand in hand.

* * *

THE GIFT OF IFA
STORY 2:3

In the beginning, Orunmila was a being of great wisdom and compassion, chosen by Olodumare, the Creator, to guide the people of the earth. One day, filled with love and devotion, Orunmila called upon Olodumare and asked, "Grant me the wisdom to lead and teach those who seek the truth." Moved by Orunmila's sincerity, Olodumare smiled and replied, "I will give you the sacred knowledge of the universe, the gift of Ifa. This will be your tool to uncover the hidden truths of life, both from the past and the future."With this blessing, Orunmila received Ifa, a powerful wisdom passed down from the heavens. Orunmila then journeyed to earth, bringing with him the sacred knowledge of Odu Ifa, unlocking the mysteries of life. He could see what others could not: the paths people walked, the choices they faced, and the destinies that awaited them. He shared this wisdom with all who sought it, sending his disciples to help illuminate the darkness. Through Orunmila's teachings, the people of the world learned that the wisdom of Ifa was not just a gift, but a guiding force that connected the earth to the heavens above.

REFLECTION & WISDOM

This story of Orunmila reminds us of the profound connection between wisdom, love, and responsibility. Orunmila, chosen by Olodumare to guide humanity, symbolizes the power of seeking truth with a pure heart. His request for wisdom is not for personal gain, but to serve others, reflecting a deep sense of duty and compassion. The gift of Ifa, which allows him to see the unseen and understand life's mysteries, is not just a tool, but a sacred responsibility to lead with integrity. Through Orunmila's teachings, we learn that true wisdom is not merely for individual enlightenment, but to illuminate the paths of others, bridging the earthly and the divine. In our own lives, may we seek wisdom not for self-interest, but to guide and uplift those around us.

* * *

THE FIRST STUDENTS OF ORUNMILA
STORY 2:4

When Orunmila descended to Earth to teach humanity the wisdom of Ifá, he needed trustworthy messengers who could help him carry and spread the divine knowledge. Olodumare granted Orunmila two spiritual sons to assist in this sacred mission: *Akoda* and *Aseda*.

Akoda was known for his discipline and strict adherence to truth. He was sharp, analytical, and firm, a guardian of the integrity of Ifá's teachings. *Aseda*, on the other hand, was gentle, patient, and compassionate, offering wisdom with kindness and understanding. Orunmila taught them both the secrets of the *odu Ifá*, the sacred verses that reveal the destiny of all things. He also gave them the power to divine, to heal, and to restore balance in people's lives. One day, Orunmila tested them. He sent both *Akoda* and *Aseda* to help two different communities. *Akoda* arrived in a town filled with corruption and used strict justice to restore order. The people feared him but respected him, and eventually peace returned.

Aseda arrived in a different town, where the people were lost and confused, but not wicked. He guided them with patience, helping them remember their values through kindness and rituals. His softness healed their spirits, and they thrived. When the two returned, Orunmila praised them both. He said: "Justice and mercy are two wings of wisdom. Without one, the other cannot fly."

. . .

The story of Akoda and Aseda reminds us that within the sacred tradition of Ifá, there are often two distinct types of Babalawos. These Ifa priests, who also serve as priests of Orunmila, follow different expressions of the same calling. Some, like Akoda, embody strictness, discipline, and a strong focus on maintaining order and structure. Others, like Aseda, reflect gentleness, compassion, and a nurturing approach to spiritual guidance. Both paths are essential in the work of a Babalawo. One offers correction and structure; the other brings comfort and support. Yet each fulfills the same divine mission to guide others with the wisdom of Orunmila. A true Babalawo learns to balance these qualities, understanding when to be firm and when to be merciful, always seeking alignment with the will of Olodumare.

INSIGHTS, OFFERINGS, RITUALS AND SPIRITUAL SIGNIFICANCE
SECTION 3

WISDOM AND OFFERINGS

Orunmila, the Orisha of wisdom and knowledge, receives divine insight from Olodumare. His followers wear beads in green and gold or green and brown, reflecting regional traditions. Stones associated with him include emerald, jade, green tourmaline, tiger's eye, and peridot, used for spiritual alignment. Offerings to Orunmila include goats, pigeons, guinea fowl, palm oil, honey, shea butter, gin, fruits, fresh water, coconuts, kola nuts, candles, incense, and cornmeal, presented with prayers for guidance, healing, or balance.

ACTIVITY: SETTING UP A CONSULTATION WITH A BABALAWO

A consultation with a Babalawo is a sacred and personalized spiritual session where the wisdom of Ifá is accessed to guide your life. The Babalawo uses divination tools such as the *opele* chain or sacred palm nuts (*ikin*) to communicate with Orunmila, the Orisha of wisdom and destiny. Through this process, a specific *Odu* (divinatory sign) is revealed. The Babalawo interprets the *Odu* to address your concerns, be it health, relationships, life path, or spiritual blockages. You may receive practical advice, spiritual prescriptions (*ebo* or offerings), or rituals to realign with your destiny (*ayánmo*). These sessions can bring deep insight, healing, and direction in times of uncertainty. Consultations may be done in person or virtually and are rooted in tradition, respect, and a deep connection to spirit.

* * *

A Prayer to Orunmila
Verse 3:2

Orunmila, divine witness to creation,
Keeper of the secrets of the universe,
You who hold the wisdom of Olodumare,
Guide us with your sacred knowledge.

Master of Ifá, interpreter of destiny,
You see the past, present, and future with clarity.
Help us walk in alignment with cosmic order,
And make choices that honor truth and balance.

Teach us to understand the signs before us,
To listen to the voice of the spirit,
And to follow the path that leads to inner peace and purpose.

Orunmila, wise and compassionate one,
May your presence bring insight to our confusion,
Light to our darkness,
And clarity to our journey.
Ase.

* * *

29. OSAIN
ORISHA OF HERBAL MEDICINE AND HEALING

A CLOSER LOOK AT OSAIN

OSAIN (ALSO SPELLED Osanyin or Ozain) is the Orisha of herbs, healing, and the mystical forces of nature in the Yoruba religion. He is the divine herbalist and guardian of all plant life, possessing deep, sacred knowledge of how every leaf, root, seed, and bark can be used for physical healing, spiritual protection, purification, and ritual power. Osain understands the hidden energies within plants and knows how to unlock their full potential. Because of this, he is considered indispensable in traditional medicine and spiritual practice. He dwells deep within the forest, far from human civilization, where wild plants grow undisturbed and rich with spiritual force. It is said that all the Orishas and human priests rely on Osain for the herbs they need in their ceremonies, as no remedy or spiritual preparation is complete without his blessing.

Without his permission, no herb is truly effective, no matter how well it is prepared. His knowledge is so powerful and secretive that only a select few are ever permitted to learn it fully. Osain is often depicted as a mysterious and wise figure who lives alone among the trees, whispering to the plants and listening to the winds. He is typically described as physically imperfect or asymmetric missing one eye, one leg, or one arm. This image symbolizes that although he lacks what others consider physical wholeness, his power is uniquely focused and spiritually complete. His strength comes not from physical form, but from his profound connection to nature. Osain is honored with offerings such as herbs, roasted yams, tobacco, rum, and sometimes a rooster. He is commonly represented by a staff or metal object known as an *Osain staff*, adorned with small hanging gourds, birds, and other symbols of nature. These ornaments represent his dominion over the invisible forces of the forest and the spirits that dwell among the trees and plants.

Osain teaches that true healing is not just about curing illness, but about restoring balance between the body, the spirit, and the natural world. He promotes humility, discipline, and reverence for the hidden wisdom of nature. Those who follow Osain must undergo deep spiritual training and prove themselves worthy to receive his teachings. As the spiritual keeper of plants and natural medicine, Osain plays a vital role in maintaining the balance of life. His influence touches every ritual involving herbs whether for healing, protection, divination, or purification. In many traditions, no herbal or spiritual work begins without first invoking his presence.

PRAYER TO OSAIN, GUARDIAN OF HERBS
VERSE I:I

Osain, wise guardian of the sacred leaves,
Master of roots, of bark, and all that heals,
I come before you with humble heart and hands.

Unlock the power hidden deep within the plants,
Grant your blessing on every leaf I use,
So healing flows, pure and true,
And spirits find protection in your sacred woods.

O Keeper of the forest's whispered song,
Who walks with one eye watching, one foot strong,
Though your form may seem incomplete to eyes of flesh,
Your spirit holds the forest's perfect breath.

Teach me your secrets, ancient and profound,
So health and light in my life abound.
Osain, without your sacred nod, no herb can cure,
No remedy holds power, no spirit endures.
Guide me through the mysteries that nature weaves,
Osain, mighty healer, guardian of leaves.

* * *

Osain's Healing Power
Verse 1:2

Deep in the forest, where wild things grow,
Lives Osain, who all the healers know.
He talks to the trees, the roots, and the breeze,
He knows the secrets of plants with ease.

With one leg, one arm, and one sharp eye,
He watches the herbs as the winds pass by.
No spell or cure can fully begin,
Unless we first ask permission from him.

He teaches that healing is more than a cure,
It's balance and spirit, deep and pure.
Osain, the keeper of nature's door,
Guarding the wisdom in every spore.

* * *

SACRED STORIES / LEGENDS
Section 2

The Story of Orunmila and the Mysterious Slave
Story 2:1

In a market filled with clamor and sound,
Orunmila, wise and revered,
walked the ground.
Vendors cried, and animals brayed,
As the bustling town in sunlight swayed.

He sought supplies for his land's need,
And laborers to plant, to till, to seed.
Among the crowd, a scene caught his eye,
A group of slaves, their spirits awry.

One man stood, frail and thin,
A mystery hidden deep within.

The sellers spoke with words of disdain,
"Too weak to work, he brings only pain."
But Orunmila, with wisdom keen,
Saw past the man's ragged sheen.

He cast his ikin, his divining nuts,
And heard the whispers of Ifa's cuts.
The odu spoke, a tale to unfold,
This slave was more than his story told.

A power lay deep within this man,
A gift of herbs, a master's plan.
Osain's knowledge, a secret untold,
Hidden in a soul, ancient and bold.

Orunmila, trusting Ifa's word,
Bought the man, though protests stirred.
Back home, Orunmila set him to task,
To toil the soil, no questions to ask.

But days passed, and Orunmila grew wise,
The slave's skill was a welcome surprise.
He knew each plant, each herb, each tree,
The secrets they held, their mysteries free.

He named them all, from root to leaf,
A healer's art beyond belief.
With every touch, the crops did thrive,
The wild herbs, too, seemed more alive.

Orunmila watched in quiet awe,
For the man's power left him in awe.
One day he asked, with a knowing glance,

"Where did you learn this herbal dance?
You know what even I don't see,
A wisdom older than the trees."
The man smiled, his eyes aglow,

"The forest's secrets I truly know.
These herbs are mine, they've been with me,
A part of my soul, eternally."

PART 2

Orunmila, curious and wise,
Asked Ifa to reveal the man's disguise.
The truth was clear, the oracle said,
The slave was Osain, with power ahead.
A master of herbs, strong and bright,
Osain tested Orunmila's sight.

With respect, Orunmila bowed,
He freed Osain, his heart proud.
Grateful, Osain shared his way,
His knowledge and wisdom
with Orunmila day by day.
Osain spoke of herbs, of their powers deep,
Of healing roots and secrets to keep.

He taught Orunmila the magic of green,
The life in each leaf, the force unseen.
Together they worked, wisdom in hand,
A bond forged in the spirit land.

Herbs became part of Orunmila's art,
In rituals and healing, they played their part.
Orunmila, wise with herbs and lore,
Now held the key to wisdom's door.

Osain, the master of earth and tree,
Shared his secrets, setting all free.
Thus, Orunmila and Osain stand,
A union of knowledge, a powerful hand.

Together they guide, heal, and teach,
The wisdom of nature, within our reach.

* * *

This story of Orunmila and Osain reveals how true power often hides beneath the surface. Orunmila, the wise diviner, sees beyond appearances when he discovers a frail slave holds deep knowledge of herbs. Through Ifa's guidance, he learns the slave is Osain, the Orisha of healing and plants. Orunmila's recognition of Osain's hidden wisdom teaches us that real strength is often overlooked. Their bond shows that wisdom isn't just about intellect but openness to new teachings. Even Orunmila, known for his wisdom, learns from Osain, whose knowledge of plants and their healing power strengthens both their spiritual practices. This partnership highlights the importance of collaboration between knowledge and nature. The story reminds us to see the sacred in the ordinary and be open to divine insights from unexpected places. It teaches that true wisdom comes from humility, connection, and respect for the natural world.

* * *

OSAIN'S LESSON
STORY 2:2

Deep within the heart of the lush, green forest, Osain, the Orisha of herbs and medicine, lived in solitude. He was the keeper of great knowledge, understanding the power of every plant, root, and leaf. But rather than sharing his wisdom, he kept it locked away inside mystical gourds that hung high in the treetops, protected by powerful spells. The other Orishas, burdened by their tasks and struggles, came to Osain with a plea. "Osain, help us! Your knowledge could ease our burdens and heal those in need." But Osain stood firm, his voice cold and unmoving. "My wisdom is mine alone. It is not meant to be given away." Disheartened by his selfishness, the Orishas turned away, frustrated. But none were more desperate than Oya, the fierce Orisha of winds and storms.

SECOND PART: OYA'S DESPERATE PLEA

Oya had a beloved son, a warrior strong and proud. But he had been struck by a terrible illness, one that no healer could cure. His body burned with fever, his breath came in ragged gasps, and the light in his eyes began to fade. Oya had heard whispers that only Osain's herbs could save him. With all her might, she traveled to Osain's sacred grove, her heart heavy with sorrow. She knelt before him, setting aside her pride. "Osain," she pleaded, "my son is dying. I do not ask for all your knowledge, just one cure, one herb that can bring him back to life." But Osain only crossed his arms. "Your son's fate is not my concern. My wisdom is mine, and I will not share it, not even with you, Oya." And this made Oya's sorrow turn to rage.

Third Part: Oya's Storm and Osain's Defiance

Summoning the fierce winds, Oya unleashed a mighty storm upon the forest. The trees bent and groaned, their leaves tearing free, but Osain's gourds remained untouched, held firm by his magic. Seeing that force alone would not work, Oya decided to outsmart him. She transformed into a beautiful woman, her eyes soft with plea, and approached Osain with gentle steps. "Great Osain," she spoke sweetly, "your wisdom is a treasure, but what good is it if no one can benefit from it?" But Osain, sharp and perceptive, saw through her deception. With a wave of his hand, he trapped her in chains, binding her power. "Foolish trickster," he sneered. "No deception can break the power I hold." Yet, even in chains, Oya's spirit was not broken. She cried out for Sango, the mighty Orisha of thunder, who heard her call and responded with a roar that shook the heavens. The Shattering of Secrets Sango summoned lightning so fierce that it split the sky in two. A single bolt struck Osain's sacred tree, shattering it apart.

The gourds cracked open, and the magical herbs inside were carried away by the rushing winds. As the herbs scattered, Oya reached out her hands. She gathered the ones she knew would heal her son and rushed home, leaving Osain to face the destruction of his hoarded knowledge. The storm did not end without cost. A heavy branch fell upon Osain, crushing him beneath its weight. In that moment, he lost an arm, a leg, and an eye, paying the price for his stubborn pride. Oya, however, wasted no time preparing the herbs she needed to heal her son.

Fourth Part: Osain's Transformation

Left broken among the ruins of his treasured secrets, Osain finally understood. He had tried to hoard wisdom, but knowledge was meant to be shared. Humbled by his fall, he vowed to teach and aid the Orishas, though he kept some secrets hidden. From that day on, his knowledge became a gift to those who sought healing, allowing the power of nature to help the world thrive. The Lesson of Osain Osain's story is a reminder that pride and selfishness can lead to downfall, but true wisdom is found in sharing knowledge with others. Like seeds scattered in the wind, knowledge grows when it is passed on, bringing healing and life to all.

REFLECTION & WISDOM

The story of Osain teaches the importance of sharing knowledge. Osain, keeper of herbal wisdom, refused to help the other Orishas, hoarding his knowledge for himself. When Oya's son fell gravely ill and Osain refused to help, her rage summoned a powerful storm that shattered Osain's defenses. With Sango's aid, Oya gathered the herbs needed to heal her son, while Osain faced the consequences of his pride. The story shows that wisdom is not meant to be hoarded. True power lies in sharing knowledge for the greater good, as healing and growth come when wisdom is passed on. Osain's fall teaches us that pride and selfishness lead to downfall, while humility and generosity lead to true strength.

* * *

THE BIRTH OF OSAIN
STORY 2:3

In the beginning, the world was young and untouched. Earth and Water lay separate, silent, still, and barren. The earth was empty and lifeless, unable to grow because there was no balance. The world could not thrive. Olodumare, the Creator, saw this desolation and knew harmony was needed. With a single act of divine will, He brought Earth and Water together. Their union was sacred and filled with energy. From this meeting, fertile soil was born, rich with potential. From this sacred soil, Osain emerged. Osain became the spirit of the land, the keeper of its green heart. Seeing Osain's power, Olodumare gave him a divine task: to watch over and protect the plants. Osain became the Orisha of herbs and medicine, the guardian of nature's greenery. With his deep connection to the Earth, Osain uncovered the secrets of every leaf, root, and flower. His wisdom vast, his power unmatched. Yet, despite holding the key to nature's healing, he remained humble and watchful, living deep in the forest where few could find him.

Legend says that Osain emerged from the soil when Olodumare combined Earth and Water at the beginning of creation. Osain is not seen as separate from the Earth, but as a part of it, emerging like a plant from the soil. He remains hidden in the depths of the forest, sharing his wisdom only with those who approach the Earth with respect and care. This teaches us that true wisdom is not easily gained; it requires humility, patience, and a sincere desire to understand. While the Earth freely offers its gifts, it is our responsibility to honor and care for it in return.

* * *

INSIGHTS, OFFERINGS, RITUALS AND SPIRITUAL SIGNIFICANCE
SECTION 3

A BRIEF INTRODUCTION TO OSAIN AND YORUBA MEDICINE

Yoruba medicine is a holistic healing system based on the belief that true health comes from maintaining balance with nature, the spirit world, and the community. The Yoruba emphasize prevention, encouraging individuals to stay in harmony with themselves and their environment to avoid illness. When imbalance occurs, the body sends warning signs. By paying attention to these signals, a person can take steps to restore balance before sickness fully manifests. Illness is seen not just as a physical problem but often as a sign of disconnection from nature, community, or the spiritual realm. Healing, therefore, involves restoring that lost harmony through herbs, rituals, prayers, and mindful living.

A key figure in this tradition is the Osainista also known as an Oloogun or Onisegun a healer initiated into the mysteries of Osain, the Orisha of plants and herbal knowledge. While Osainistas and Babalawos typically have different roles, many Babalawos also undergo initiation into Osain, blending divination with herbal healing. Yoruba healing methods are diverse and can include herbal teas, spiritual baths, incantations, offerings, prayers, amulets, and observing taboos. Often, healing requires the combined efforts of several priests with specialized knowledge, showing the spiritual depth and complexity of Yoruba medicine.

Offerings to Osain typically include items like flowers, leaves, and tobacco, given with reverence. His sacred staff, the opere, represents his healing power and is used in rituals. Practitioners may also offer honey, fruits, kola nuts, roasted corn, and alcohol to honor him and ask for his support in healing. Osain's power is found throughout the natural world, and through these gifts, healers seek his blessings for health and spiritual alignment.

* * *

30. OSHUN
ORISHA OF LOVE AND BEAUTY

A CLOSER LOOK AT OSHUN

OSHUN (ALSO SPELLED OSUN, Ochun, or Oxum) is one of the most beloved Orishas in the Yoruba religion. She rules over love, beauty, sensuality, and all fresh water sources, rivers, streams, and lakes. As the guardian of these vital elements, Oshun deeply influences how we experience love, understand ourselves, and develop compassion and intimacy with both ourselves and others. She is often shown as radiant and graceful, dressed in gold, a symbol of wealth and beauty. The Osun River in Nigeria is a sacred place for Oshun's followers, serving as the heart of the annual Osun-Osogbo Festival. This lively two-week event attracts thousands who come to honor Oshun, celebrate, pray, and seek her blessings.

Oshun brings love, emotional closeness, and joy into people's lives, but she is also respected for her powerful and complex nature. She balances kindness with strength. While she grants healing, blessings, and abundance to those who honor her, she can also bring justice and hardship when disrespected. This duality reminds people to approach her and the forces she embodies with care, reverence, and humility. Her sacred waters reflect this nature; they can gently heal, cleanse, and provide abundance, but they can also flood and cause destruction, symbolizing the balance of creation and power in nature. Oshun's influence centers on beauty, love, and emotional connection. She inspires both physical attraction and deep emotional bonds. Many turn to her for help attracting love, repairing relationships, and deepening intimacy. She teaches her followers to enjoy life's sweetness, which is why honey, a natural symbol of sweetness, is especially sacred to her.

In rituals, Oshun is honored with sweet offerings like honey, sugar, fruits, and flowers, symbolizing her love of beauty and joy. She is closely associated with yellow and orange fruits such as oranges and bananas, along with gold and mirrors, which are often offered to her. As a true bringer of abundance, Oshun leads people toward prosperity, pleasure, and harmony. Her vibrant energy encourages self-love, emotional openness, and a life rich in joy, sweetness, and happiness.

THE SWEET WATERS OF OSHUN
A Prayer and Poem
VERSE I:I

Oshun, Orisha of rivers wide,
Your waters flow where dreams reside.
With love and light, your reign is sweet,
In your embrace, our hearts shall meet.

You bring the wealth of joy and grace,
A healing touch, a gentle place.
Protector strong of women, child,
Within your care, our souls run wild.

From deep within your flowing heart,
You guide us, never to depart.
Your energy, like purest air,
Surrounds us all with tender care.

Oshun, your presence fills our veins,
The pulse of life, the love that reigns.
Bring light to shadows, day and night,
Be with us in your sacred light.

We call upon your sacred name,
With humble hearts, we fan your flame.
Guide us in your sweet embrace
Oshun, giver of love and grace.

* * *

OSHUN, LIGHT OF LOVE
A Prayer and Poem
VERSE 1:2

Oshun, queen of rivers bright,
You bring love, joy, and light.
With golden grace, your waters heal,
Our hearts you touch, our spirits feel.

Guardian of love and life's flow,
In your care, we bloom and grow.
Teach us kindness, teach us peace,
From your sweet waters, our troubles cease.

Oshun, radiant, strong, and true,
We honor and call on you.
Fill our lives with beauty's song,
In your love, we all belong.

* * *

SACRED STORIES / LEGENDS
SECTION 2

THE VULTURE'S ASCENT
STORY 2:1

Long ago, the Orisha gathered with pride, boasting among the mountains and clouds. "We are powerful," they declared. "We need no guidance not even from Olodumare, the Supreme Creator!"But Olodumare heard their arrogance and withdrew his blessings. The rains stopped, rivers dried, crops withered, and the world fell into famine and sorrow. The Orisha cried out, but the heavens remained silent. Among them was Oshun, goddess of love, beauty, and fresh water often seen as delicate and unimportant. Yet within her was quiet strength. Moved by the suffering on earth, Oshun said, "I will go to Olodumare and ask for forgiveness." The others mocked her. "You? This task needs strength, not softness!" Undeterred, Oshun spread her golden wings and flew toward heaven. The journey was harsh, the sun scorched her feathers, and fierce winds battered her. By the time she reached Olodumare's throne, she had transformed into a vulture worn, dark, yet unbroken. She bowed and spoke of the earth's pain, the people's thirst, and the regret of the Orisha. Olodumare, moved by her humility and courage, restored his blessings. Rain returned, rivers flowed, and life blossomed once again. Oshun returned not as the goddess they once dismissed, but as a symbol of true strength. Olodumare named her his messenger on earth, reminding all that power can be gentle, graceful, and unshakable. And from that day, the vulture became sacred, and Oshun's flight a legend passed through generations.

REFLECTION & WISDOM

This story reminds us that true strength lies not in pride, but in humility and compassion. While the powerful Orisha were silenced by their arrogance, it was Oshun gentle and overlooked, who had the courage to act. Her transformation into a vulture symbolizes sacrifice and resilience. What seemed like weakness became divine power. Oshun's journey shows that quiet determination and love can restore what pride destroys. In the end, the story teaches that strength isn't always loud, it's often found in grace, persistence, and the willingness to serve others.

* * *

OSHUN TURNS THE RIVER SWEET
STORY 2:2

A river cursed by war and hate,
Stood bitter, black, and desolate.
No bird would sing, no child would play,
Its poison drove all life away.

But Oshun came with tears that healed,
With quiet love her heart revealed.
She cried into the angry stream,
And turned its pain into a dream.

The waters danced, the people sang,
With drums and honey offerings rang.
What once was death now flowed so sweet,

Renewed by love at Oshun's feet.
Where hatred reigned, now blossoms grow
Because her grace began to flow.

REFLECTION & WISDOM

This story shows that love heals what hate destroys. Oshun didn't fight the poisoned river she wept into it, and her compassion brought it back to life. True power lies in gentleness. Even the bitterest places can be made sweet with kindness and care.

* * *

OSHUN AND THE SPIRIT OF THE FOREST
STORY 2:3

A forest deep, by spirit sealed,
Its sacred herbs remained concealed.
The strongest Orisha faced defeat
No force could make the spirit yield.

But Oshun came with honey sweet,
And sang a song both soft and fleet.
She bowed, she smiled, she gave no threat
And with her peace, the spirit wept.

The forest opened, wide and free,
Its secrets shared with harmony.
The people healed, the land was blessed
All through her voice and tenderness.
She showed the path no blade can find:
That gentle hands can calm the wild.

REFLECTION & WISDOM

Oshun's story reminds us that calm and compassion can overcome resistance. Where force failed, her sweetness and respect opened hearts and minds. In a world often driven by conflict, her message is clear: gentleness can transform even the most stubborn challenges.

* * *

THE RIVER'S BLESSING
STORY 2:4

Oshun, the Orisha, so graceful and kind,
With love in her heart and beauty to find,
By the river each day, her dress she would wash,
The water turned yellow, so bright, like a flash.

She worked by the river, with children to feed,
Washing the clothes was the only way she could succeed.
For every garment, a coin she would earn,
Each coin, a small treasure, a way to return.

But one fateful day, as the current did rush,
A coin slipped from her hands, with a soft, gentle hush.
It floated away, swept far out of sight,
The last of her coins, her food for the night.

Desperate and worried, she called out with might,
To Yemoja and Olokun, in the deep water's light.
"Please return my coin, it's all that I have,
Without it, my children will suffer and starve."
The deities heard her and gathered the sea,
They parted the waters, as vast as can be.

Treasure was shown from the ocean's deep floor,
Gems and gold, and riches galore.
But Oshun, so wise, did not take them all,
She reached for the coin and answered the call.

Her heart full of honor, she only took one,
The coin she had lost, her work now undone.
Yemoja and Olokun, impressed by her grace,
Blessed Oshun with treasures, to her they gave space.

They declared the river would now be her home,
A sacred domain where she'd always roam.
They spoke words of wisdom, so deep and so true,

"Never give all you have, keep some for you."
And from that day forward, Oshun did reign,
A ruler of rivers, with love in her name.

REFLECTION & WISDOM

Oshun, a kind Orisha who washes clothes by the river, loses her last coin to the current. She calls on Yemaya and Olokun, who part the waters to reveal ocean treasures. Yet Oshun only takes back her lost coin, showing integrity. Impressed, the deities bless her, making the river her sacred domain and teaching her the value of saving. Oshun then becomes the loving ruler of rivers.

* * *

INSIGHTS, OFFERINGS, RITUALS AND SPIRITUAL SIGNIFICANCE
SECTION 3

OFFERINGS TO OSHUN

Oshun is honored with offerings that reflect sweetness, beauty, fertility, and emotional healing. These include pure fresh water, golden or yellow flowers such as sunflowers and marigolds, and sweet fruits like melons, oranges, and bananas. Sacred items like honey, brown sugar, mirrors, and yellow candles are offered to invite her blessings and delight. Eggs represent fertility and purity, while incense lifts prayers to the heavens. Animals such as goats, turtles, guinea hens, and pigeons are sometimes sacrificed with reverence. Precious materials like amber, citrine, gold, and topaz are also associated with Oshun's radiant energy. These offerings are best placed by rivers, especially calm or gently flowing waters, where Oshun's presence is strongest and most receptive. Each item is given with love, humility, and the hope of receiving her joy, sweetness, and grace in return.

* * *

THE MANY FACES OF OSHUN

Oshun is a beloved Orisha known for her beauty, sweetness, and deep wisdom. She has many different forms, called caminos or paths, each showing a unique side of her spirit. Some paths reveal Oshun as a gentle healer and nurturer, while others show her as a fierce protector, a powerful witch, or a wise river mother. In the Yoruba tradition, Oshun is the Orisha of love, rivers, fertility, and abundance. Her many paths reflect how she moves between joy and sorrow, strength and tenderness, always guiding her children with grace. Each path reminds us of Oshun's ability to bring prosperity, heal emotional wounds, and fight fiercely for justice when needed. Some of the most well-known paths of Oshun include:

- **Oshun Ibú Ikolé:** Represented by the vulture, Ibú Ikolé embodies power born from poverty and struggle. She dwells in the forest and is revered as the oldest of the Aje (witches). She brings deep wisdom through life's difficulties and serves as a guardian of the home and those in distress.
- **Oshun Ibú Akuaro:** Ibú Akuaro, symbolized by the quail, is a youthful and hardworking path of Oshun. She lives near waterfalls, heals the sick, and protects against curses. Gentle but fiery, she dances with Shango and hunts with Ochosi.
- **Oshun Ololodí:** Ololodí, the wife of Orunmila, is a master diviner who shares the power of the cowrie-shell oracle. After observing Orunmila's practice, he entrusted her with the sacred cowrie shells, enabling her to perform divination in his absence.
- **Oshun Ibú Añá:** Ibú Aña, the guardian of rhythm and drumming, bridges earth and heaven through music. She resides where rivers drum, their rushing waters creating a rhythmic sound.
- **Oshun Ibú Yumu:** Ibú Yumu is the oldest path of Oshun. She resides where the river is calm, clear, and gentle, bringing wealth, healing, fertility, and peace to those who make offerings to her.

* * *

RIVER RITUAL TO HONOR OSHUN

The purpose of this ritual is to honor Oshun, and to invite her blessings of emotional healing, love and abundance into your life.

Materials Needed

- Fresh honey or Brown Sugar
- An offering for Oshun, preferably yellow flowers, or an edible yellow or orange fruit that you are sure you do not have any allergies to.
- A small yellow or gold candle
- You may want to bring a small container with you to collect some of the fresh river water, which you can bring home with you if you desire.

Location: a river

Choose a peaceful spot by a river where you can sit quietly and remain undisturbed.

* * *

Step 1: Prepare the Space

1. *Sit quietly by the river and take a moment to connect with the sound of the flowing water and to nature.*
2. *Lay out your offerings near the riverbank.*
3. *Light the yellow or gold candle in honor of Oshun.*

Step 2: Opening Prayer

Take a moment to speak to Oshun from the heart, sharing your thoughts, desires, and gratitude. If you prefer, recite the following prayer with sincerity and reverence:

Oshun, sweet mother of river and light,
Lady of gold, shining bright,
Flow through my spirit, dance in my soul,
Bring joy, bring healing, make my heart whole.
With sweetness and love, your blessings I seek,
I honor you humbly, with spirit and speech.
Oshun, O mother, O river divine,
With all that I am, I offer what's mine.

*　*　*

STEP 3: PERSONAL CONNECTION

Take a moment to connect deeply with Oshun by speaking freely from the heart. Share your thoughts, emotions, and any burdens or joys you may be carrying. Express your gratitude for her presence, acknowledging the beauty, love, and abundance she brings into your life. Share your wishes, whether they are for emotional healing, love, or the manifestation of specific blessings. This is your time to openly communicate with Oshun, trusting in her ability to hear and understand your heart's desires. Speak with sincerity and openness, allowing the flow of words to come naturally, as you invite her gentle yet powerful energy into your life.

STEP 4: MAKE THE OFFERINGS

1. *Taste a small amount of the honey, sugar, or fruit, as its customary to do so before offering them to Oshun. Only taste the edible items and be mindful of any food allergies. Offer something you're certain you can consume safely. Do not taste the flowers.*
2. *Drizzle a bit of honey or sugar into the river while whispering your prayers.*
3. *Gently place the flowers or edible fruit in the water or by the river's edge.*

STEP 5: BLESS YOURSELF

Take a small handful of river water and sprinkle it over your head, chest, and hands. Ask Oshun to bless you with her love, sweetness, and guidance.

STEP 6: LISTEN AND REFLECT

Sit quietly by the water for a few more minutes if you desire. Listen for any insights, emotions, or messages. You can use a notebook to write down anything you sense or feel if you desire.

STEP 7: CLOSING

Thank Oshun sincerely for her presence and the blessings. Extinguish the candle if it's still burning and clean up your space, leaving no trash behind.

Approach this ritual with love, humility, and deep respect.
Repeating this ritual regularly can strengthen your bond with Oshun.

* * *

31. Osumare

Orisha of Rainbows, Transformation and Renewal

A Closer Look at Osumare

Osumare (also spelled Osumare, Ochumaré, or Oxumaré) is a powerful and sacred Orisha in the Yoruba spiritual tradition, revered as the spirit of the rainbow, transformation, and the eternal cycle of life. Osumare embodies movement, fluidity, and change not just in nature but in the soul's journey through existence. Often depicted as a radiant rainbow-colored serpent or a snake coiled into a perfect circle, Osumare symbolizes infinity, unity, and the constant dance between beginnings and endings. The circular form mirrors the cycles of birth, death, and rebirth, and highlights the connection between the earthly and the divine.

Osumare stands for balance and harmony across all dualities, light and darkness, masculine and feminine, the material and the spiritual. This Orisha transcends binary identities, carrying both male and female aspects in perfect harmony. As such, Osumare serves as a spiritual archetype for wholeness, reminding us that true power lies in the union of opposites. Osumare's energy brings deep transformation, healing from within, and the promise of abundance and renewal. Just as a rainbow appears after the storm, Osumare's presence signals that hardship has passed and that beauty, clarity, and hope are returning.

According to Yoruba cosmology, when Olodumare, the Supreme Creator, finished shaping the heavens and the earth, it was Osumare who was called upon to mark the moment with a divine gesture. In response, Osumare stretched a radiant arc of color across the sky: the first rainbow. Since then, the rainbow has been a sacred sign of Osumare's presence, a celestial reminder that every ending opens the way to a new beginning. The rainbow is not just a natural phenomenon but a spiritual bridge, a vibrant thread linking the human world to the heavens above. Osumare is also closely connected to the umbilical cord, which in Yoruba belief is more than just a physical structure; it is a sacred lifeline between the living and their ancestors. It symbolizes our spiritual connection to where we come from, both in human lineage and divine origin. Just as the rainbow bridges the sky and the earth, the umbilical cord links each person to their family, heritage, and spiritual roots. Both serve as powerful reminders that we are never truly separate from our beginnings.

OSUMARE'S LIGHT
A Prayer and Poem
VERSE 1:1

Osumare, the serpent divine,
In colors of rainbows, you brightly shine.
A symbol of change, of new beginnings,
You bring forth hope with your rainbow winnings.

From the storm, you bring calm,
A gentle touch, a soothing balm.
After the chaos, you lead the way,
Turning darkness into light of day.

With Olodumare's word so true,
You painted the sky in every hue.
A sign to all that the earth was done,
A work of creation under the sun.

You rule the cycles of the sky,
The sun, the clouds, the rain that's high.
From condensation to the morning dew,
Osumare, we look to you.

In your dance, we find release,
From negativity, there comes peace.
Purification flows like rain,
Cleansing our hearts from every pain.

So when you see the rainbow bright,
Remember Osumare, the guiding light.
For in your path, we are reborn,
A new day rises, fresh and sworn.

* * *

THE SHAPER OF THE EARTH
VERSE 1:2

Born of Nana, wise and old,
A brother to Obalu-aye, bold.
An ancient being, strong and bright,
He shaped the world with endless might.

Coiling tight around the land,
He carved the rivers with his hand.
A serpent grand, he bites his tail,
A circle of life that will never fail.

With every turn, the earth was made,
Through hills and valleys, light and shade.
Bringing rain to help things grow,
Guiding waters as they flow.

Osumare, ruler of the sky,
Lifts the ocean, sends it high.
Clouds take shape, the rain comes down,
A rainbow shines above the ground.

A sign of peace, a promise true,
Colors stretching, red to blue.
Osumare's gift for all to see,
A world in balance, wild and free.

* * *

SACRED STORIES / LEGENDS
SECTION 2

OSUMARE'S GIFT
STORY 2:1

In the beginning, before the day,
Olodumare made light to stay.
The earth was vast, the sky was wide,
But no bridge linked the two inside.

Then Osumare, with grace and might,
Slithered through the endless night.
A serpent bright, both fierce and free,
Its colors swirled for all to see.

Guardian of cycles, wealth, and flow,
Bringing balance high and low.
After storms, when rains would cease,
Osumare brought the world peace.

A bridge was formed, a shining glow,
A path where blessings flow below.
It is through the rainbow bridge so wide,
That spirits travel, side by side.

A sacred path from earth to sky,
Where souls ascend and Orishas fly.
With every hue so bold and bright,
They turned the dark into the light.
A promise made, both old and new,
That life would always start anew.

REFLECTION & WISDOM

This story explains Osumare's role in connecting heaven and earth, bringing balance and renewal to the world. In the beginning, when the sky and land were separated, Osumare took the form of a radiant serpent and created a colorful bridge, the rainbow. As the guardian of cycles and transformation,

Osumare ensures the flow of energy, prosperity, and peace, particularly after storms. This rainbow bridge serves as a sacred path for spirits and Orishas, symbolizing the eternal promise of renewal, transforming darkness into light.

* * *

OSUMARE AND THE GREAT DROUGHT
STORY 2:2

The earth was dry, the sky was clear,
No rain in sight, no clouds near.
The people prayed, their hopes held high,
But still, the land was cracked and dry.

Shango called the thunder loud,
Summoning storms from the darkened cloud.
But rains fell fast, then went away,
Leaving the earth to thirst and sway.

Then Osumare, serpent bright,
Coiled through the clouds, a shining light.
With Oya's winds to guide the way,
They brought the rains to help the day.

Oshun's rivers sang below,
Nourishing the earth to make it grow.
The rainbow's arc, so bold and wide,
Marked the end, with peace beside.

The drought had passed, the crops did rise,
And abundance filled the earth and skies.
Through balance, patience, and harmony,
The land was healed, so all could see.

Together they worked, the forces strong,
To bring prosperity all along.
Osumare taught, with wisdom clear,
That unity brings what we hold dear.

Reflection & Wisdom

This story highlights the collaboration between powerful Orishas to bring life and balance to a drought-stricken land. Despite Shango's efforts to summon storms, the rains fell briefly and left the earth thirsty. It is Osumare, with the help of Oya's winds, who brings the much-needed rains, restoring fertility to the land. The rainbow that follows marks the return of peace and abundance. Through unity and patience, the Orishas work together to heal the earth, teaching that harmony and collaboration are key to prosperity and renewal.

* * *

THE GENEROUS FARMER
STORY 2:3

A farmer once lived with land so wide,
But greed in his heart he couldn't hide.
He kept his harvest, and would not share,
Leaving others hungry, unaware.

One day, Osumare, wise and old,
Asked for food, his story told.
The farmer refused, his heart was cold,
Unaware of the lesson about to unfold.

Osumare, in anger, made a choice,
Transformed the farmer with a powerful voice.
He became a snake, shedding skin each year,
Learning humility and shedding his fear.

Through time and change, the farmer grew,
Learning kindness and compassion too.
When Osumare saw the farmer's heart was true,
He gave him back his form, fresh and new.

The farmer now shared, with love and care,
A lesson of renewal, he chose to share.
Osumare's gift was clear to see,
That through transformation, we all can be free.

This story is about a greedy farmer who refused to share his harvest, even when Osumare asked for food. In response, Osumare transformed the farmer into a snake, teaching him humility and compassion over time. As the farmer shed his old, selfish ways and learned kindness, Osumare saw the change in his heart and restored him to his human form. Transformed by his experiences, the farmer chose to share his abundance with others, showing that through personal growth and transformation, we can all become better and more generous people

* * *

OSUMARE AND SANGO'S TRICK
STORY 2:4

One day, Osumare appeared in the sky, shining brightly with vibrant colors, creating a rainbow for all to see. Sango, watching with envy, wanted to capture this beauty for himself.

Knowing that Osumare wouldn't remain in the sky for long, Sango devised a plan to trap him. He invited Osumare to his palace, surrounded by guards and soldiers. Once Osumare entered, Sango shut the doors, trapping him inside. Sango chased him around the palace, but there was no way out. In fear, Osumare called to Olorun for help.

Olorun heard Osumare's plea and transformed him into a serpent. With new, shimmering scales, Osumare slipped away, causing Sango to retreat in fear of the snake. Osumare managed to escape through a small crack and fled to safety. Now in Orun, Osumare's role is clear—to bring the rains when the clouds appear. Sango, however, would never be able to catch him again.

REFLECTION & WISDOM

The story of Osumare and Sango teaches that not everything can be controlled by force. Sango tries to trap Osumare, but Osumare's transformation into a serpent shows that true freedom comes from adaptability. The story empha-

sizes the importance of trusting life's natural flow and letting go of control for growth and transformation.

* * *

INSIGHTS, OFFERINGS, RITUALS AND SPIRITUAL SIGNIFICANCE
SECTION 3

OFFERINGS TO OSUMARE

Osumare is honored with offerings that symbolize life, abundance, and spiritual connection. Common gifts include fresh water, bright flowers, and sweet fruits like watermelon and mango. Yellow candles and incense are used to invite light and purification, while eggs represent rebirth and new beginnings. Ducks may also be offered, and stones such as quartz and moonstone are closely linked to Osumare's energy. Other offerings like honey, seeds, sugar, gold, coconuts, and herbs are given to bring prosperity, protection, and cleansing. These offerings are usually placed in special natural places on mountaintops, near waterfalls, by rivers or lakes, or wherever rainbows often appear - reflecting the vibrant and flowing energy of Osumare.

* * *

32. OYA
ORISHA OF WINDS, STORMS & TRANSFORMATION

A CLOSER LOOK AT OYA

OYA (ALSO KNOWN AS *YANSA, Iansa,* or *Yansan*) is a powerful Orisha in the Yoruba spiritual religion, who governs winds, storms, and transformation. Her name likely comes from the Yoruba phrase *"o ya,"* meaning "she tore," reflecting her fierce connection to strong winds and sudden change. Like Shango, the Orisha of thunder and lightning, she is a fierce warrior and Shango's devoted wife. Together, they form a fiery pair: Oya's wind, rain, and storm fueling Shango's lightning and fire. Symbolizing the natural balance between wind, fire, rain, and forces that can both create and destroy.

Oya is deeply connected to the forces of change, both in nature and in people's lives. She oversees the upheaval and sudden shifts that happen when someone faces spiritual stagnation or struggles to grow. To help, she first sends subtle warnings, like a soft breeze, signaling that a part of their life is about to fall apart. If the person resists change, she may unleash a powerful storm that tears away everything no longer serving them, clearing the way for spiritual growth and fresh beginnings. Oya also fiercely protects her followers from oppression, guiding them toward better paths and shielding them from harm. In nature, this process is reflected as well; her winds sweep away old trees and debris, while her rain cleanses and nourishes the soil, encouraging new growth. Her presence carries both destruction and healing, reminding us that growth often follows life's storms.

Oya is also believed to govern the marketplace and the flow of trade and commerce. In Nigeria, she is seen as the guardian of the Niger River, an essential resource for farming and trade. This connection highlights her dual role as both a force of transformation and a protector of business and markets. As the Orisha of transformation, Oya oversees upheaval, growth, and renewal. She rules over all movement, whether it's the busy activity in the marketplace or the passage between life and death at the cemetery gates. Always in motion, like the flowing Niger River, she represents the endless flow of life and constant change. As the guardian of cemetery gates, she watches over souls as they move from the living world into the ancestral realm.

In rituals and at her shrines, items such as red and purple fabrics, copper, and buffalo horns are displayed. These objects represent her legends and stories and are considered sacred to her. People often call on Oya for support during major life changes, especially when they need to remove obstacles or restore balance. She reminds us that even amid chaos, transformation is possible and that every storm can bring new growth.

OYA, QUEEN OF STORM AND SKY
A Prayer and Poem
VERSE I:I

Oya, queen with winds so high,
You ride the storm across the sky.
With thunder's roar and lightning's flash,
You clear the past in one bold crash.

You bring the rain, you bring the change,
You help our lives to rearrange.
You lift us up when things feel tough,
And teach us all to be strong enough.

You walk the markets, full of life,
And guide us through our pain and strife.
At gates where life and death both meets,
You help the lost find rest and peace.

Oya, you speak through winds that blow,
Through swirling leaves and rivers' flow.
You guard the spirits, old and wise,
And keep their wisdom in your eyes.

You fight for justice, fierce and true,
You stand by those who can't break through.
A warrior mother, bold and kind,
With strength and vision sharp in mind.

We call your name in times of need,
When storms arise or hearts must bleed.
Help us grow and stand up tall,
And find our power through it all.

* * *

OYA'S EMBRACE
VERSE 1:2

Trust your heart, feel the breeze,
Oya's power comes with ease.
Though it may seem like chaos around,
In change, new beginnings are found.

A whirlwind spins when you've been blind,
Oya comes to clear your mind.
But in her eyes, a mother's care,
She'll protect you from despair.

A warrior strong, a love so deep,
In Oya's arms, you can always sleep.
A witch, a queen, so fierce and wise,
She sees through your heart, beyond your eyes.

* * *

SACRED STORIES / LEGENDS
SECTION 2

HOW THE BUFFALO HORNS BECAME A SYMBOL OF OYA
STORY 2:1

Ogun went hunting in the forest one day,

When a buffalo came charging his way.
He raised his spear, ready to fight,
But something happened that changed his sight.

The buffalo shed its rough, thick skin
A beautiful woman appeared from within!
It was Oya, so clever and wise,
With a spark of power deep in her eyes.

She hid her skin and went to the town,
Where Ogun saw her walking around.
He asked her to marry, drawn by her grace,
And Oya agreed, with a careful embrace.

They lived in joy with children nine,
Their hearts were full; their love did shine.
But Ogun's wives, with envy and hate,
Uncovered her secret to change her fate.

They sang a song while Oya was gone,
A song that told what had been hidden long.
When Oya heard it, she knew right then,
Her buffalo skin must be hers again.

She found her skin and became her true form,
A buffalo fierce, strong as a storm.
She fought her rivals and left them behind,
But gave her sons a gift to remind:
"These horns will protect you, call my name,
And I'll return to guard you again."
Now buffalo horns bring strength and cheer,
With Oya's power always nearby.

REFLECTION & WISDOM

This story tells of Ogun, the great hunter, who encounters a buffalo charging through the forest, only to discover that beneath its skin is the beautiful and powerful Oya. After she transforms into her human form, they marry and have nine children, but Ogun's jealous wives expose Oya's secret. In her true

form, Oya returns to reclaim her buffalo skin, becoming a fierce buffalo to
protect her children and confront her rivals. She gifts her sons buffalo horns,
symbolizing her enduring power and protection. The story highlights Oya's
strength, wisdom, and motherly love.

* * *

How Oya Became the Queen of the Dead
Story 2 2

Babalú-Ayé, once a king, so strong,
Returned to his village where the orishas belong.
A grand celebration, filled with cheer,
But his terrifying form brought him near.

With skin so marked, and limbs so thin,
He stood alone, not able to join in.
Ogun, the mighty, saw his plight,
And cloaked him in cover, out of sight.

He brought him in, to join the dance,
But still, no one dared to give him a glance.
Babalú-Ayé stood in the crowd,
A quiet figure, unseen, unbowed.

But Oya, the wind, with heart so kind,
Saw his sorrow, and she designed
A plan to help him, without delay,
To bring him joy on that lively day.

When the moment was right, Oya took flight,
Using her powers, she called on the night.
With a swirl of wind, a gentle sweep,
She turned his ailments into a shower so deep.

Popcorn rained down, soft and bright,
Revealing his beauty, his handsome light.
Babalú-Ayé, in awe, gave a smile,
Grateful for Oya, who made it worthwhile.

In return, he shared his kingdom wide,
And Oya, with joy, danced by his side.
Her movements, powerful, graceful, and free,
Showing the spirits, how strong she could be.

With each step, she called on the dead,
Her winds swirling, where spirits were led.
And so, Oya became queen, so grand,
With Babalú-Ayé's love, and power in hand.

Now, with the dead, Oya reigns supreme,
A queen of spirits, like a powerful dream.
Her dance forever entwined with his,
A bond of affection, where the dead live.

REFLECTION & WISDOM

This story tells how Oya became the Queen of the Dead. When Babalú-Ayé, a once-powerful king, returns to his village for a celebration but is shunned due to his terrifying appearance, Oya takes pity on him. Using her wind powers, she transforms his ailments into a shower of popcorn, revealing his true, handsome form. Grateful, Babalú-Ayé shares his kingdom with Oya, and in return, she dances joyfully, demonstrating her power over the spirits. Oya's powerful connection with Babalú-Ayé leads her to become the queen of the dead, a position she holds with strength, love, and grace.

* * *

OYA, GUARDIAN OF SOULS
STORY 2:3

Oya, the wind, both fierce and wise,
Guides the souls that must arise.
She stands at the gates where shadows lie,
A guardian of the dead, with watchful eyes.

Through the cemetery's quiet gates,
She leads the lost, through the afterlife's fates.
Her winds blow soft, yet firm and true,

Helping souls find paths to start anew.

With every whisper, every breeze,
Oya holds the key to mysteries.
She transforms the dead with loving grace,
Guiding them gently to their rightful place.

Between life and death, she stands so tall,
A force of nature who answers the call.
Her role is one of both ends and start,
A cycle of life that heals the heart.

REFLECTION & WISDOM

This poem tells the story of Oya, the powerful and wise wind, who serves as a guardian and guide for the dead. Standing at the gates of the cemetery, she watches over the souls as they transition from life to the afterlife. With her soft yet firm winds, Oya helps the lost find their way, transforming their spirits with loving grace. She bridges the realms of life and death, offering peace and renewal. As a timeless force, Oya ensures that the souls she guides are made whole, moving them gently to their final resting place.

* * *

INSIGHTS, OFFERINGS, RITUALS AND SPIRITUAL SIGNIFICANCE
SECTION 3

OYA'S SACRED GIFTS
VERSE 3:1

Oya, the wind, with power so strong,
Her offerings call to her all day long.
Plums and eggplants, ripe and sweet,
Grapes and raisins, a sacred treat.

Honey drips, and incense burns,
Wind chimes tinkle as the world turns.
Cowries and copper coins so bright,

Red wine flows, a gift of light.

Jewelry glimmers in the evening's glow,
Amethyst and copper stones below.
Pigeons and goats, a humble plea,
Guinea hens, to set her free.

Ram is forbidden, a sacred rule,
But Saint Theresa stands by her side, so cool.
The number nine, a symbol divine,
In Oya's hands, all things align.

Brown river stones, red and bright,
Amethyst and ruby, a glowing light.
Her colors shine in red and brown,
Purple hues that swirl around.

In plants, geraniums dance in the breeze,
Basil and plums, offering with ease.
Oya, fierce and wise and true,
Her gifts surround, her spirit anew.
Ase!

* * *

OYA'S SACRED WIND INCENSE

PURPOSE

Oya's Sacred Wind Incense is designed to invoke and honor the powerful energy of Oya, the Orisha of winds, transformation, and protection. This blend of Sandalwood, Dragon's Blood, Myrrh, and Clove is carefully crafted to channel Oya's transformative winds, bringing strength, courage, and protection into your space. The incense is intended to clear negativity, open pathways for change, and create an environment of empowerment and ancestral connection.

* * *

Ingredients needed

- *Two parts Sandalwood (calming, grounding strength)*
- *One part Dragon's Blood (empowerment, storm energy, courage)*
- *One part Myrrh (ancestral connection, protection)*
- *One part Clove (fiery strength, protection)*

* * *

Preparation Steps

Step 1: Gather Your Materials
Ensure you have all ingredients in resin, powder, or finely ground form. You'll also need a clean mortar and pestle (or a bowl and spoon) for mixing.

Step 2: Set Your Intention
Take a moment to center yourself. Focus on connecting with Oya's energy her transformative winds and protective power.

Step 3: Measure the Ingredients

1. Add 2 parts Sandalwood as the grounding base.
2. Add 1 part Dragon's Blood,
3. Add 1 part Myrrh,
4. Add 1 part Clove.

Step 4: Grind and Blend

1. Gently grind the ingredients together using a mortar and pestle.
2. Blend thoroughly with respect and mindfulness. Visualize Oya's winds clearing negativity and opening pathways.

Step 5: Store or Use Immediately

- To store: Place the finished incense in an airtight container.
- To use immediately: Burn a small pinch on a charcoal disc in a heat-safe incense burner.

Step 6: Offering to Oya

- Once the incense is burning, place the incense burner near an open window or outdoors to offer it to Oya's winds.
- You can say a prayer, chant, or speak from your heart, inviting Oya's energy into your space.

Step 7: Say a Simple Prayer

Here is an example prayer you can use: *Oya, queen of winds and change, with your power, guide us through the range. Protect us through storms, both fierce and true,*

We offer this smoke in honor of you.

Step 8: Burn with Reverence

- As the incense burns, ask Oya for her blessings, and for her winds to sweep away negativity and protect your space.
- You may pray, chant, or simply sit in silent connection with her energy, feeling her presence.

* * *

33. Shango
Orisha of Thunder, Strength, and Leadership

A Closer Look at Shango

Shango is one of the most powerful and revered Orishas in the Yoruba religion, known as the Orisha of thunder, lightning, fire, and justice. He symbolises strength, masculinity, leadership, and moral authority. Often depicted as a king, Shango represents both spiritual and earthly rulership. His energy is fierce and dynamic - capable of destruction and renewal, bringing thunderous storms that cleanse and rejuvenate the land. As a protector, he defends against evil and injustice, while his fiery nature embodies vitality, passion, and transformative change. Revered for his courage and authority, Shango upholds moral order and ensures balance within the community. Devotees call on him for guidance in leadership, protection, and the strength to face challenges with resolve.

According to Yoruba mythology, Shango was also a real king, the fourth Alaafin of the Oyo Empire in present-day Nigeria, known for his formidable power and fiery temperament. He wielded a double-headed axe called the Osé, symbolising his dominion over thunder and lightning. This ability to command the forces of nature made him both awe-inspiring and fearsome to his people. In Yoruba culture, Shango balances destruction with protection. He punishes wrongdoers by sending lightning bolts, enforcing truth and justice. Beyond his warrior role, Shango is linked to fertility, prosperity, and social stability, reflecting his multifaceted influence.

Shango's worship is lively and vibrant, involving drumming, dancing, and offerings like palm wine and fruits. Central to his ceremonies is the bata drum, whose thunder-like rhythms summon his presence. Another important symbol is the thunderstone, a sacred rock believed to form where lightning strikes the earth. Shango's legacy has travelled far beyond Africa, continuing to inspire Afro-diasporic religions such as Santería and Candomblé in the Americas, where he is syncretised with Catholic saints Santa Barbara in Cuba and Saint Jerome in Trinidad.

SHANGÓ, FLAME OF JUSTICE
A Prayer and Poem
VERSE I:I

Shangó, king with thunder's crown,
Your fire burns when truth is drowned.
You rise where lightning splits the skies,
With fierce red eyes and battle cries.

You once walked earth in mortal frame,
A king of Oyo, feared by name.
With axe in hand and voice like flame,
You brought down liars cloaked in shame.

But envy struck with poisoned tongue,
Your foes conspired while war drums rung.
You vanished fast, but not in flight,
You soared as storm, as a god, as light.

O Shangó, Lord of fire and sound,
Shake injustice to the ground.
If fear should rise within my chest,
Strike it down, let courage rest.

Let thunder speak where I am weak,
Let lightning guide the truths I seek.
Stand with me when I must decide,
And plant your strength deep in my stride.

You dance through rain, through roaring flame,
And all the world resounds your name.
A warrior king, yet just and wise,
A guardian beneath the skies.

Your drums still call in sacred night,
Your winds still howl for what is right.
When battles rise and faith is thin,
Your fire kindles strength within.

O Shangó, I call to you
To lead me when I'm breaking through.
To guard my soul from coward's fate,
And hold me to the path of great.

With storm and spark, O king, descend,
My guide, my shield, my blazing friend.
Let fire renew, let falsehood fall.
Shangó, lift me and hear my call.

* * *

SHANGÓ: LORD OF THUNDER AND JUSTICE
A Poem and a Prayer
VERSE 1:2

Shangó, O mighty lord of flame,
We call upon your sacred name.
Orisha bold, with thunder's might,
You ride the storm you blaze the night.

Once crowned a king, with power wide,
You ruled with strength, with heart and pride.
Your double axe, both swift and true,
Cuts down the wrong, defends the few.

In robes of red and banners bright,
You shine with fire; you lead the fight.
The bata drums begin to rise,
And you descend from blazing skies.

Shangó, flame that lights the way,
Come guide us through the storm today.
Bring justice down like driving rain,

And cleanse this world of hate and pain.

Where we are weak, make us stand tall.
When shadows come, break through them all.
Let your fire within us burn,
And teach the hearts of men to turn.

O warrior, dancer, lord of sound,
In every bolt your truths resound.
Your passion shakes both earth and sky,
Your fury makes oppression fly.

With fearless heart and noble fire,
You lift the low, you strike the liar.
You are the storm that sets things right,
You are the roar that births the light.

Shangó, protector, fierce and wise,
With justice flashing in your eyes
Stand with us now, through fight and flame,
And make us worthy of your name.

So, when the thunder drums the land,
We know it's you who takes a stand.
And through the storm and fire's breath,
You bring us life, you conquer death.

* * *

SACRED STORIES / LEGENDS
SECTION 2

SHANGO: THE KING WHO BECAME AN ORISHA
STORY 2:1

A long time ago, in the powerful kingdom of Oyo, there was a great ruler named Shango. He came from a family of strong warriors and was known for his incredible strength and fiery spirit. When Shango spoke, his voice rumbled like thunder, and his eyes burned with energy. Whenever Shango

224

got angry, flames would appear around him, and the sky seemed to answer his mood. But Shango wasn't just a mighty warrior he was also a wise and fair king. Under his rule, Oyo grew strong, and the people lived happily and safely. Shango had three special wives. Oshun was smart, beautiful, and charming. Oba was loyal and strong, always standing by his side. Oya was wild like the storm and understood Shango's restless heart better than anyone.

But as Oyo became more powerful, jealousy started to grow among Shango's warriors. Some of them spread lies, saying Shango used dark magic to hurt the land. Fear spread among the people, and soon they turned against their king. Shango was heartbroken. Sad and angry, he called on the storms. The sky turned dark, thunder rolled, and lightning struck the ground. Fire spread through the kingdom, but it was too late, the people no longer stood with him. Shango left his throne and disappeared into the sacred forests. His wives searched for him, calling his name. Oshun and Oba cried, but Oya stood strong in the storm, her winds mixing with Shango's fire. They looked at each other one last time before Shango lifted his eyes to the sky. In a flash of lightning, he vanished. But Shango didn't really die. His spirit became part of the thunder and fire. Even today, when storms roar and lightning flashes, people remember Shango the powerful king who never truly faded.

REFLECTION & WISDOM

The story of Shango shows that true strength lies not just in power, but in how we face betrayal and loss. Though he ruled Oyo with wisdom and might, envy led his warriors to rebel against him. Rather than cling to a fallen throne, Shango embraced transformation, rising beyond death to become the living force of thunder and fire. Shango, with his powerful wives, Oshun, Obá, and Oyá, built a thriving kingdom. But jealousy turned his people against him, and as rebellion spread, Shango unleashed storms in his sorrow. After one final meeting with Oyá in the sacred woods, he vanished in a flash of lightning. Though his mortal reign ended, Shango's spirit endures, honored in every storm as a symbol of courage, dignity, and renewal.

* * *

SHANGO AND THE RAM
STORY 2:2

Long ago, when the Orishas roamed the Earth, there was a powerful god named Shango. He was the Orisha of thunder and lightning, known for his immense strength and fearless nature. Among his followers was a proud ram. At first, the ram was loyal, but as time passed, jealousy began to grow in his heart. He envied Shango's power and dreamed of ruling the skies himself. Determined to take that power for himself, the ram formed an alliance with a clever rooster. Together, they devised a plan to steal Shango's sacred tools.

One night, while Shango slept, the ram quietly snuck into his room and stole his sword, axe, and the tools that controlled the thunder. With the tools in their possession, the ram and the rooster taunted, "Come face us, Shango! Let's see who is truly stronger!" Shango was initially surprised and didn't immediately realize he had been betrayed. Seeking guidance, he visited the wise Orisha, Orunmila. Orunmila advised him, "Make an offering with a pure heart, and you will prevail." Shango followed Orunmila's advice and made a heartfelt offering. As he prepared for battle, he discovered his weapons were gone. But he didn't lose hope. Nearby, he found an old wooden bat. With the bat in hand, Shango stood firm and ready. The ram charged at him, confident of victory. But with one powerful swing, Shango struck the ram to the ground. The rooster, terrified by the defeat, fled in fear. Shango stood over the ram and declared, "Because of your betrayal, your kind will be sacrificed to me forever." From that day forward, the ram became a sacred offering to Shango. This story teaches us that loyalty and honor are far stronger than jealousy and greed.

REFLECTION & WISDOM

This story of Shango and the ram teaches the consequences of betrayal and the power of loyalty. The ram's jealousy and greed led him to betray Shango, only to face defeat. Shango, instead of reacting with anger, sought wisdom from Orunmila and approached the situation with sincerity, using a simple wooden bat to defeat the ram. This shows that true strength comes from within, not from material tools. The ram's fate as a sacrifice underscores the consequences of dishonor. The story reminds us that integrity and wisdom lead to true power, while betrayal and greed lead to downfall. It teaches that power earned through righteousness is far more lasting than that gained through deceit.

* * *

INSIGHTS, OFFERINGS, RITUALS AND SPIRITUAL SIGNIFICANCE
SECTION 3

SHANGO'S GIFTS AND SACRED OFFERINGS

Thunder stones and flint so rare,
Obsidian and chert, with power to share.
These stones are sacred, to Shango they belong,
Their strength and magic echo in his song.

We offer him red wine and rum,
Gin and tobacco, gifts to come.
Red and white candles light the way,
Roasted yams to honor the day.

Red peppers, bitter kola, and porridge sweet,
Okra, bananas, a feast complete.
Water, incense, and palm oil too,
Guinea hens and roosters, gifts for you.

But be careful of the red kola nut,
In some places, it's a forbidden cut.
These offerings show our love and grace,
To Shango, the king who rules in space.
Ase!

* * *

THE MANY FACES OF SHANGO

Shango is a powerful and respected Orisha, known as the spirit of thunder, lightning, fire, and leadership. He has many different forms, called caminos or paths, each revealing a different side of his strength and character. Some paths show Shango as a fierce warrior and king, others as a wise judge, a protector of justice, or even a healer through fire and energy. In the Yoruba tradition, Shango represents courage, authority, passion, and the power to overcome obstacles. His many paths reflect his ability to rule, defend, and inspire his followers in all aspects of life. Each path teaches us about bravery, the balance of power and wisdom, and the importance of standing strong in the face of challenges. Some of the most well-known paths of Shango include the following:

- **Shango Obadimeyi:** Shango and Aganyu are brothers in this path and should be honored equally.
- **Shango Oban Shola:** A wise and peaceful king who prefers diplomacy over conflict.
- **Shango Lubbe o Lubbeo:** Walks with the dead and uses lightning to fight evil. Linked to Eggun and may appear through possession.
- **Shango Alafin Ajuani:** A warrior king born of spiritual forces, representing mystery and inner strength.
- **Shango Olufina Kake:** Moves between heaven and earth, protects the innocent, and punishes with fire.
- **Shango Alafi:** A just king who holds thunder and lightning in his hands to fight injustice.

* * *

SHORT MEDITATION TO CONNECT TO SHANGO

PURPOSE:

This meditation helps you connect with Shango, the Orisha of thunder and lightning, to invite his powerful energy and guidance into your life.

ITEMS NEEDED FOR THIS MEDITATION

- *Red and white candle (Shango's colors)*
- *Pen and paper (for jotting down insights)*

Step 1: Prepare your space

1. Sit in a comfortable, strong posture with your back straight and chest open.
2. Light the red and white candle.

Step 2: Visualization

1. Close your eyes and imagine lightning striking the Earth.
2. Visualize it entering through the top of your head (your crown chakra) and filling your body with vibrant red energy.

Step 3: Prayer to Shango

You can recite the prayer to Shango below or speak from your heart using your own words.

Prayer:

Shango, King of Thunder and Fire, Mighty protector and ruler of justice, Fill me with your strength and courage. Clear my path with your thunder, renew my spirit with your fire, and guide me to lead with wisdom and boldness. I honor and thank you, great Shango. May your power live within me. Ase.

After the prayer, take a moment to speak with Shango and share whatever your intuition guides you to say or do.

Step 4: Focus on your heartbeat

Tune into your heart, feeling your pulse and the rhythm of your "internal drum" awakening.

Step 5: Meditation

Stay in meditation for 10-15 minutes, focusing on your breath, breathing deeply and calmly.

Step 6: Thank Shango

Before closing, thank Shango for his presence and guidance. You can say something like: *"Thank you, Shango, for your strength, wisdom, and protection. I am grateful for your energy."* Optional: You may also leave an offering near a tall tree outdoors as a sign of gratitude.

STEP 7: RECORD INSIGHTS

Keep pen and paper nearby to jot down any thoughts, ideas, or intuitions you receive during your meditation.

* * *

34. Yemoja, Yemaya
Orisha of the Fish, Ocean and Motherhood

A Closer Look at Yemoja

Yemoja is a powerful and revered Orisha. Her name comes from the Yoruba words *Yeye* (mother), *Omo* (child), and *Eja*(fish), meaning "Mother of Fish Children." This name reflects her deep, ancient connection to water and to life itself. Originally, Yemoja was honored as the goddess of the Ogun River in Nigeria. However, as West African peoples were forcibly moved across the Atlantic, her worship spread to the Americas. In places like the Caribbean and South America, Yemoja's role shifted; she became primarily associated with the vast ocean and emerged as a central figure in spiritual traditions such as Santería, Candomblé, and Umbanda.

Yemoja is revered as the divine mother of all Orishas and, by extension, of all humanity. She embodies unconditional love, nurturing care, steadfast protection, and immense strength qualities akin to a powerful and loving mother. Her domain is the vibrant, sunlit surface of the ocean, where light penetrates, and marine life flourishes, distinguishing her from Olokun, another Orisha who governs the ocean's dark and mysterious depths. Many turn to Yemoja for healing, protection, and emotional solace. She holds a special place in the hearts of women and children, offering profound comfort during times of grief and acting as a fierce protector of the vulnerable. Yemoja's nature mirrors the ocean itself: she can be as gentle as calm waves or as formidable as a storm, her dual capacity for kindness and power making her a trusted guide.

Yemoja's preferred colors are the serene blues and whites that reflect the ocean's own hues, its deep waters, cresting waves, and delicate seafoam. She shares a powerful connection with the moon, and many believe her influence is drawn from both lunar and oceanic energies. As a potent water

Orisha, she lovingly oversees the ocean and all its inhabitants, demonstrating kindness and protection toward fish and other marine creatures, including mermaids, one of her common forms. Devotees often show their reverence by placing offerings at the water's edge, including flowers, fruits (especially watermelon), and seashells. Ritualistic bathing in the ocean or using sea salt are common practices for cleansing and purification, symbolically washing away negative energy and ushering in freshness. Yemoja can manifest to her devotees in various forms, with the majestic mermaid being one of the most frequently recognized.

YEMOJA, GUARDIAN OF LIFE AND LOVE
A Prayer and Poem
VERSE 1:1

O Yemoja, great mother of the sea,
Your waves reach far and tenderly.
In the flowing river and ocean's tide,
Your spirit moves, with love as guide.

You are the breath of gentle care,
A presence felt in sea and air.
With hands of healing and heart so wide,
You walk with us, right by our side.

You lift the broken, soothe the soul,
You pour in joy and make us whole.
Matriarch strong, with grace you lead,
And meet us in our time of need.

You carry the gift of life and birth,
Bringing peace and joy to earth.
In storms, your strength does not depart,
You calm the waves and still our hearts.

Your love is deep, your arms are wide,
In you, dear Mother, we safely hide.
A symbol of power, soft and kind,
A light in the dark we always find.

O Yemoja, we offer this prayer,
Wrapped in devotion, spoken with care.
Protect us, guide us, bless each day,
Forever in your flow, we stay.

* * *

YEMOJA, QUEEN OF THE WAVES
VERSE 1:2

Yemoja, the queen of the ocean's wide,
Ruler of waves and the saltwater tide.
A mermaid so graceful, with a heart full of care,
She watches the seas, both calm and fair.

Her waters are gentle, her spirit so bright,
Balancing Olokun, who rules the deep night.
Where the sun's rays can touch and shine,
Yemoja's power grows, pure and divine.

But when anger stirs in her calm, blue sea,
Her waves can crash wild and violently.
Yet, she's a mother, nurturing and strong,
Guiding us gently where we belong.

Called upon for comfort and grace,
Yemoja's protection is a warm embrace.
With her energy, the world feels whole,
A symbol of life, love, and soul.

She's the mother of fish, the giver of life,
Helping women in times of strife.
Her calming waters, her soothing sway,
Guide us all through night and day.

* * *

SACRED STORIES / LEGENDS
SECTION 2

YEMOJA AND THE FISHERMAN'S OFFERING
STORY 2:1

A fisherman, poor and tired,
Prayed to Yemoja, his heart inspired.
He asked for fish, to fill his net,
But had no gift, no offering yet.
One day he found, so pure and bright,
A blue stone shining in the light.

He tossed it back into the sea,
A humble gift, as he did plea.
Yemoja saw, and in her grace,
She filled his nets with fish to chase.
But greed soon grew inside his mind,
He wanted more than he could find.

A storm then raged and sank his boat,
The waves crashed high, the winds did gloat.
He knew his heart had lost its way,
And begged for mercy, where he lay.
With lessons learned, he bowed his head,
No longer greedy, he was fed.

He brought her gifts, both pure and true,
Watermelons, beads, and skies so blue.
Yemoja smiled, her heart so kind,
She blessed him with a peaceful mind.
From that day on, he lived with grace,
Honoring her in every place.

REFLECTION & WISDOM

This is a cautionary tale about a poor fisherman who, in his humility, offers a simple yet sincere gift to Yemoja, the goddess of the sea. Moved by his devotion, she blesses him with abundant fish, but when greed clouds his heart, he

234

demands more, angering the goddess. A violent storm punishes his arrogance, sinking his boat and teaching him a painful lesson. Humbled, he repents and brings Yemoja true offerings, earning her favor once more. In the end, he finds peace by living with gratitude and honoring the goddess with sincerity.

* * *

YEMOJA, MOTHER OF THE SEA
STORY 2:2

Long ago in a land so bright,
Lived Yemoja, bathed in light.
Her home was lush, her heart was strong,
She ruled with love, she knew no wrong.

Olodumare, wise and grand,
Gave her life and blessed the land.
She cared for all, both big and small,
A mother's heart she loved them all.

But trouble came, dark as the night,
Her husband turned from love to spite.
He sought to harm her children dear,
And filled her gentle heart with fear.

With her favorite child in tow,
She ran where wild rivers flow.
Through valleys deep, past hills so steep,
She ran until her feet grew weak.

Then, oh no! She tripped and fell,
And something strange began to swell.
Her womb broke open, wild and wide,
A mighty wave burst from inside!

Rivers danced and lakes appeared,
And then the ocean, vast and clear!
The waters roared, the tides did rise,
The sea stretched far beneath the skies.

Now Yemoja, so strong and free,
Made her home beneath the sea.
She swore to guard both land and wave,
To help the lost, protect the brave.

She calms the storms, she hears our cries,
She lifts our prayers to the skies.
Mother of oceans, kind and true,
Yemoja watches over you.

REFLECTION & WISDOM

Yemoja was one of the first Orishas, created by Olodumare, the Supreme God. She once lived in a beautiful and abundant kingdom, but betrayal disrupted her peace. Her husband, driven by cruelty, sought to harm her children. To protect them, she fled with her most beloved child. However, in her desperate escape, she stumbled and fell. In that moment, her womb burst open, and from her waters, rivers and lakes began to flow, eventually giving birth to the vast ocean, her new and eternal home. Through this transformation, Yemoja became the mother of all life, the protector of women, and the guardian of the seas. Her story teaches us about resilience in the face of adversity and the power of sacrifice. Her sorrow, reflected in the salt of the ocean, reminds us that even pain can give rise to something vast and life-sustaining. Her broken womb, from which the waters flowed, symbolizes the endless cycle of creation and renewal.

* * *

YEMOJA AND THE LOST CHILD
STORY 2:3

A mother wept beside the shore,
Her child was lost forevermore.
The waves had taken him away,
And left her heart in dark dismay.

She called to Yemoja, strong and wise,
With tears that sparkled in her eyes.
"Oh, Mother Ocean, hear my plea,
Bring my child back home to me!"
Yemoja heard the mother's cries,
And felt her pain beneath the skies.

She dove beneath the waters deep,
Where hidden secrets swayed and sleep.
Through coral caves and silver sands,
She searched with gentle, careful hands.

Until at last, a soul so bright,
Glowed softly in the ocean's light.
She placed the soul within a shell,
A shining pearl inside its dwell.

Then rose above the rolling sea,
To face the mother's agony.
"This shell now holds your child's soul,
No longer lost, but healed and whole.

Life begins and ends in me,
A cycle like the endless sea."
The mother held the shell so tight,
Its glow was warm; its song was light.

She felt her child, so near, so true,
A love that never fades from view.
From that day forth, she lived to teach,
The lessons Yemoja would preach.

A priestess strong, with heart so wide,
Her child became a spirit guide.
And to this day, when waves do call,
And ocean breezes rise and fall,
We hear the voice of love so free,
Whispered softly by the sea.

Grief-stricken, a mother pleaded with Yemoja to return her drowned child. Moved by her sorrow, Yemoja dove into the ocean, retrieving the child's soul and placing it in a seashell. She reminded the mother that life flows in cycles, beginning and ending in her waters. This story teaches us about acceptance, transformation, and the eternal bond between loved ones. Though the child was lost to the sea, his spirit lived on as a guide. The mother, embracing Yemoja's wisdom, became her priestess, finding purpose in grief and strength in the rhythms of life.

★ ★ ★

INSIGHTS, OFFERINGS, RITUALS AND SPIRITUAL SIGNIFICANCE
SECTION 3

YEMOJA BATH WITH SEAWEED AND SEA SALT

This bath is intended to remove negative energy and spiritual blockages, serving as a deep cleanse for the spirit. The sea salt draws out heavy emotions, stagnant energy, and anything that weighs down the soul. At the same time, the minerals in the seaweed nourish both the body and the aura, promoting healing, emotional balance, and inner peace. The purpose of this bath is to recreate the ocean's natural cleansing and renewing energy.

YOU WILL NEED:

- *A handful of dried organic seaweed (such as kelp or wakame)*
- *1/2 to 1 cup of sea salt*
- *A large bowl or bathtub filled with fresh water*
- *(Optional) Some seashells and a natural organic sponge for washing*

★ ★ ★

STEP 1: PREPARE THE SEAWEED
Soak the dried seaweed in warm water for a few minutes to soften it. It will expand and release its minerals into the water.

STEP 2: PREPARE THE BATH WATER

Fill your bathtub (or large bowl) with fresh water. Add the sea salt and stir it clockwise with your hand, setting your intention as you do.

STEP 3: ADD THE SEAWEED

Place the softened seaweed into the water. The minerals from the seaweed will help cleanse and bless your body.

STEP 4: BLESS THE BATH

Stand over the bathwater, gently dip your finger in, and say:
"Yemoja, mother of the oceans, Bless this water with your healing power. Cleanse my spirit, calm my heart, and surround me with your love and protection. I give thanks for your blessings, Yemoja. Asé."

STEP 5: TAKE YOUR BATH

Soak in the water, letting the seaweed touch your skin. Visualize the ocean waves washing away all negativity, stress, and sadness, and imagine the ocean surrounding you with its healing energy.

STEP 6: AFTER THE BATH

Let your body air dry naturally, allowing the blessings of Yemoja to remain on your skin. If you're near the ocean, consider offering a small gift to Yemoja at the shore as a gesture of gratitude.

* * *

THE MANY FACES OF YEMOJA

Yemoja, the mother of all waters, is a powerful protector of life, family, and emotional well-being. She is known to appear in many forms, called *caminos* or "paths," each expressing a unique aspect of her divine nature. Some of these paths present her as a fierce ocean warrior; others show her as a gentle, nurturing mother or a wise and powerful matriarch. In the Yoruba tradition, Yemoja's many paths reflect her role as a source of creation, emotional strength, and divine protection. Each path offers lessons in resilience, love, and the healing power of compassion. Some of the most well-known paths of Yemoja include:

- **Yemoja Awoyo** – Considered the oldest path of Yemoja, she is associated with great wealth and ancient wisdom.
- **Yemoja Akuara** – A male aspect of Yemoja, dwelling where saltwater meets freshwater, embodying balance and transition.
- **Yemoja Ibu Konla** – A masculine manifestation found along the shoreline where sea meets land. He is linked to sea foam and guides maritime travel, known as the owner of sea vessels.
- **Yemoja Yemú (Yembó)** – Revered as the primordial mother, she is honored as the mother of all Orishas.
- **Yemoja Ibu Akinomi** – Resides at the crest of ocean waves, symbolizing power, movement, and natural rhythm.
- **Yemoja Asesu** – Acts as a divine messenger to Olokun, bridging deep ocean mysteries and surface life.
- **Yemoja Ibu Gunle** – Dwells within coral reefs, representing hidden beauty, protection, and underwater life.
- **Yemoja Ibu Osaguá** – A calm and nurturing path, she fosters peace, emotional balance, and family harmony. She is often invoked for protection within the home.

Each of Yemoja's paths offers a different way to understand and connect with her timeless wisdom and sacred presence.

* * *

OFFERINGS TO YEMOJA
VERSE 3:1

To Mother Ocean, vast and free,
We bring these gifts upon the sea.
White flowers drift on waves so wide,
A gentle prayer upon the tide.

Sweet melons, full of waters true,
A gift of life, so fresh and new.
Golden honey, thick and bright,
To bless the soul with love and light.

Molasses dark and rich with grace,
A token sweet in time and space.

Cool coconut with milk so pure,
A healing touch, a heart's cure.

Cowrie shells and seashells white,
Whispers of the ocean's might.
Jewels that shimmer, beads so fine,
In blue and white, her colors shine.

Candles flicker, soft and high,
Blue like waters, white as sky.
With pigeons sent to soar above,
We ask for peace, we pray with love.

O Yemoja, strong and true,
Accept these gifts we bring to you.
Mother who guards both near and far,
Guide us like the evening star.
Ase!

REFLECTION & WISDOM

Offerings to Yemoja include white flowers, melons, coconuts, molasses, honey, and white rice with fish. Symbols of the sea cowrie shells, beads, coins, and mirrors, honor her essence. Oils, Florida Water, soap, combs, and feminine items are also used. Some offer fish, paper boats, sweet drinks, or written prayers. In certain rites, pigeons are included. All offerings should be made with respect and clear intention.

* * *

VARIOUS PRAYERS

1. PRAYER OF GRATITUDE TO YEMOJA
O Yemoja, Mother of the Waters, You who nourish all life, I thank you for your constant presence. For the flow of love in my life, For the protection you offer without asking, And for the wisdom you whisper like waves on the shore. May I always remember your grace, And walk in the rhythm of your tides, Ase.

2. PRAYER FOR HEALING

Yemoja, gentle mother, healer of hearts, Wash over me with your sacred waters. Cleanse my spirit, soothe my pain, Bring peace to my mind and balance to my soul. May your cool embrace carry away all sorrow, And may your tides return joy and strength to my being. Let your love be the medicine I need, Ase.

3. PRAYER FOR PROTECTION

O Divine Mother Yemoja, Wrap me in your flowing skirts of sea and foam. Shield me from harm, seen and unseen. Guard my home, my family, and all I hold dear. Let your deep waters drown all ill intentions, And your waves wash away fear. With your shell and mirror, reflect only truth. With your wisdom, protect my path, Ase.

4. PRAYER FOR GUIDANCE

Mother of the Deep, You who knows the currents of time and fate, Guide me through life's shifting tides. When I am lost, show me the way. When I am still, speak through the silence. When I must act, give me strength. Let me move as the ocean moves, With purpose, with grace, with power, Ase.

* * *

35. YEWA
ORISHA OF THE GRAVE,
DECOMPOSITION AND TRANSFORMATION

A CLOSER LOOK AT YEWA

YEWA (EWA, Yegua, Yegba, or Eua) is an Orisha in the Yoruba tradition who embodies purity, modesty, mystery, and inner beauty. Originally linked to the Yewa River in present-day Benin, her role later expanded to include cemeteries and the quiet, transformative power of death. Yewa is believed to reside among graves, gently guiding and protecting the souls of the departed as they begin their journey to the afterlife.

In traditional Yoruba society, it was common for families to bury their dead beneath the home. This practice helped protect graves from robbers and kept ancestors close. Because of this, Yewa was originally viewed more as a river deity linked to purity and chastity, rather than to the cemetery itself. However, with urbanization, modern burial laws, and the influence of Christianity and Islam, this practice has largely disappeared, especially in cities. Today, home burials are rare, and Yewa's association with the cemetery has grown more centralized in modern religious worship. There are different understandings of Yewa's role in the afterlife. Some lineages say that Oya opens the gates of the cemetery and guides the spirits inside, and Yewa receives them afterward. Others say it is Yewa who first receives the dead and then passes them on to Oya. In both versions, Yewa plays a key role in helping souls cross over and begin the spiritual transition. She is believed to oversee the unseen process of the body's decay and renewal, embodying the silence, calm, and sacred mystery of the cemetery.

One well-known myth speaks to Yewa's deep commitment to chastity. In this story, she is seduced by another Orisha; many say it was Shango, the powerful Orisha of thunder and lightning. Overcome with shame and sorrow after losing her innocence, Yewa withdraws from the living world and finds refuge among the dead. Her retreat into the cemetery is said to mark the beginning of her deep connection to death and the spirit realm. In many legends, Yewa is portrayed as a quiet and solemn figure, mourning the purity she once had. She is often shown living alone among tombs, surrounded by shadows and silence, lost in deep thought and sacred grief. Her solitude in the cemetery symbolizes both a spiritual withdrawal from worldly life and a powerful connection to the mysteries of death, transformation, and the unseen world.

THANKING YEWA AT THE CEMETERY
A Prayer and Poem
VERSE I:1

Yewa, protector of sacred ground,
You watch over graves where our ancestors are found.
With gentle hands, you guard the night,
Keeping their spirits safe in your light.

You hold the past with quiet care,
Watching over those who rest there.
Thank you for your strength so true,
For guiding the dead and watching through.

Bless us as we honor those gone,
With your protection, we journey on.

REFLECTION & WISDOM
When I enter the cemetery, I first pray and leave an offering for Oya at the gates, honoring her as the guardian of the entrance. Then, once inside, I recite a prayer and offer flowers to Yewa, honoring her as the protector of the graves.

* * *

GUARDIAN OF THE SILENT GROUND
VERSE I:2

Yewa, Ayaba, mysterious and wise,

A queen of the earth beneath quiet skies.
She dwells in the cemetery, calm and deep,
Where the silent dead in stillness sleep.

Associated with beauty, soft and rare,
She rules the ground with a gentle care.
Where the earth embraces all that dies,
Yewa watches with knowing eyes.

She guides the cycle, from life to decay,
Where bodies return to the earth to stay.
In her realm, the mysteries unfold,
Of death's secrets, both quiet and bold.

Her presence is soft, yet powerfully true,
In the soil, where life and death renew.
Yewa, the Orisha of earth and grace,
In the cemetery, she holds her place.

* * *

SACRED STORIES / LEGENDS
SECTION 2

YEWA'S SACRED TALE
STORY 2:1

Yewa lived in a garden so grand,
With flowers she grew by her gentle hand.
Pure and graceful, her heart was true,
A beauty admired by all she knew.

Her father kept her safe inside,
A world of peace where she could hide.
But Elegua, the trickster sly,
Decided to test Shango's pride.

"Shango," he said, "so strong and bold,
Can you win Yewa, pure as gold?"

Shango laughed, "I'll prove my might,
Her heart will be mine by the end of the night."

Shango went with his charm and fire,
Speaking words that sparked desire.
Yewa, cautious but unaware,
Fell for his spell and love's sweet snare.

But soon she found, with growing dread,
A child within her Shango had fled.
She turned to Boromu, wise and kind,
Hoping for a solution she might find.

Boromu gave her a potion to drink,
Yewa's heart sank; she began to think.
The child was gone, her guilt ran deep,
She buried it under a tree to keep.

Ashamed and broken, she fled away,
To the quiet tombs where the spirits stay.
There in the stillness, she wept and prayed,
Hoping her pain would somehow fade.

Olofin, the ruler, heard her cry,
And called her forth beneath the sky.
She told her story, her sorrow, her shame,
And begged to leave the world's cruel game.

"Yewa," Olofin said with care,
"You'll find redemption waiting there.
Among the dead, your task will be,
To guard their rest for eternity."

So Yewa became the cemetery's queen,
With wisdom and strength, calm and serene.
A guardian of spirits, both lost and near,
Her presence demanded hearts pure and clear.

But the child she lost was not in vain,

Boromu and Olokun eased her pain.
They raised its spirit from death's deep sea,
Naming it Borosia, strong and free.

Now Borosia guards the ocean's tide,
A symbol of life reborn with pride.
And Yewa, in her quiet domain,
Found purpose and peace after her pain.

REFLECTION & WISDOM

The story of Yewa tells of a pure and gentle woman, guarded by her father, who is tricked by Shango into falling in love with him. After discovering she is pregnant and abandoned by Shango, Yewa seeks help from the wise Boromu, who assists her in ending the pregnancy. Ashamed, Yewa retreats to the tombs, where she finds solace and is called upon by Olofin to become the guardian of spirits in the cemetery. Though she is broken, Yewa's pain is eased when the spirit of her lost child, Borosia, is raised by Boromu and Olokun and becomes a guardian of the ocean. Through her journey, Yewa finds redemption, peace, and a purpose in her quiet domain.

* * *

INSIGHTS, OFFERINGS, RITUALS AND SPIRITUAL SIGNIFICANCE
SECTION 3

MEDITATION WITH YEWA

Visit a peaceful cemetery where you can quietly connect with the Orisha Yewa. Choose a serene, undisturbed spot away from foot traffic. Out of respect, avoid stepping directly on graves. Simply being present in this sacred space is part of the experience. Once you've found your spot, take a few deep breaths and relax. Reflect on death not as an end, but as a natural transformation. Consider the cycles of life, death, and rebirth. Yewa, Orisha of stillness and guardian of the dead, watches over these sacred transitions. Sit quietly. Let your breath flow naturally and observe your thoughts without judgment. When you feel centered, offer a prayer to Yewa. You may say this or speak from your heart:

A Short Prayer to Yewa

Yewa, Orisha of silent ground,
Guardian of mysteries where the dead are found,
I come before you with reverence deep,
Seeking your wisdom where the shadows sleep.

You hold the peace of the grave in your hand,
And the wisdom of transformation, vast and grand.
Guide me through cycles, life's ebb and flow,
Help me embrace the stillness where secrets grow.

Grant me courage to face each change I must meet,
And the peace to honor those who rest at your feet.
May your grace bring solace, gentle and pure,
As you watch over spirits, forever secure.
Ase.

* * *

After your prayer, leave a simple offering flowers, cowrie shells, incense, fruit, water, or a small candle (if allowed). Be respectful and clean up afterward, leaving the space as you found it. Sit a few more minutes in silence. Feel the stillness. Listen. Yewa's presence is subtle and quiet, often felt more than heard. If you like, bring a notebook and write down any thoughts or feelings that arise. When you're ready to end your visit, say:

Closing Words

Yewa, thank you for your wisdom and presence.
I honor you as the guardian of transitions and the protector of spirits.
May I carry the quiet peace of your grace with me, now and always.
Ase.

Returning to the World

When you feel ready, begin your return to everyday life. As you leave the cemetery and pass through its gates, remember that you carry with you the peace, clarity, stillness, or other blessings you received.

OFFERINGS TO YEWA
VERSE 3:1

Cowrie shells gleam soft and bright,
Flowers bloom in gentle light,
Water flows, pure and clear,
Incense rises, sweet and near.

Candles flicker, pink and white,
Herbs of power calm the night
Holy basil, geranium's grace,
Mugwort whispers, fennel's embrace.

Female pigeons soar with peace,
Young virgin goats stand at ease,
Female fowl in quiet line,
Offered now with hearts divine.

With humble hands and open heart,
We bring these gifts to do our part,
To honor Yewa, calm and clear
Guardian of the threshold here.

* * *

36. SACRED CYCLES
EXPLORING THE YORUBA
CALENDAR AND FESTIVALS

UNDERSTANDING THE YORUBA CALENDAR

THE YORUBA PEOPLE have long used a profound and ancient system of timekeeping known as the *Kojodá* Calendar, which translates from Yoruba to English as *"may the day be clearly foreseen."* While the modern version of the *Kojodá* calendar is lunisolar, combining the cycles of the moon and the sun, historical evidence suggests that the original Kojodá was strictly a lunar calendar, consisting of 13 months. Today, many Yoruba communities use the Kojodá Calendar alongside the Gregorian calendar, which was introduced from Europe during the colonial era. Long before this outside influence, the Yoruba tracked time through the moon's phases, seasonal shifts, agricultural cycles, and the timing of sacred rituals. Days were not simply counted; they were lived in harmony with the Orisha, ancestral wisdom, and the rhythms of the cosmos. Though its exact origins are unclear, some scholars suggest the Yoruba calendar is over 10,000 years old. According to this view, the year 10,000 in the Yoruba system aligned with 1958 in the Gregorian calendar. This reflects a sophisticated understanding of astronomy. For the Yoruba, timekeeping was not just practical; it was spiritual, guiding planting, divination, and ritual life.

THE FOUR-DAY SACRED WEEK

The Yoruba calendar has a week that lasts only 4 days. Each month has seven of these weeks, so there are 28 days in a month. Unlike the Gregorian calendar, which has 12 months, some experts think the old Yoruba calendar had 13 months, making 364 days in a year. The extra day was probably celebrated during the New Year festival. Many places celebrate this festival in early June, often with the Ifá festival, but some celebrate it in August. The Yoruba year usually started with either the new moon or the full moon. Most believe the full moon was used more often to begin a new month. Each day in the four-day week is named after a main Orisha, but other Orishas are also honored on those days. The four days and their main Orishas are:

Day of Obatala (Ojo-Obatala)

On this day, we honor Obatala, the Orisha of purity and wisdom, along with Egungun, Iyaami, Aje and Babalu-Aye. This day seeks spiritual clarity, strength, and healing.

Day of Orunmila (Ojo-Orunmila)

This day is dedicated to Orunmila, the Orisha of wisdom, and includes Esu, Oshun, Yemoja, Aje, Ifa, and Olokun. It focuses on gaining guidance and blessings for destiny and spiritual growth.

Day of Ogun (Ojo-Ogun)

On this day we celebrate Ogun, the Orisha of iron and strength, along with Oshosi and Oko. It invokes power for protection, courage, and success in work and justice.

Day of Sango (Ojo-Sango)

On this day we honor Sango, the Orisha of thunder, and Oya, the Orisha of the winds. This day seeks protection, transformation, and balance in the face of challenges.

This four-day cycle is central to Yoruba religious practice and reflects the spiritual connection between time and divine forces.

Traditional Offerings and Practices

Offerings are an essential part of Yoruba spiritual practice. Each of the four days provides an opportunity to connect with the Orishas and other spiritual beings associated with that day. Common practices include meditating or sitting quietly at an Orisha's shrine, praying or spending time in contemplation, and sometimes performing divination. Other activities may include presenting offerings to the Orisha, cleaning the shrine, conducting readings for clients, and performing rituals such as consecrations, cleansings, and other sacred ceremonies specific to that day.

What is Itadogun?

Itadogun is a sacred period in the traditional Yoruba calendar that occurs every 16 days, with the main observance on the 17th day. During this time, followers of Orúnmìlà and Ifá seek guidance and blessings through divination and perform rituals to align with their destiny and gain personal insight. Many practitioners visit temples or consult a Babalawo (Ifá priest) for spiritual guidance on this day. Different communities observe Itadogun on varying schedules some once a month, others every 16 or 17 days.

The Four Kojoda Days and Their Spiritual Significance

Kojoda is more than just a calendar. It is a spiritual guide that helps you focus on different parts of your personal and spiritual life. Each day in the four-day cycle highlights a specific area to reflect on whether it's clarity, wisdom, action, or release. By following this rhythm, you can grow spiritually, find balance, and live with greater purpose and awareness.

Day 1: Day of Obatala (Ojo Obatálá)
Use this day to slow down and reflect on your life. Set clear intentions and spiritual goals for the week. Visualize the person you want to become, and send your intentions into the world through focused thought or prayer.

Take part in spiritual practices that help you manifest your goals or gain clarity and insight into a challenge or desire. This is a time to plant spiritual seeds and begin the new cycle with peace, purpose, and clear direction. The main themes of this day are *purity, intention, calmness, mental focus, and clarity.*

Day 2: Day of Orúnmìlà (Ojo Orúnmìlà)
Use this day to seek insight and spiritual guidance. Focus on understanding your destiny and acquiring the wisdom needed to achieve your goals. It's a time for learning, planning, and figuring out the steps required to bring your vision to life. Reflect on your path and prepare yourself for the actions

ahead. The main themes of this day are *insight, destiny, learning, planning, spiritual guidance, and wisdom.*

DAY 3: DAY OF OGÚN (OJO OGÚN)

Use this day to focus on action and discipline. It's a time for putting your plans into motion through hard work, physical effort, and determination. This day encourages healing and protection as you face challenges and obstacles. Channel your energy into executing your goals with strength and focus. The main themes of this day are *action, discipline, physical effort, and how to carry out your plans effectively.*

DAY 4: DAY OF ṢÀNGO (OJO ṢÀNGO)

Use this day for reflection and emotional release. It's a time to look back on what you've accomplished and celebrate your progress. This day encourages you to let go of anything that no longer serves your growth or well-being. Embrace transformation by releasing old habits, thoughts, or feelings, making space for new energy and opportunities. The main themes of this day are *reflection, emotional release, transformation, and celebration.*

* * *

THE SEVEN DAY WEEK CYCLE
(COMMONLY USED OUTSIDE AFRICA)

OJO-AIKU (SUNDAY)
This day is often dedicated to seeking blessings and health, and it honors Obatala, Ori, Olodumare, Orunmila, and Ifa.

OJO-AJE (MONDAY)
This day is focused on prosperity, and it honors Eleggua/Eshu and Orisha Aje for wealth and abundance.

OJO-ISEGUN (TUESDAY)
This day is for victory, and it honors Ogun and Oshosi to help overcome challenges and achieve success.

OJO-IRU (WEDNESDAY)
This day is dedicated to honoring ancestors, and it honors Oya, Egungun, Babalu-Aye, and Egbe for their guidance and blessings.

Ojo-Bo (Thursday)
This day is for new projects and celebrations, and it honors Shango and Ori for strength and inspiration in starting new ventures.

Ojo-Eti (Friday)
This day is focused on cleaning and removing obstacles, and it honors Oshun, Eshu/Elegua, Ori, and Egungun to clear away negativity.

Ojo-Abameta (Saturday)
This day is for finishing projects and honoring mothers, and it honors Yemoja, Olokun, Osain, and Egungun for completion and maternal blessings.

* * *

Using the Moon for Spiritual Practices and Rituals

In Yoruba cosmology, the moon is a sacred force that guides emotion, intuition, and the right timing for spiritual work. Each phase of the moon carries its own energy and purpose:

New Moon
New Moon rises, dark and wide, A call to start, to step, to guide. We honor Egbe and kin now passed, Their wisdom whispers, deep and vast.

Spiritual Meaning: A time for fresh starts. Offer prayers to Egbe (spiritual companions) and honor ancestors who guide your path.

Waxing Moon
Waxing Moon with growing light, We plant our dreams in steady flight. Intentions bloom, goals begin The fire of purpose grows within.

Spiritual Meaning: A period of growth and momentum. Focus on building your intentions and nurturing new goals.

FULL MOON

Bright and clear, the wisdom flows, Clarity and insight, as the moonlight grows. A moment to honor your Ori's light, Guiding you through the day and night.

Spiritual Meaning: A moment of clarity and illumination. Deepen your connection with your Ori and seek spiritual insight.

WANING MOON

Waning Moon begins the fall, We shed old skin, release it all. What no longer serves, we leave behind, Creating space for peace of mind.

Spiritual Meaning: A powerful time for release. Let go of what no longer serves you and begin the process of renewal.

DARK MOON

In silence, we rest, reflect, and heal, A time for introspection, deep and real. The dark moon whispers, calm and still, Inviting rest, as we heal at will.

Spiritual Meaning: A sacred pause. Rest, reflect, and tune in to your inner world. Use this time for deep listening and healing.

* * *

THE THIRTEEN SACRED ORISHA MOONS

In some Yoruba lineages throughout West Africa and the diaspora, each *full moon* is spiritually guided by a specific Orisha. These moons are not just points in time but powerful portals for ritual, reflection, and transformation. The Yoruba calendar is lunar-based, with each month carrying the unique energy and teachings of an Orisha. These sacred moons invite us to reconnect with nature, the divine, and our ancestors.

1. **January Full Moon - *Obatala:* *Purity and Wisdom***
2. **February Full Moon - *Sopona (Babalú-Ayé):* *Wellness and Protection***
3. **March Full Moon - *Yemoja:* *Emotional Renewal***
4. **April Full Moon - *Oshun:* *Love and Prosperity***
5. **May Full Moon - *Egungun:* *Ancestral Remembrance***

6. **June Full Moon - *Orunmila:*** *Destiny and Insight*
7. **July Full Moon - *Eshu:*** *Open Roads and Choices*
8. **August Full Moon - *Shango:*** *Power and Renewal*
9. **September Full Moon - *Ogun:*** *Work and Victory*
10. **October Full Moon - *Oya:*** *Change and Ancestral Winds*
11. **November Full Moon - *Iyaami / Osoronga:*** *Mystery and Power*
12. **December Full Moon - *Obaluaye:*** *Healing and Completion*
13. **13th Full Moon (Oṣù Olódùmarè) - *Olodumare / Spirit Source:*** *Unity* and Divine Alignment, called the "Moon of Divine Power" or *Oṣù Àṣẹ,* the thirteenth full moon calls us to reflect deeply and align with the Source.

* * *

CELEBRATING THE YORUBA FESTIVALS

Yoruba festivals provide a time for family and friends to come together and celebrate, both in Nigeria and the diaspora. Some major festivals where the Orishas are honored include:

THE IFA FESTIVAL
This festival honors Orunmila, the Orisha of wisdom and divination, through offerings and rituals that seek spiritual insight and guidance. It is celebrated in Ile-Ife, Osun State, typically in late spring to early summer.

THE OLOJO FESTIVAL
Commemorating the creation of the universe, this festival honors Olojo, the deity of the sun and life, with prayers and rituals for spiritual renewal. It is held in Ile-Ife, Osun State, during early fall.

THE EYO FESTIVAL
A grand cultural event in Lagos, this festival features a procession of white-clad figures and honors important historical figures and newly appointed royalty. It usually takes place in late winter to early spring.

THE SANGO FESTIVAL
This vibrant celebration in Oyo honors Sango, the Orisha of thunder, fire, and leadership. It features drumming, dancing, and offerings made for strength, protection, and guidance. The festival is held at the Alaafin's palace in August, during the Yoruba New Year, which marks the beginning of the festival season.

THE OSHUN OSOGBO FESTIVAL
Devotees gather in Osogbo, Osun State, to honor Oshun, the Orisha of love, fertility, and rivers, through a sacred pilgrimage to the Osun River for blessings of health and prosperity. This takes place in late summer.

THE ORO FESTIVAL
A secretive and male-only ceremony, this festival honors deceased monarchs and spiritual leaders with rituals for protection and guidance. It is observed in various towns across Ogun, Oyo, and Kwara States during the dry season.

THE EGUNGUN MASQUERADE FESTIVAL
This ancestral festival involves colorful masquerades, dances, and rituals to welcome the spirits of the ancestors and seek their blessings. It is celebrated across Yoruba communities, often during the dry season.

THE FESTIVAL OF YEMOJA
Held along Brazil's coastal regions like Bahia and Rio de Janeiro, this festival honors Yemoja, the Orisha of the sea, with ocean offerings symbolizing prayers for healing, protection, and fertility. It typically occurs in the winter.

* * *

In conclusion, the moon's phases and Yoruba festivals both play pivotal roles in spiritual life, marking significant times for rituals, honoring deities, and reflecting on life's cycles. These traditions offer a deep connection to the past and present, providing guidance, renewal, and spiritual alignment.

* * *

GLOSSARY

A

- **Aganju**: Orisha of strength, transformation, and perseverance, associated with volcanoes, deserts, and mountains. Called upon for stability in difficult times.
- **Aje-Shaluga**: Orisha of wealth, prosperity, and abundance, governing financial success and commerce. Invoked for business blessings.
- **Ajogun**: Negative spirits believed to cause misfortune. They are often seen as obstacles to personal and communal well-being in Yoruba belief.
- **Ayangalu**: Orisha of the talking drum, seen as the first drummer and conveys spiritual messages through rhythm.
- **Ayelalá**: An Orisha of justice and truth, known for punishing criminals and exposing lies. She is invoked to seek justice and fight against injustice and criminality.

B

- **Baba**: "Father" (a respectful term used in family and religious contexts).
- **Babaloricha/Babalocha**: A respected Santero with extensive initiation knowledge.
- **Babalawo**: A skilled diviner and spiritual guide, also known as a priest of Orula.
- **Babalú-Aye**: Orisha of earth, illness, and healing, with the power to cure or bring diseases. Tied to death and nature's cycles.
- **Batá**: A set of three double headed drums resembling an hourglass, each with specific roles and spiritual significance.

- **Bembé**: A lively drumming ceremony held in honor of the Orishas.
- **Boveda**: An altar dedicated to ancestors and spirits, used for offerings and prayers.
- **Burukú**: Moral flaws or bad character ("iwá burukú").

C

- **Calabash**: A gourd used in Yoruba rituals for offerings, divination, and as containers for sacred items.
- **Chango / Changó / Sango/ Shango** – One of the major orishas, associated with thunder, fire, lightning, masculinity, drumming, and dance.
- **Cowrie**: A type of seashell used in divination and ceremonies, symbolizing wealth, money and used as currency by the ancient Yoruba.

D

- **Dada**: Orisha of motherhood, fertility, and the well-being of unborn children. Revered for her role in childbirth and nurturing.
- **Derecho**: Payment made to Olorisha or Babalawo for their services or out or respect.

E

- **Ẹbọ (Ebo)**: Sacrifice or offering made to orishas or ancestors for guidance, protection, or blessings.
- **Egbe**: Refers to a group, society, or community in heaven.
- **Egún**: Spirits of deceased ancestors, often honored and revered for their guidance and protection.
- **Egungun**: Masquerade costumes worn to honor the Egun (ancestor) spirits in ceremonies.
- **Ẹlẹ́dá (Eleda)**: Creator; refers to Olodumare, the supreme deity in Yoruba cosmology.
- **Erinle**: Orisha of health, medicine, hunting, and estuaries. Syncretized with Archangel Raphael, protector of marginalized communities.

- **Esu/Elegua**: Messenger of the Orishas, owner of all roads and paths. A trickster and gatekeeper who facilitates communication between realms.

I

- **Ibeji**: Orisha of twins, symbolizing duality and balance. Revered for the sacred bond between twins.
- **Iroko**: Spirit inhabiting the Iroko tree, linked to spiritual connection. Harm to the tree brings misfortune.
- **Iyami Osoronga**: powerful female spirits in Yoruba tradition who guard nature, enforce justice, and punish those who act disrespectfully or unjustly.

N

- **Nana Buluku**: Supreme goddess of creation, grandmother of all life and Orishas. Rules over life cycles, fertility, and abundance.

O

- **Oba**: Orisha of marriage and relationships, known for her tragic story with Shango. Transformed into the Oba River.
- **Obatala**: Father of all Orishas, symbolizing purity, wisdom, and justice. Creator of humans and associated with moral character.
- **Ochosi**: Orisha of hunting, justice, and truth. Protector of hunters, called upon for fairness and protection.
- **Oduduwa**: Father of the Yoruba people and civilization, credited with world creation and establishing order.
- **Ogun**: Orisha of war, iron, and technology. Known for strength and endurance, Ogun serves as a protector and guide.
- **Oke**: Orisha of high mountains and elevated places, often linked to Obatala. A protector during travel.
- **Oko**: Orisha of agriculture, farming, and abundance. Invoked for prosperous harvests.
- **Olodumare** : The supreme creator deity, also referred to as God in Yoruba tradition.
- **Olokun**: Orisha of the deep ocean, wealth, and prosperity.

Associated with hidden treasures, beauty, and the ocean's mysteries.
- **Olori-Merin**: Orisha who governs the four cardinal points and maintains balance across all creation.
- **Ori**: The head or spiritual consciousness of an individual. It represents one's destiny and essence.
- **Oro**: Historical king and an Orisha of justice. Also represents a spiritual force associated with divine communication.
- **Orunmila**: Orisha of wisdom, knowledge, and divination. The first Babalawo, consulted for guidance on destiny.
- **Osain**: Orisha of herbs, healing plants, and herbal medicine. Protector of healers and the forest, with knowledge of all plants' healing properties.
- **Oshun**: Orisha of love, beauty, and sensuality. Protector of women and children, bringing wealth and emotional healing.
- **Osumare**: Orisha of rainbows and serpents, symbolizing renewal and transformation. Protects children and creative individuals.
- **Oya**: Orisha of wind, tornadoes, and hurricanes. Known for her fierce protection of the dead and as a guardian of the marketplace, she is associated with sudden changes and heightened intuition.

S

- **Santería:** also known as Santería or Lucumí, is an Afro-Cuban religion rooted in Yoruba traditions. It originated in Cuba and spread to other parts of the Americas, blending elements of Catholicism, Taino (Indigenous Caribbean) beliefs, and other spiritual traditions alongside its Yoruba foundation.
- **Shango**: Orisha of thunder, lightning, fire, and drumming. A symbol of masculinity and protection, revered for his power to overcome obstacles.

T

- **Taiwo:** A name often given to the first-born of twins.
- **Tutu**: Coolness.

U

- **Umbanda:** Originating in Brazil, Umbanda combines elements of African, indigenous, and Christian beliefs. It centers on the worship of the orishás.

V

- **Vodou**: Also known as Voodoo, Vodou is a syncretic religion that originated in Haiti. It centers on the worship of loas, spirits who represent various aspects of nature and human life and incorporates elements of West African religions.

W

- **Warriors**: An initiation ceremony where the Orishas Elegua, Ogun, Ochosi, and Osun are bestowed upon individuals to assist them on their spiritual journey.

Y

- **Yemaya**: Orisha of the ocean and motherhood. Represents fertility, protection, and nurturing, often invoked by women seeking to conceive.
- **Yewa**: Orisha associated with earth and death. Guards the boundary between life and death and governs the decomposition of corpses.

* * *

May Olodumare continue to bless you, give you support and guide you on your journey.

* * *

The End

* * *

BIBLIOGRAPHY

1. Adepegba, C. O. *Yoruba Egungun: Its Association with Ancestors and the Typology of Yoruba Masquerades by Its Costume.* University of Ibadan, 1984.
2. Adeoti, Adeola Abiodun, and Daniel Odekunle Odetayo. "The Artistic and Aesthetics Analysis of the Costume of Egungun Elewe in Igbomina Land." *African Journal of Social Sciences and Humanities Research*, vol. 7, no. 3, 2024, pp. 48–61.
3. Akinsemoyin, Kunle. *Twilight Tales.* Illustrated by Prue Theobalds, African University Press, Lagos, 1965.
4. Angarica, Nicolás Valentín (Obá Tolá). *Manual de Orihaté: Religión Lucumí.* 1955, Cuba.
5. Balogun, Wande Abimbola. "Ifá: A West African Cosmological System." *Lumina*, vol. 20, no. 2, Oct. 2009, pp. 1–10.
6. Bascom, W. R. "Social Status, Wealth and Individual Differences among the Yoruba." *American Anthropologist*, vol. 53, no. 4, 1951, pp. 490–505. https://doi. org/10.1525/aa.1951.53.4.02a00040.
7. Beier, Ulli. *Yoruba Myths.* Cambridge University Press, 31 Oct. 1980.
8. Belt, Lida M. "Ritual Objects Associated with the Worship of Shango among the Yoruba." *Folklore Forum Bibliographic and Special Series*, no. 11, Studies in Yoruba Folklore, Department of Folklore and Ethnomusicology, Indiana University, 1973, pp. 17–30.
9. Bolívar Aróstegui, Natalia. *Orishas del panteon afrocubano.* Quorum Editores. ISBN 8488599986.
10. Brown, David H. *Santería Enthroned: Art, Ritual and Innovation in an Afro-Cuban Religion.* University of Chicago Press, 2003.
11. Calvo, Rafael Garcia. "The Ritual Dialogue in the Òrìṣà Religion: A Linguistic Approach." *Axis Mundi*, vol. 2, 2022, pp. 14–22.
12. Centers for Disease Control and Prevention. "Shapona, the Yoruba God of Smallpox." David J. Sencer CDC Museum, U.S. Dept. of Health & Human Services, last reviewed 30 Apr. 2021, www.cdc.gov/museum/history/shapon a.html. Accessed 10 June 2025.
13. Cohen, Peter F. "Orisha Journeys: The Role of Travel in the Birth of Yorùbá-Atlantic Religions." *Archives de Sciences Sociales des Religions*, vol. 117, Jan.–Mar. 2002, pp. 17–36. OpenEdition Journals. Accessed 15 June 2025, https://pu.edu.pk/images/journal/phill/pdf_files/Paper-3_36_16.pdf.
14. Coletanea, D. *Ìyàmì Òsòróngà: Poder Feminino no Contraste de Amor e Medo.* Independently published, 2004.
15. Dayrell, E., and A. Lang. *Folk Stories from Southern Nigeria.* Longmans, Green, and Co., 1910.
16. Drewal, Henry John, John Pemberton, Rowland Abiodun, and Allen Wardwell. *Yoruba: Nine Centuries of African Art and Thought.* Center for African Art, 1989. PDF. ISBN 978-0-8109-1794-1.

17. Ellis, A. B. *Yoruba-Speaking Peoples of the Slave Coast of West Africa: Their Religion, Manners, Customs, Laws, Language, etc.* Chapman and Hall, 1894.

18. Falola, Toyin. *Esu: Yoruba God, Power, and the Imaginative Frontiers.* Carolina Academic Press, 2013.

19. Falola, Toyin, and Akintunde Akinyemi, editors. *Encyclopedia of the Yoruba.* Indiana University Press, 2016.

20. Famiyesin, Mike. "Controlling the Boundaries of Morality: The History and Powers of Ayelala Deity." *Yoruba Studies Review*, 1 Jan. 2021. Accessed 9 Oct. 2023.

21. Gershon, Livia. "How Does the West African Talking Drum Accurately Mimic Human Speech?" *Smithsonian Magazine*, 27 July 2021. Accessed 4 Aug. 2021.

22. Greene, Sandra E. "Religion, History and the Supreme Gods of Africa: A Contribution to the Debate." *Journal of Religion in Africa*, vol. 26, no. 2, 1996, pp. 122–138. Brill Academic Publishers, https://doi.org/10.1163/157006696X00037.

23. Idowu, E. Bolaji. *Olodumare: God in Yoruba Belief.* Longmans, Green, and Co., 1962.

24. Ifagbemi, Awo [Michael Perez]. *The Yoruba Spiritual Training Manual: The Ultimate Resource Guide to the Yoruba Religion.* Barnes & Noble Press, 24 July 2024.

25. Lindsay, Arturo, editor. *Santería Aesthetics in Contemporary Latin American Art.* Smithsonian Institution Press, 1996.

26. Lopes, Nei. *Enciclopédia Brasileira da Diáspora Africana.* Selo Negro Edições, 2004, pp. 266–267. ISBN 9788587478214.

27. Ojo, Olufemi Dada Matthias. "Incorporation of Ayelala Traditional Religion into Nigerian Criminal Justice System: An Opinion Survey of Igbesa Community People in Ogun State, Nigeria." *Etnoantropološki problemi / Issues in Ethnology and Anthropology*, vol. 9, no. 4, 8 Dec. 2014, pp. 1025–1044. University of Belgrade, Faculty of Philosophy. https://doi.org/10.21301/eap.v9i4.11.

28. Ogaiya, Adeyinka Olaiya. *The Yoruba Esu: An Analysis of the True Messenger of Olódùmarè According to Adeyinka Olaiya.* 2021. PDF.

29. Ogumefu, M. I. *Yoruba Legends.* Forgotten Books, 1929, p. 10. ISBN 978-1-60506-017-0.

30. Ologundudu, Adedayo, and Awotunde Aworeni. "Ìwòrì Méjì." *The Original Major Odu Ifá: Ilé-Ifẹ̀*, Center for Spoken Words / Institute of Yoruba Culture, 2008, pp. 103–135.

31. Olusegun, Oladosu. "Title of the Article." *European Scientific Journal*, vol. 11, no. 5, Feb. 2015, Obafemi Awolowo University, Ile-Ife, Nigeria, pp. [insert pages if available], https://core.ac.uk/download/pdf/236409049.pdf.

32. Orunmila, Awo Osa She. *Centro de Estudios de las Reglas Africanas: Regla de Osha, De Iyawo a Orihaté.* Centro de Estudios de las Reglas Africanas, n.d.

33. Oruene, T. O. "Cultic Powers of Yoruba Twins: Manifestation of Traditional and Religious Beliefs of the Yoruba." *Acta Geneticae Medicae et Gemellologiae: Twin Research*, vol. 32, 1983, pp. 221–228. The Mendel Institute / Alan R. Liss, Inc. Cambridge University Press. PDF. Accessed 10 May 2025.

34. Probst, Peter. *Osogbo and the Art of Heritage*. Indiana University Press, 2011, p. 17. ISBN 978-0-253-22295-4.

35. Rodríguez P., Edgar A. *Diccionario de los Orishas*. Publicación independiente, n.d.

36. Salami, Ayò. *Teología y Tradición Yorùbá: El Hombre y la Sociedad*. Instituto Superior de Ciencias Religiosas San Dámaso, 2003.

37. Santería: An African Religion in America. U.S. Department of Justice, Office of Justice Programs, NCJ 137194, 1992, https://www.ojp.gov/pdffiles1/Digitiza tion/137194NCJRS.pdf. Accessed 15 June 2025.

38. The Chicago Manual of Style. 18th ed., The University of Chicago Press, 2024.

39. Veneration of Egbe/Egbe Orun by Babalawo Obanifa. *Sun & Planets Spiritualities*, 2019. PDF.

40. Wyndham, John. *Myths of Ífè*. E. Macdonald, 1921.

* * *

ABOUT THE AUTHOR

Michael Perez, known as Awo Ayodele Ifagbemi, is a priest of the Yoruba spiritual tradition and a devoted practitioner of Orisha spirituality and Ifa divination. With a background in social work and over two decades of experience in spiritual exploration, he is committed to guiding others on their journey of healing, self-discovery, and personal transformation. Through his teachings, he shares the wisdom of the Orishas, offering a path to spiritual alignment and deeper understanding. In addition to *The Sacred Teachings of the Orishas,* he has authored several other books and is passionate about preserving and teaching the Yoruba spiritual tradition.

OTHER BOOKS BY THIS AUTHOR

The Yoruba Spiritual Training Manual: The Ultimate Resource Guide to the Yoruba Religion — This book is a practical, hands-on guide for both beginners and experienced practitioners, offering clear, step-by-step instructions for learning and practicing Yoruba spirituality. This book offers guidance on connecting with the Orishas and integrating Yoruba spiritual principles into daily life, enabling readers to deepen their spiritual practice, foster personal growth, and cultivate balance and purpose.

Living the Sacred Orisa Path: A Complete Guide to the Orishas, Yoruba Wisdom, and the 256 Sacred Odu Ifa — This guide offers a clear and accessible introduction to the 256 Odu Ifa, including the herbs and plants associated with the 16 major Odù families, along with their meanings and practical uses within Yoruba spiritual practice.

Keep learning and growing.

Best Wishes!

Awo Ifagbemi

www.ingramcontent.com/pod-product-compliance
Lightning Source LLC
Chambersburg PA
CBHW070548130626
46556CB00001B/66